Dear Doc,

I know a our neighborly shop.

With Fond Best Wishes

Gwendolen

9/26/11

Gwen Chen
(Deng Yuan-yu)
with Rudi A. Carboni

SHADOWS IN THE LOTUS POOL

Printed in the United States of America.

BookLocker.com, Inc.
2011

First Edition

The China map is reproduced with the kind permission of the University of Texas Libraries, the University of Texas at Austin.

To my sixth grade teacher
who first recognized and inspired me
to see that I could excel as a student.
He was a key factor in my transformation.

The sun-kissed lotus rises from its muddy bed,
Symbol of love and redemption.
But a cloud floats by before the sun,
Casting sinister shadows in the lotus pool.
                    -- R. Carboni

Contents

Author's Note ix
Characters in the Story xi
Chapter 1 - The Beginning- From Countryside to Moscow 1
Chapter 2 - A General at 22! 19
Chapter 3 - Wen-yi and the Bandits 33
Chapter 4 - Chiang vs. the Warlords and Wen-yi 44
Chapter 5 - Chiang and Wen-yi in Exile 54
Chapter 6 - A Powerful Force Emerges 69
Chapter 7 - Wen-yi's Intelligence and Strike Force 80
Chapter 8 - Disgrace, Vindication 91
Chapter 9 - Wen-yi, Military Attaché in Russia 100
Chapter 10 - A Kidnapped Generalissimo, a Disgraced
    Rescuer 111
Chapter 11 - Amid the Horror a Bundle of Joy 125
Chapter 12 - Goodbye Mother, Now I Am a Weed 133
Chapter 13 - Reprimand, Promotion, and a New Wife 142
Chapter 14 - WWII, Wen-yi in the 3rd War Zone 149
Chapter 15 - A Weed in the Wind 159
Chapter 16 - Taiwan - Shangri La on the Island of Sadness 171
Chapter 17 - One War Ends, Another Begins 197
Chapter 18 - Goodbye China 208
Chapter 19 - The Civil War - Part 1 216
Chapter 20 - Civil War - Part 2, Bad News, Like Falling
    Snowflakes 228
Chapter 21 - The North and Beiping in Jeopardy 236
Chapter 22 - Defeat and Exodus 241
Chapter 23 - My Two Lives in Taiwan 250
Chapter 24 - Taiwan and Wen-yi in Transition 268
Chapter 25 - Wen-yi: Entrepreneur, Diplomat 275
Epilogue 286
Notes 291
Selected Bibliography 303
Discussion Questions 317

China

International boundary
Province-level boundary
★ National capital
⊛ Province-level capital

Author's Note

My Chinese name is Deng Yuan-yu. As is customary in the Chinese language, my surname, Deng, is given first. This story is, in part, about my journey to becoming Gwen Chen.

My father, Deng Wen-yi, became a major general at twenty-two, and a member of Chiang Kai-shek's inner circle of trusted officers and staff. His relationship with China's leader was tempestuous. My father had no time for his children. I felt no love or closeness to him. I was just one of his seven daughters. The only bond between us was the love we shared for the mother I never knew, since she died when I was two years old.

There is a Chinese proverb, "A child with a mother is a jewel and a child without a mother is a weed." I was left to fend for myself and became the ward of an aunt who ignored me and an uncle who repeatedly molested me. Through the recognition of a sixth-grade teacher, I was able to enter good schools and gain self-esteem by studying earnestly. Eventually I placed my harsh childhood behind me and felt only a slight pang of guilt for having no filial feeling toward my own father.

My stepmother, now 80 years old, spent many hours with me talking about my father and life in those earlier days. She had served over twenty years as a member of the National Assembly in Taiwan. My father had died at the age of 93, after a long career under Chiang Kai-shek. My stepmother urged me to write a book about my father and his experiences. I wondered whether recalling the events of the past would bring pain or liberation. I also knew I could not write this book by myself. I turned to my friend Rudi Carboni, whose professional book and published poetry I admired, to write the book with me. He knew of my past and he inspired me to write a memoir of my father and my life during the turbulent days of China's war with Japan, and the subsequent civil war between Chiang's Nationalists and Mao Ze-dong's Communists. After much prodding, Rudi agreed to help me write the book. It was a fortunate choice. There would be no book without him.

I was also fortunate to have my father's memoirs and other writings, as well as my conversations with him and family members including my stepmother and my brother, historian and author Deng Yuan-zhong.

Characters in the Story

Borodin, Mikhail Markovich Russian agent in China between 1923 and 1927, sent to aid and build an alliance between the Soviets and the emerging China.

Bai Chong-xi Able Nationalist general, a leader on the Guangxi Clique.

Chen Cheng Nationalist War Minister, close associate and potential successor to Chiang.

Chen Jiong-ming Early rival of Chiang for Sun Yat-sen's favor. As Guangdong warlord he was defeated by Chiang Kai-shek in two Eastern Expeditions.

Chen Li-fu A leader of the powerful anti-Communist CC Clique, with brother Go-fu.

Chiang Ching-kuo (1910-1988) Chiang Kai-shek's son. Held many important positions in preparing to succeed his father and became the able president of the Republic of China on Taiwan.

Chiang Kai-shek (1887-1975) China's leader over twenty years, and later, president of the Republic of China on Taiwan.

Chiang Kai-shek, Madame (Soong, Mei-ling) Beautiful, US-educated, wife and active partner of Chiang.

Dai Li Powerful, feared leader of China's secret police. Among the most trusted subordinates of Chiang

Du Yue-sheng Leader of powerful underworld Green Gang in Shanghai. Dealt extensively with Chiang.

Fu Zuo-yi Commander of Nationalist forces in North China. Surrendered his troops and Beiping to the Communists.

Galen Able Soviet general and Chiang's military adviser.

Gu Zhu-tong Field general, commander-in-chief of the Nationalist army.

He Ying-qin Ambitious general and Minister of War.

He Zhong-han Regarded as one of the Three Most Outstanding Whampoa Military Academy graduates. Ambitious and skilled politician, wielded much influence as General Secretary of the Blue Shirt Society.

Hu Han-min Early ally of Chiang, leader of the Legislative Yuan, finally opposed Chiang.

Hu Zong-nan Nationalist army commander, among the more capable generals.

Li Zong-ren Leader of Guangxi Clique. Sometime ally and enemy of Chiang. Became vice president, then acting president of the Nationalists during the final days in mainland China.

Lin Biao Chinese Communist general and political leader. Lin was trained at Whampoa Academy. He later commanded the Communist military offensive in the northeast against Chiang Kai-shek. Lin was appointed defense minister of the People's Republic in 1959.

Mao Fu-mei Chiang's first wife and mother of Chiang Ching-kuo.

Mao Ze-dong (1893-1976) Communist Party leader. Spearheaded the Communist victory over the Nationalists. Chairman of the People's Republic of China.

ShenWen-ying Wen-yi's wife, member of the National Assembly in Taiwan.

Song Zi-wen (Soong, T. V.) Trained at Harvard and Columbia Universities. Brother-in-law of Chiang, served as chief of the Central Bank of China, minister of finance, minister of foreign affairs, and prime minister of the Executive Yuan.

Sun Yat-sen Chinese revolutionary and political leader. Recognized as the "Founding Father of the Republic of China."

Wang Jing-wei Chiang's rival, and leader of the left wing of the Nationalist Party. Later a collaborator with the Japanese during Sino-Japanese war.

Wang Ming Rival of Mao Ze-dong for Communist Party leadership. Member of the Soviet Communist International (Comintern).

Wu Pei-fu Chinese general and major warlord who controlled much of central and northern China, including Beiping between 1918 and1926.

Xiao Zan-yu Co-founder of the Lixingshe (Blue Shirt Society). Served as Chiang's personal secretary. Close friend of Deng Wen-yi. Xiao, He Zhong-han, Liu Yong-yao, Yuan Shou-qian, and Deng Wen-yi, all members of the first class graduated from Whampoa Military Academy and all from Hunan Province, were considered by some the Hunan Clique.

Yan Xi-shan Chinese warlord who served in the government of the Republic of China. Ruled the province of Shanxi until the Communist victory in the Chinese Civil War.

Zhang Xue-liang A.k.a. the Young Marshal. Initially a warlord, inheriting control of Manchuria from his father. Later Chiang's commander of North China forces, and finally kidnapped Chiang to force unification with the Communists against the Japanese invader.

Zhou En-lai (1898-1976) Among the most successful and influential officers of the Communist party. Suave, diplomatic, and Mao Ze-dong's right-hand man. Also respected by the Nationalists.

The Family

Deng Kuang-shuin Wen-yi's father, my paternal grandfather
Ho Shui-tseng Wen-yi's mother, my paternal grandmother
Pan Wen-yi's mother-in-law, Li Bai-jian's mother, my maternal grandmother
Deng Wen-yi (1904-1998)
Li Bai-jian (1908-1939) Wen-yi's wife, my mother
Shen Wen-ying (1917-2007) Wen-yi's second wife, my stepmother
Deng Yuan-zhong (b.1930) Wen-yi and Bai-jian's eldest son
Deng Yuan-yu (b.1937) also named Gwen Chen, Wen-yi and Bai-jian's youngest daughter, the author
Deng Wen-shi (1906-1992) Wen-yi's brother, my uncle and adoptive father
Chung Ke-ming Wen-shi's wife, my aunt and adoptive mother

Deng Yuan-cheng Wen-shi and Ke-ming's adopted son, my cousin

Deng Bi-xia (1919-2005) Wen-yi's youngest sister, my aunt

Deng Wen-jie Wen-yi's youngest brother

May One of Wen-jie's three wives

Chapter 1

The Beginning
From Countryside to Moscow

It was time to say goodbye. Although my father could hardly wait to begin his journey, he could not restrain a sense of sadness to be leaving Liling, a small town in Liling County in the eastern end of Hunan Province where he had lived his entire life. Located in southeast-central China along the southern banks of the Yangtze River, the province was surrounded by hills and mountains on three sides, and on the fourth by a fertile river plain, which, combined with its mild climate, had made Hunan a major rice producer for the country. The large majority of the people of Liling were poor, some nearly destitute. There were also a small number of merchants, and there was a much smaller but influential group of landlords.

As my father Deng Wen-yi approached the end of his senior year in high school, his parents and relatives assumed he would seek a job teaching in the village. His father wanted to arrange a marriage for him. This was understandable since, in the traditional Confucian ethic, family and self interest took priority over the outside laws and edicts of the Central government. However, Wen-yi had no interest in the limited opportunities offered locally. Marriage held no attraction at this point. He wanted to explore, if not "conquer," the world. There was nothing to keep him in Liling. He had developed a romantic resolve to serve the nation.

In 1903, my grandfather, Deng Kuang-shuin, then 18, was married to my grandmother, Ho Shui-tseng, a village girl of fourteen. She was illiterate, petite, and regarded as beautiful and graceful, with a simple and sweet personality. Her hair was always combed back into a bun. Her bound feet forced her to take small steps, adding to her appeal. In 1904, before she

1

turned sixteen, Grandmother Ho gave birth to her first son, my father, Deng Wen-yi. Two years later, she had a second son, Deng Wen-shi. My grandparents had a third son and two daughters in close succession.

Wen-yi's elementary education had been supported by a small income provided by his grandfather. At the age of eight he was organizing little gambling sessions with his young schoolmates, using small coins and other barter as stakes. When he was ten Wen-yi began to help out at the family store. He was responsible for doing some relatively simple book keeping and accounting. Wen-yi soon noticed that when people could not pay what they owed, his father would often tell him to forget the debt. The young boy would carry a sense of generosity toward his friends to an extravagant degree throughout his career.

During the winter of 1916, my grandfather suffered a shattering reversal in the family's fortunes. While he was engaged in a lengthy gambling session with friends, bandits cut a hole through the wall of his store and stole all the goods. There were many such bandit groups throughout the provinces who turned to stealing and brigandage, especially in country districts where authority was lax. The family was suddenly penniless. They were forced to move in with my grandmother's family in the remote village of Dongxiang. The expanded household barely survived by making and selling bean curds. Wen-yi and his mother were reduced to pushing a heavy stone "bean grinder" for a large part of each day.

Wen-yi had shown early indications of high intelligence. He was liked and admired by his family and friends. To his dismay, he was forced to quit school after fifth grade to contribute to the family's livelihood. However, there were no paying jobs for a child his age. Then, he heard that a distant relative was supervising a mining project in a remote mountain area one hundred miles away. After much argument, his parents gave their reluctant consent for their young son to travel with four villagers to the mining site. Twelve-year-old Wen-yi arrived at the site after a three-day trek. The small group was quickly hired. My father was given the tasks of bookkeeping, distributing wages to the crew, and weighing the iron ore. He received one silver dollar a month.

The work was not demanding. Wen-yi was able to study lessons in the school books used by the sixth grade. He satisfied his wanderlust by exploring the pristine mountain with its variety of flowers, trees, and caves.

Nights were different. Young Wen-yi could hardly sleep amidst the howling of wild animals that seemed to be just outside the thin walls of the mining camp's simple housing. There were no children of his age, and he was lonely. He kept asking himself, "Do I really want to spend the rest of my life like this...as a bookkeeper... forever?" "No," he decided, "definitely not!" He needed to get an education if he were to make something of himself. He began to plan his departure. After eight months, with ten dollars in his pocket (two dollars as bonus money), he finally got permission to return home. The experience helped to establish the adventurous, defiant attitude he carried into his adult years.

Once home, he gave five dollars to his family and saved the other five for schooling. Fortunately, the school had competent teachers and received some financial support from the community and the government. The schoolmaster, impressed with Wen-yi's determination and book studying during his job at the mine, decided to allow Wen-yi to skip a grade and enter the seventh grade directly. A grateful Wen-yi limited his playtime, stayed late at school, and studied at night. He finished seventh grade fifth in his class of sixty pupils. His schoolmaster, a graduate from a famous military academy, had story sessions each day, holding the children's rapt attention as he described the derring-do and righteous deeds of the "heroes of the green wood" (the Chinese version of Robin Hood). This teacher encouraged his students to set ambitious goals, and to brave leaving the home village to pursue their promise in the great world outside. This would have a profound influence on my father. Wen-yi loved to read historical and martial novels, and was determined to go to high school in Liling, though attendance was costly.

Wen-yi and the Goose

Wen-yi had been invited to join some friends from wealthier families in tutoring sessions to prepare for the high school entrance exams. Their tutor, Mr. Zhou Shu-fen, was a knowledgeable and highly respected retiree who had studied in Japan. Zhou held young Wen-yi in some favor because of his earnest approach to school work.

During recess the boys often swam in a creek near a flock of geese. One day, on an impulse, the boys decided to steal one of the geese and cook it for a small feast. Wen-yi dove into the water and snared one, which was quickly transferred to a makeshift sack. The boys started a fire with straw and twigs, then carefully roasted the goose. It was a great treat. Wen-yi set his friends to work removing any evidence of their mischief by throwing the ashes and bones into the dung in the outhouse. However, one student had observed this activity and immediately informed the goose owner, a relative, of the episode. The outraged owner charged to the school, berating Mr. Zhou for poor discipline, demanding compensation for the goose and assurances there would be no repetition of the misdeed. When Zhou vigorously denied the incident had occurred, he almost came to blows with the owner in front of all the students.

The boys angrily denied any wrongdoing. To reinforce their case, Wen-yi urged Zhou to insist on a formal apology if the owner could not produce tangible evidence of the crime. The teacher threatened the owner. Without evidence or a witness (his student relative having been silenced by threats), the owner had no option but to apologize. Wen-yi and the other young culprits watched with glee and fear as the poor fellow lit firecrackers and kowtowed to Mr. Zhou as an apology for his faulty accusation. Wen-yi wondered at how easily they had fooled their teacher and the well-to-do landowner. Two years later, Wen-yi decided to confess his perfidy to teacher Zhou who, with a mixture of anger and amusement, reprimanded his young charge.

Wen-yi passed the entrance exam, a major hurdle, and was accepted in high school. The tuition and living expense was fifteen dollars per semester. After the first year, his family could no longer provide the money. Fortunately, the local Deng Community Association, aware that only three hundred children of the five thousand Deng descendants in Liling County went to school, with fewer than twenty advancing to high school and college, granted Wen-yi ten dollars each semester. Without such help he could not have continued his education. Nevertheless, obtaining the balance of the tuition presented serious problems.

With the realization that he could not count on his family for financial support, he resorted to playing in small gambling sessions in town. He usually won and was able to meet the school fee requirements with his winnings. Through it all, he studied hard and slept less than his classmates. Despite the time "invested" gambling in town, he managed to remain in the upper fifth percentile in his class. His teachers were fond of him and praised him openly as a bright and hard-working student. Two envious students told the teachers of Wen-yi's extracurricular activities, of how he would sneak out to engage in gambling. The teachers refused to believe the stories, and defended Wen-yi. My father knew he had to continue his nocturnal activities; but he would become more circumspect about his forays in town.

In the spring of 1923, news circulated at the school that General Cheng Qian, a leading revolutionary hero originally from Liling of Hunan, was recruiting young men to be trained as cadets for a new Jiangwu Military Academy in Guangzhou. Wen-yi and several other seniors felt this was an opportunity that could not be ignored. He believed a military career was the only option available to him to advance his future.

Journey to Guangzhou

After tearful goodbyes with family and neighbors Wen-yi set out on his new adventure. In their anxiety to depart, Wen-yi and several of his classmates missed their high school graduation. They agreed to meet in Changsha so they could journey together 430 miles to the metropolis of Guangzhou. Wen-yi took a train to Changsha and proceeded by boat with his companions to the city of Hankou. The seven young adventurers were stunned by the beautiful new world they had entered. As Wen-yi and his companions strolled along Hanzheng Street in the center of town, they stared in awe at the buildings and the variety of goods in shops and markets along the ancient thoroughfare. Everything seemed so new and grand to the country boys. For three days they roamed the city absorbing one wondrous scene after another. As they approached the crowded areas of the city they held hands, lest they be separated and lost. One day they discovered the Liling County Association building. To their delight and relief, they met a military officer who was going to Guangzhou. He agreed to guide their group to that city.

When they arrived in Shanghai, their emotions, overloaded from their experiences in Hankou, soared even higher as they gawked at the architecture, wide roads, electric trolleys, automobiles, and the hustle and bustle of droves of people hurrying in every direction. It was almost too much to absorb. The bewildered young men would stop in the middle of the road not knowing how to dodge oncoming vehicles. They were equally confused by night markets, the lights and sounds of the amusement park, and the aggressive approach of prostitutes offering pleasures Wen-yi could not afford. The more affluent young men agreed to each give Wen-yi one dollar, in return for which he would guard their luggage in the small hostel where they were staying while they indulged themselves. Two of his pleasure-seeking traveling companions contracted a sexually transmitted disease. But Wen-yi used his money toward purchase of a boat ticket to Guangzhou.

On August 17, 1923 the group finally arrived in Guangzhou. The city was filled with troops and local militia men. The Cheng Qian Military Training Camp was still recruiting but would soon be converted into the Jiangwu Military Academy. Since Wen-yi had run out of money, he immediately applied for the Camp. He completed the entrance procedure, pawned his belongings to pay the hostel, and began his military training.

He was assigned to a military camp as a student soldier under the command of General Cheng. Wen-yi and his fellow recruits soon discovered life in the camp was Spartan, with meager supplies. Each student soldier received two sets of uniforms. Two soldiers shared a wooden bed with three blankets. There were no showers. With the crudest of hygiene facilities the trainees stank with sweat, and were infested with lice. Wen-yi was punished frequently because he talked too freely, criticized the system, and once, deliberately kicked a soccer ball into the river. He awoke one morning to find that his bed-fellow had died in his sleep...from the filth, thought my father. No one was allowed to leave camp during the first three months. Thereafter, student soldiers were given a one-day leave on weekends, on a rotating basis. The grim training conditions hardened Wen-yi, providing a sound foundation for his future military career.

At this point, fate stepped in. There had been much talk in Guangzhou about a new Military Academy being established at Fort Whampoa, on an island in the Pearl River, twelve miles south of Guangzhou. The academy had been a high priority for Sun Yat-sen, the revolutionary leader and national hero who had played a key role in the overthrow of the Qing Dynasty. He had founded and become the first provisional president of the new Republic of China and founder of the Nationalist Party.[1] Sun Yat-sen realized that a well-trained military force was needed if he were to deal successfully with the powerful warlords[2] who controlled many of the provinces. Sun enlisted the support of Soviet Russian military and political officials from Communist International (Comintern[3]) to help establish a

Military Academy, based on the Russian model. Sun's young protégé, General Chiang Kai-shek, had recently returned from Russia where he had studied its military structure and arms. Chiang was determined to be appointed Commandant of the new Academy.[4] The Academy would be the source of trained officers to carry out the missions of the new government, officers who would be loyal to him, personally and ideologically.

Wen-yi decided that this was an opportunity that could not be ignored. With twenty fellow student soldiers he surreptitiously took the preliminary recruiting examinations for Whampoa Military Academy in February 1924. Four of them, including my father, passed the tests. When the Jiangwu Academy administrators learned of the students' unauthorized action they were furious. They pressured and threatened the renegade students, and tried to dissuade them from taking any further action. Wen-yi was not to be denied. The current school had placed no emphasis on political, ideological, and spiritual training. Wen-yi considered these to be important for his future. In March, the four students defiantly took and passed the final recruiting examination for Whampoa. School officials refused to release the four. Wen-yi suddenly developed an illness, feigned so convincingly that he was taken to a local hospital. He escaped from the hospital and hid in a rundown hotel until the opening of the new Academy. The other three also attempted to escape. One was re-captured and placed in prison at the school. He died three months later.

On May 4, 1924, the first class of five hundred cadets, including 160 provisional cadets on the waiting list, reported to the Military Academy to begin their training. Facilities were primitive. Many of the cadets were forced to live in tents. Commandant Chiang Kai-shek had developed a curriculum with the close guidance and supervision of several military advisers from Moscow. On June sixteenth, Dr. Sun Yat-sen, as the titular leader of the Republic of China, the Nationalist Party, and the Academy, arrived to officiate at the delayed opening ceremonies and to meet with the cadets. He emphasized that the sole purpose of the Military Academy was to create a strong revolutionary army. They, the future officers, would build a united Republic of China, based on his "Three People's Principles" of nationalism, democracy, and people's livelihood. My father was ecstatic, and full of fervor.

Two months after the opening of the Academy, a Norwegian ship sailed up the Zhu River carrying military equipment ordered by the Mercantile Guild in Guangzhou for their Merchants' Militia. The Guangzhou businessmen had formed a militia to protect their interests against radical workers and other agitators. Sun Yat-sen, suspicious of their intent, ordered Chiang Kai-shek to intercept the ship. The raid was carried out successfully using Whampoa cadets and personnel. Confiscated rifles and ammunition were taken to the Whampoa Military Base. The cadets had achieved their first success. The outraged Mercantile Guild insisted the weapons were for defensive reasons only, and ordered a series of shop strikes throughout the city. After much negotiation and many threats, an agreement was reached. Whampoa would release half of the weapons for payment.

The cadets soon developed two factions, the pro-Communist "Federation of Young Soldiers" with sixty members and the non-Communist "Sun Yat-sen Society." The two groups did not get along. My father became one of the five leaders of the non-Communist group. This did not go unnoticed by Commandant Chiang. To maintain a sense of neutrality and order, Chiang made a deliberate effort to become personally acquainted with each member of the class. He invited each cadet to his office for a chat. It was here that a curious, special bond began to form between the leader and Wen-yi that would remain despite the ups and downs of their relationship over the years. Chiang decided to form an intelligence group to do surveillance on the Communist contingent at Whampoa. He asked Wen-yi to lead the intelligence network to keep Communist activity under observation.

Wen-yi Joins Sun Yat-sen on His Northern Expedition

Shortly after the opening of the Whampoa Academy, President Sun Yat-sen initiated a northern expedition to seize power from the warlords and unite China. The expedition was strongly opposed by his erstwhile aide Chen Jiong-ming and the Beiping government. My father was among the 124 cadets assigned to guard the president, Dr. Sun, who established his division headquarters in Shaoguan, Guangdong Province. During the trek, the 59-year-old leader discussed concepts of war strategy with the Whampoa cadets though he was not an accomplished military man. It did not matter to my father and the other cadets. This was "the Father of the Chinese Revolution" ... provisional president of the new Chinese republic. It was a great honor to serve him. Living conditions at headquarters were poor, with mosquitoes, insects, and unsanitary conditions. Wen-yi contracted dysentery followed by malaria. He was relieved when the assignment was over and they went back to the Academy in early October.

To meet the urgent need for officers, the one-year training program of the first class was condensed into eight months. Amid intensified training and political pressure, Wen-yi became seriously ill and was sent to a military hospital at the end of October. Food at the hospital was poor. A nurse took a special interest in the dashing cadet. She loaned Wen-yi her personal blankets and brought him nutritious foods during her visits several times a day. This relationship helped him get through an otherwise dismal month in the hospital. He would always remember her with affection.

Wen-yi's hospitalization caused him to miss the final field exercises. Now he was fearful he might not be graduated and he would have to stay behind with the second class. However, Commandant Chiang gave specific instructions that the cadets in the hospital who had not participated in the final field exercise would graduate with the class. A great weight was lifted from Wen-yi's shoulders. He graduated, and was assigned to the Second Brigade as a junior officer.

In November, Dr. Sun journeyed north again to discuss the future of China with the warlords, with little success. He then proceeded to Beiping for similar discussions with local leaders, again with discouraging results. Suffering from deteriorating health, Sun must have been severely tested by the journey. On March 12, 1925 Sun Yat-sen died of liver cancer in a Beiping hospital.

Wen-yi Faces Combat, the Eastern Expedition

Sun Yat-sen had relied on two aides, Chen Jiong-ming, known as the Hakka General, and Chiang Kai-shek, to oversee all military matters of the new government. There was no love lost between the two men. Each was jealous and suspicious of the other's relationship with their leader. Chen Jiong-ming was an unusually able military leader and administrator. He considered Sun unqualified to organize any military expedition. He also feared that Chiang Kai-shek was pressing Sun to dismiss him. With the support of an important warlord, Wu Pei-fu, Chen revolted and declared himself commander-in-chief and governor of Guangdong Province, i.e. a warlord.

The Hakka general prepared for an attack on Guangzhou. Chiang vowed to fight Chen with the Whampoa force even though the first class had hardly completed its training. Chiang's chief military adviser, a skillful, battle-hardened Russian general known as Galen, urged Chiang to launch a preemptive strike against Chen's forces. Two Nationalist training regiments were established, assigning graduates of the first class to various duties as interim officers in the 1st and 2nd Regiments. My father was appointed as a platoon leader. All levels of Whampoa personnel, including instructors and staff, were pressed into service. The expeditionary force consisted of only three thousand troops who would be facing the warlord army of 30,000. This would be Kai-shek's and the cadets' first battlefield campaign. Although loyalty among the drafted troops was in doubt, the spirit and pride of the new officers were high. The officers were told that only victory was permitted. Almost all officers wrote their wills prior to departure, and pledged to sacrifice their lives for the cause.

On February 3, 1925 the troops left Guangzhou and marched eastward. My father commanded a platoon of raw recruits with no training. To his consternation, many hardly knew how to aim and fire a rifle. His troops spoke different dialects, making it difficult for him to pass on orders.

At first, the troops encountered minor resistance. The first significant objective, the Guangzhou-Kowloon railroad station, was captured with little difficulty. However, the first ten days in the field served to toughen and increase the confidence of Wen-yi and his fellow cadet officers. The officers and troops were sternly warned, under severe penalty, not to loot, rape, or cause any destruction among the people and their homes.

The young Whampoa officers and troops were temporarily stymied when they arrived at the walled town of Danshui. However, the young troops used bamboo ladders to climb up and over the wall. Wen-yi's good friend, Company Leader Yeh, leaped directly up the closest ladder and eventually reached the top, seizing the enemy's flag. He took seven bullets, falling from the wall. His enraged followers and Whampoa officers howled and rushed upward, paying little heed to gun fire, bullet wounds, and the mortal wounds of their comrades. The Brigade overpowered the stunned enemy and opened the gate for the Whampoa troops. Danshui was captured in three days and Whampoa revolutionary troops became the idol of the country. My father and his platoon of raw recruits were assigned to combat duty to replace battlefield losses. Fortunately, the enemy was now on the run. Wen-yi's platoon had experienced only minor encounters and the experience of pursuing the enemy.

On March 20, Wen-yi's 7th Company was ordered to attack Xianlin, another stronghold of Chen Jiong-ming. The city was protected by a moat filled with water on three sides. Wen-yi's platoon dived into the water and waded through the moat approaching the west gate. For the first time, the platoon engaged in serious combat on the streets outside the wall, with gunshots pouring down from the roof tops. Two thirds of his troops were wounded. My father was shot in the leg, and was carried to the infirmary on a stretcher.[5] That evening Xianlin fell. The Easter Expedition was over. The enemy had fled across the border into Fujian Province, leaving large stores of weapons behind. Warlord Chen Jiong-ming escaped to Hong Kong. Chen Jiong-ming later proclaimed that the expeditionary force directed by Chiang Kai-shek did not fight with guns, they fought with their blood. General Galen had provided the plan and tactics that permitted the campaign to proceed with impressive speed. The victory of the expeditionary army over a grossly superior force became legend. The status of Chiang and General Galen was now considerably enhanced.

Wen-yi and other wounded officers were taken by two small boats to a hospital in Shantou. The trip took 2 ½ days. Chiang Kai-shek came to visit his wounded officers. With tears in his eyes, Chiang stopped to chat privately with each of the young officers. Wen-yi's eyed filled when he saw the Leader. Chiang held my father's hand and expressed his admiration and affection. He gave each officer a cash award of thirty dollars for their bravery. The visit and gesture increased Wen-yi's considerable admiration for and unflinching loyalty to the Commandant. Chiang wrote an emotional introduction to the Year Book of the first Whampoa class cadets, "*...It is not even a year since the commencement of the Academy. The surviving comrades are fewer than 70 percent ...The wounded ones like ...Deng Wen-yi suffered from broken limbs, punctured organs, and even more serious, permanently disabling injuries. When I saw them, we could only cry together...I often relive our battle field devastation deep into the night. I regret that I did not die earlier to follow Premier (Sun Yat-sen) and our dear students, to travel far and above the abyss of misery to spare me deep sorrow and pain... Now a month after the warfare,* *my family is still startled by my screaming and howling nightmares. When I wake up, I am as dazed and bewildered as ever. Actually I am saddened and despondent in mourning my brave, deceased comrades.*"[6]

My Father Marries

Wen-yi remained in the hospital for a month for treatment of his gunshot wound. However, as the wound healed, doctors realized he was also suffering from an infection that may have resulted from the water, food, lice, or some other source. His convalescence would not be a short one. The excitement of battle and subsequent euphoria were now behind him. In the quiet environment of the hospital he became restless. He was homesick. He missed the closeness of his family, and the tranquility of his home village. He was eager to tell his folks about his adventures and the excitement he had lived through. He began to imagine how it would be to be married, to experience the comfort of a beautiful wife. He requested and received permission for a medical leave. The doctors had been reluctant to agree to Wen-yi's leave, fearing he had not sufficiently recovered. Wen-yi ignored their warning. He obtained a three-month leave. Though not fully recovered, he began the arduous journey home to Hunan.

Traveling great distances was difficult and hazardous. Train and boat routes often were not conveniently connected. This required Wen-yi to do a considerable amount of walking. When he finally arrived home he was stunned by the enthusiastic hero's welcome from the villagers. He was greeted with exploding firecrackers and banners. Loud music from a local makeshift band resounded throughout the village. The villagers were proud that one of their own was now an officer wounded in a glorious, victorious campaign. All this in less than two years! They were sure great things were in store for him. They also hoped if he continued to rise, he would protect the village from bandits and warlords. Wen-yi would later achieve a large measure of their expectations.

Almost every night my father was the honored guest at a dinner or small party, however humble. The villagers listened with rapt attention to his adventures, demanding minute details of each incident he had encountered. However, the constant festivities proved to be too much for his still weakened condition. His health regressed and he became ill. Wen-yi's parents were alarmed at the fragile state of their son. They resorted to an old Chinese remedy. *The happiness of marriage would expel the sickness, and bring back health and vitality to the sick man.* As was the custom, marriages were arranged by parents. They had already taken initial steps to arrange the engagement of their son to a young village girl. Now they moved expeditiously to complete marriage arrangements for their son with sixteen-year-old Li Bai-jian (my mother). Wen-yi was not enthusiastic since he had not even seen the girl. However, he obediently accepted his parents' decision. Brides and grooms customarily did not see or know each other until the wedding day.

Finally, it was time for the couple to meet. Wen-yi stared at Bai-jian, suddenly pleased. He had seen her before, from a distance. He only remembered she was pretty and seemed a spirited girl. Bai-jian looked quickly then lowered her eyes. Wen-yi was considered quite handsome, with large expressive eyes, sensuous lips, a straight nose, and a light complexion. He was of above average height, with a garrulous and engaging personality. Much later, she confided to her husband that she had been secretly taken by the good looks of her young prospective husband. This quick appraisal had not gone unobserved by Wen-yi's parents. They were pleased.

The wedding preparations, ceremony, banquet, and entertainment all went by in a blur for Wen-yi. The activity had taxed his still delicate health. He had a relapse, drifting in and out of consciousness for several days. The two mothers were frantic. They turned to an ancient "sex-therapy" strategy, which included collecting various bedroom concoctions for the young bride, and seeking the advice of the experienced women in the village. Bai-jian was a bright, cool, and spirited girl. She understood the situation and the importance of her role. She listened to the torrent of advice from her mother and mother-in-law, and patiently accepted the gadgets and sex advice of a thousand years. She remained constantly by Wen-yi's side as he floated in and out of consciousness. As his health improved, he began to enjoy the tender ministrations of his wife. He became fully aware of the beautiful girl who faithfully tended his needs. He was touched by the sight of his lovely young bride gazing at him, eyes full of adoration. He later told his mother, "Fortune has smiled on me." My father recalled that it was on the fifth day after the wedding that they finally consummated their marriage, though tentatively. The intimacy and loving relationship was a new phenomenon for him, and it deeply touched him. As Bai-jian shyly presented the stained cloth to her mother and mother-in-law, signaling the consummation of marriage and loss of her virginity according to Chinese custom, the entire household responded with a sigh of relief. Bai-jian was now fully accepted by his family.

Wen-yi's leave expired. He must now return to Whampoa with no idea regarding his next assignment. He was low on money, and the family was heavily in debt from the wedding. He decided to ask for help from his powerful Leader. He wrote a carefully composed letter to Chiang Kai-shek, explaining his sickness and awkward financial situation. To his surprise, the reply came quickly, ordering him to report to Whampoa Military Academy. Thirty dollars was attached for his travel expenses. Wen-yi bid a sad farewell to his new wife and family. He knew it would be harder for Bai-jian, as a new member of the Deng household, to adjust to living as an intimate stranger in the family, without her husband, and subject to her mother-in-law's wishes.

He set out for Guangzhou, accompanied by his brother, Wen-shi, and four young villagers who hoped to find better job opportunities in the outside world. When they arrived in Guangzhou, Wen-yi spent three days arranging for the young men to be placed as student soldiers in a military camp. Once Wen-yi reported for duty at the Academy he learned he had been promoted to first lieutenant, in charge of a group of cadets at the Academy. The cadets were smart, knowledgeable, and ambitious, quite different from the simple soldiers he had previously supervised as a platoon leader.

One day early in September, Wen-yi was inspecting his cadets on guard duty at the Nationalist Central Party Department in Guangzhou. He noticed a document on the bulletin board inviting cadets to interview for special studies in Moscow. The Russian Communist International (Comintern) had established training and schooling facilities in Moscow for the further development of selected young candidates from China. Visitors would be assigned either to the "military and aviation academies" or the "Sun Yat-sen University." This provided the Soviets with a great opportunity to indoctrinate the Chinese student with Lenin-Stalinist concepts. The Comintern had an important stake in influencing the outcome of the struggle between the Chinese Communist Party (CCP) and the right-wing Nationalist Party. Russia carefully kept its relationship with both groups. Many Soviet agents were sent to China to apply their policies to the Chinese Communist Party and to the country. The prospect of such an adventure excited Wen-yi. This was an opportunity to receive college-level training in new military techniques at the power center of Russia! However, the offer was for cadets only. Wen-yi ignored the restriction and decided to apply. The contingent to Russia would consist of three hundred recruits from Shanghai, Guangzhou, Tianjin, and Beiping. He passed two competitive exams, and was among the 300 applicants selected for the openings.

But a problem developed. The provost of the Whampoa Military Academy insisted Wen-yi should not have applied for the assignment without prior approval. He was in no mood to give it now. My father was angry and frustrated. He wanted the assignment. He turned to his mentor, Chiang Kai-shek, for assistance in obtaining a release from the Academy. Chiang quickly intervened in Wen-yi's behalf, and the obstacle was removed. However, Chiang had come to my father's assistance for reasons of his own. Chiang was suspicious of the intent of the staff at the politically-oriented Sun Yat-sen University. He was anxious to place someone loyal to him in Moscow to evaluate the situation. Wen-yi's appeal had come at an ideal time. Chiang instructed Wen-yi on the kind of information he wanted and urged Wen-yi to be thoughtful and clever. Wen-yi was assigned to Sun Yat-sen University.

Chapter 2

A General at 22!

My father left Whampoa for Moscow in November 1925. The group was delayed for almost a month in Guangzhou awaiting the ship that would take them on their journey. With much free time Wen-yi soon made many new friends and indulged himself in the many amusements offered by the city. By the time he finally boarded ship, he had squandered nearly all of his travel money. The ship docked for two days in Shantou for supplies. By coincidence, Chiang Kai-shek was in the port town attending to government matters. He invited the Russia-bound cadets to dine with him. Chiang took Wen-yi aside for quick instructions. When Wen-yi, embarrassed, informed Chiang that his funds were depleted, Kai-shek gave him 200 dollars for traveling expenditures.

Wen-yi began the long journey with a bit of homesickness. The Academy had become his home. The outside world appeared unfamiliar and strange. The sea journey took him north to Shanghai, Korea, and finally Vladivostok, a large port near Russia's border with China and North Korea.

Never had the group felt such an intense cold. They boarded an old Siberian train for the long journey to Moscow, making endless stops along the way. However, these were often welcome since the train was unheated and it was difficult to keep water from freezing. There was little to do to keep their minds off the numbing cold other than exchanging reading material and playing impromptu card games. Stops offered the opportunity to buy food and liquids, and above all, to use the station toilets. It took two weeks for the westbound train to reach its final destination. Finally, in late December, the train pulled into a somber Moscow Station. They were greeted by Mif Pavel, vice provost of the Sun Yat-sen University. After his brief welcome address, the group was loaded onto buses for the final short drive to dormitories where each would be assigned a room.

The students were divided into groups of 35-40, based principally on their ideological association. Wen-yi soon became one of the leaders of his conservative group. Food at the University was surprisingly good compared to that of the local population, varying between Russian and Chinese-style dishes. Each student was given a Russian name. My father was surprised to discover that Kai-shek's son, Chiang Ching-kuo, who had arrived a month earlier, had joined a Chinese Communist group.

Wen-yi's first impression of the city was one of fierce coldness. Snow and ice were everywhere. He had been raised in a semi-tropical climate, so the adjustment was difficult. He found the 30-minute walk from the dormitory to school and back each day in the frigid weather almost nightmarish. He told himself a good military person should be able to brave cold, heat, and hardship. The severe environment was truly a conditioning experience for him.

The curriculum at the University focused on economics, geography, politics, world revolutionary history, evolution, Nationalism, and Russian language. Classes were small, 16-18 students per class. Translators were provided for the classes. The learning process was effective, and most students progressed well.

The Comintern discouraged contact between Russian citizens and foreigners, including the Chinese students. The Russians treated foreigners with distrust and suspicion, and the Chinese in particular, with contempt. The situation was aggravated by serious ideological conflicts among the Chinese enclaves at the University. Conservative Nationalist members were in the minority compared to their Communist classmates. They became targets of intense recruitment to the Communist cause. This included threats, distortions, segregation, and isolation. Wen-yi, mindful of his mission and Chiang Kai-shek's admonition, took pains to present himself as politically neutral.

This impressed the Comintern officials who believed his sympathies were really with the Communists, and that his neutral demeanor was to avoid retribution from Nationalist students. His "reasonableness" made him popular with the sizeable Communist contingent. However Wen-yi, fiercely anti-Communist, was meeting secretly once or twice every week with a Nationalist committee with several cells, headed by He Zhong-han. My father served as one of the cell coordinators. Wen-yi knew he was in a dangerous position, but he felt an excitement mixed with fear. Two Nationalist students had been caught engaged in anti-Communist activity and were removed from the University to some undetermined fate. My father stayed busy and involved in many activities. He was elected to the student commune committee, and given the task of coaching the women's rifle team.

Wen-yi appeared to be popular among the few female students. He even had a casual affair with one of them. However, he missed his wife terribly. He wrote to her once a week expressing his love. He anxiously awaited her letters that never came. Friends observed his hurt and disappointment, and felt his wife Bai-jian was cold and unreasonable. They suggested Wen-yi forget her and be rid of her. Wen-yi continued to write faithfully. Unknown to Wen-yi and his friends, Bai-jian received each letter with joy and reread them endlessly. She wanted desperately to respond to each letter, but felt ashamed she could not express eloquently what she wanted to say. Her sense of inadequacy was misplaced, since she had grossly underestimated her ability to write an appealing letter. This would become evident in a later exchange of letters to Wen-yi and his friend Xiao Zan-yu.

Chiang Kai-shek Launches the First Northern Expedition

As the Chinese students were carrying out their studies and intrigues at Sun Yat-sen University, they were made aware by their teachers that Chiang Kai-shek had launched an expedition against the northern warlords on July 9, 1926. Chiang's Nationalist Army of 100,000 was outnumbered 5-to-1 by northern militarists. However, the warlord armies consisted largely of untrained, illiterate peasants and unemployed workers, poorly armed and without artillery. They were no match for Chiang's trained, disciplined troops. The expedition ended in a great military success for Chiang. But it had also intensified the sense of disunity between Communists and Nationalists, though they had been nominal allies in the campaign.

The liberal wing of the Nationalists was encouraged by Russian adviser Borodin to move the center of government north to the Communist-friendly area of Wuhan. This could be a major factor in the success of the Communist revolution. However, Chiang, who had now captured the city of Nanchang, was determined to make it the provisional capital, and ultimately Nanjing the permanent center of government. At this point, Russian General Galen, who had served Chiang so ably in the eastern and now northern campaigns, concluded he could no longer be associated with Chiang's anti-Communist determination. Their three-year association ended. Galen remained in Wuhan. Wang Jing-wei, Chiang's liberal competitor for leadership of the Nationalist Party, returned from Europe to establish the left wing of the Nationalist Party in Wuhan. The Chinese Communist leaders decided to form an association with Jing-wei, however reluctantly.

Wen-yi Returns to China with a Communist Group, Undercover

Suddenly, in January 1927, word spread that a contingent of 100 Communist Chinese students would be selected to return to China for a special assignment, led by Comintern agent M.N. Roy. Forty Chinese students from Sun Yat-sen University were selected, 37 Communists and three Nationalists. Wen-yi was astonished to learn he had been selected to be in this special group. He was now faced with the option of continuing his education at the University or becoming part of the Communist group selected for some unspecified mission. Mindful of his promise to Chiang, Wen-yi accepted the offer. He would try to learn as much as he could about the purpose of the mission.

This time the train trip to Vladivostok took only one week. Wen-yi learned with alarm that the group would be involved in some sort of "revolution" that would bring the Communist Party in control of China. What revolution? When? Where? At Vladivostok, they boarded ship for the journey home. During the sea voyage, he engaged in many "casual" conversations with members and group leaders, speculating on the nature of their mission. The Communist students were euphoric, certain they would play an important part in a revolutionary action whose success was inevitable. Gradually, the skimpy base of information began to take form. Wen-yi was shocked to learn his contingent was to function as a cadre leading a broad uprising by workers and Communist sympathizers in various cities in an attempt to take over the government! Wen-yi could hardly wait to pass the information on to senior Nationalist officials.

At last, after six days at sea, the ship arrived in Guangzhou. Wen-yi was fully aware of his precarious situation. If the Communists discovered his mission for Chiang Kai-shek, there would be severe repercussions for him and his family. If the Nationalists believed he had been turned by the Communists, the consequence would be no better. Wen-yi began to consider ways to slip away from the group, so he might alert Nationalist authorities about the Communist plan.

The Whampoa Academy staff and cadets, many of whom were Communists, prepared a reception for the returning comrades. There were speeches of welcome. Then, to Wen-yi's amazement, a Comintern official asked him to give a response of thanks on behalf of the returning contingent. "Why me, of all people?" Wen-yi wondered. Was it to flatter him into a stronger association with the Communist group? Or would a Whampoa graduate, who had been a Nationalist leader at Whampoa, now

23

speaking for a Communist group, sway some of the current Whampoa cadets? Carefully, Wen-yi gave a short, noncommittal "Thank you" for the cordial reception then sat down.

The contingent was scheduled to remain in Guangzhou for a week then move to Wuhan. As soon as possible, my father approached the provost of the Academy and summarized what he had learned. The provost agreed Wen-yi must not go to Wuhan. He must report his findings to the Nationalist authorities in Guangzhou.

Wen-yi quickly put his plan into action. To separate himself from his Communist group, he pretended to have fallen quite ill. Wen-yi had never appeared robust physically, and had had a record of illness. He was allowed to stay in Guangzhou temporarily, and plan to rejoin the group in Wuhan later. Free from the scrutiny of the Communist contingent, Wen-yi hid himself in a small hotel in Guangzhou. It was urgent he make contact with the Nationalist officials in Guangzhou to tell them what he had learned. The Communists were planning wide-scale riots to overthrow the Nationalist Government!

When the time came, Wen-yi reported his findings to officials gathered at the Home Command Headquarters of the Revolutionary Army in Guangzhou. His information was treated seriously. For security reasons, Wen-yi moved in with the Acting Chief of the Political Department of the Home Command Headquarters, Zeng Yang-fu. Zeng arranged briefing sessions for Wen-yi with the Nationalist leaders in Guangzhou. Among these were Qian Da-jun, Wen-yi's former teacher in Whampoa and now Commander of the 20th Division of the National Revolutionary Army. Wen-yi also met with Li Ji-shen, Chief-of-Staff and Acting Chief of the Home Command headquarters. The information and recommendations, including Wen-yi's, were sent to Chiang Kai-shek, who was still engaged in the Northern Expedition.

Wen-yi suddenly became an object of interest among his Nationalist contacts. He received several job offers. Zhongshan

University proposed an assistant professorship to do research in political and social science. Acting Chief Zeng Yang-fu put in a bid to hire him on staff in the Political Department of the Home Command Headquarters. Whampoa Military Academy offered Wen-yi the post of political section leader with the rank of lieutenant colonel! My father was wary of the job offer from the Academy, since it was heavily infiltrated with Communists.

Then Chiang Kai-shek trumped all other offers by appointing my father to dual positions as Chief of the Political Department of the Nationalist 20th Division, and Chief of the Political Department of Guangzhou Defense and Police Affairs with the rank of full Colonel, reporting to Commander Qian Da-jun. From 1st Lieutenant to Colonel!

Stunned, my father accepted the appointment, but not without trepidation. He could hardly believe this amazing turn of events...a colonel, at 22! He was also painfully aware of his inexperience in this work. He reported to his new job in mid-February 1927. The Nationalist Party had high expectations for him. The Communists had begun to place him under surveillance.

Wen-yi formed a tight surveillance network monitoring the increasing activities of Communist-led worker organizations.[1] He collected and analyzed incoming intelligence data, and passed summary reports to the division commander. Wen-yi and his operatives continued to collect a list of Communist members and sympathizers seen with worker and activist student groups, preparing for a future action. He participated in regular secret meetings with officials to establish strategies to counteract mounting unrest. In his new position, he made frequent reconnaissance visits throughout Guangzhou City. He felt the popular discontent simmering beneath the surface was about to erupt, openly and violently.

Wen-yi moved to the headquarters of Defense and Police Affairs, located in the center of the city, close to the pro-Communist labor union headquarters. He could hear the roar from the martial drills and exercises of hundreds of activists and union workers under the supervision of Communist agents. Intelligence information confirmed the Communists were plotting a riot in Guangzhou on April 16th. He urgently pressed his superiors for action guidelines.

Meanwhile, Chiang's Northern Expedition had resulted in a dazzling series of victories extending from July 1926 to March 1927. This placed the entire country south of the Yangtze River, including Wuhan, Nanjing, and Shanghai[2] within control of the Nationalist government. Chiang was now a national hero. The Communists, however, were convinced the loose organizations of Nationalists in the south were ripe for easy take-over. A massive gathering of peasants and laborers was planned on April 16th in key cities including Shanghai and Guangzhou. Under the pretense of celebrating the victory of the Northern Expedition, the Communists would overthrow the Chiang-controlled Nationalist government.

The Shanghai Insurgency

Chiang had been made aware of the gravity of the situation, based on intelligence received from several sources, including Wen-yi. His troops had occupied Nanjing and were now poised at the gates of Shanghai, intent on taking control of the city. There had been several general strikes and mass demonstrations by union workers and students, abetted by Communist officials. A very large demonstration had been planned for April 12. However, those plans were preempted by an attack on hundreds of Communists as well as workers by the Green Gang, a powerful underworld organization centered in Shanghai. The gang was a frequent ally of Chiang. The Communist Party called for a general strike as a protest against this anti-Communist coup. At noon, April 13, more than 100,000 workers filled the streets .[3] Chiang then turned his troops against the Communist-led workers, killing and imprisoning thousands of participants and bystanders. The purge persisted several days. Kai-shek, his army, and allies had caused one of the truly tragic events in the history of the civil war. Following the attacks, Kai-shek broke his alliance with the Communist Party, formed a Nationalist Chinese government with Nanjing as the capital, and started the golden ten years known as the Nanjing Decade.

Guangzhou

Meanwhile in Guangzhou, tens of thousands of peasants, laborers, and Communist Party members had been gathering in and around the city to display their power through open protests and demonstrations. This aggressive display reflected the confidence of the Communists that they would be successful. Since all major organizations in Guangzhou and Whampoa were well infiltrated with their people, the Communists did not expect any serious resistance from Nationalists.

However, the Nationalist Central Command Headquarters was ready to execute quickly the plan that had been developed to quell the Communists. General Qian Da-jun was placed in charge of military activities. It was a risky task, but the Nationalists had an advantage in their ability to coordinate their political and military forces speedily, and to provide flexibility of action.

The major concern, however, was the officer corps, which was infiltrated by left-wing elements. At the time, only the 59th Regiment of the 20th Division was stationed in Guangzhou. Regiment Commander Chiang Chao-xiong, a Whampoa first class graduate, was sympathetic to Communists, and would most likely not follow orders regarding the Purge. At General Qian's dinner meeting with officers, Wen-yi approached Chiang Chao-xiong to assess his position. He asked Chao-xiong now that the Purge had begun in Nanjing and Shanghai, how should they proceed in Guangzhou? Chao-xiong said, "Under no circumstances would we just kill the Communists." Wen-yi persisted, "What if the Communists started a riot to kill the Nationalists and overthrow the Party, how should we proceed then?" Chao-xiong responded, "That would not happen."

Chiang Chao-xiong's pro-Communist position was established. Commander Qian placed him under house arrest in the regiment, and assigned a loyal battalion commander to lead the military force in forestalling the uprising. Chiang Chao-xiong was later executed.

On the evening of April 12th, Commander Qian Da-jun met secretly with Wen-yi to firm up their strategic action plan. The search-and-arrest phase would be carried out by the network Wen-yi had painstakingly built in the past month. Military action would be led by General Li Ji-shen. An energized Wen-yi spent the entire night of April 12th contacting network leaders to develop lists of active Communists to be arrested. Action teams for the arrests were deployed to pre-assigned locations. In less than 24 hours the emergency plan was in place, and ready to be activated.

At 2:00 a.m. on April 14th, martial law was imposed on Guangzhou. Wen-yi's search-and-arrest action proceeded calmly but forcefully citywide. Over ten thousand Communists and workers were arrested within eight hours, and herded into eight theaters. Wen-yi led police and soldiers to the medical school and Hospital of Zhongshan University, where they arrested scores of high-level Communists. Although Wen-yi described the purge as anti-Communist, most of those arrested were probably workers and peasants who had been incited to demonstrate.

The military phase that followed was conducted with ruthless and bloody efficiency. General Li Chi-sen's military force subdued or gunned down those who actively resisted. The whole city was suddenly caught in an atmosphere of terror and disbelief! This was not what the workers had been expecting. A delegation of Soviet trade unionists en route to Hankuo arrived at Guangzhou on April 14. They reported that, on the following day, they witnessed raids on the trade unions, mass arrests, and executions in the streets carried out at the orders of General Li Ji-shen.[4] Many Communist and pro-Communist participants fled. The threat of rebellion was over and martial law was lifted. The Communist plan to overthrow the Nationalists was in shambles. Communist reports claimed Nationalist forces had killed 2100 Communists and labor activists, secretly executed another 100, and expelled over 2000.[5] Although the Communist Headquarters in Guangzhou was destroyed, the remaining Communists went underground and continued to pose problems for the Nationalists in Guangzhou. Gradually, news arrived of blows struck at the Communists in Ningbo, Fuzhou, Xiamen, and Santou.

Whampoa Purge

On orders from the Military Commission, various branch military training units in the provinces were dissolved and reconstituted at Whampoa. The Academy population increased to almost 10,000 including 1,000 Communists. Many of the political workers and instructors were Communist. Provost Fang Ding-ying was easygoing and tolerated military and political cadres for the Communist Party. On April 16, Xiong Xiong, Acting Chief of the Political Department, and other high-level Communist members boarded a steamboat in an attempt to escape. The boat was captured and Xiong was killed, leaving the Political Department without a chief. At 6:00 a.m. April 18 the entire complement in the Fort was corralled in the parade grounds. Communist cadets and staff members were segregated from Nationalists and imprisoned in concentration camps. Later, additional Communist members were arrested. Some escaped, as did many non-Communist cadets.

General at 22!

At the end of April 1927, Generalissimo Chiang Kai-shek, citing Deng Wen-yi's extraordinary contributions in the Guangzhou Purge and his avid anti-Communist activities, appointed him Assistant Chief and Acting Chief of the Political Department of Whampoa Military Academy with the rank of major general! This position was held by Zhou En-lai two short years earlier, and more recently by the now defunct Xiong.

From first lieutenant when Wen-yi left for Moscow in the winter of 1925, to colonel in February 1927, and now major general, at the age of twenty two!! Wen-yi was overwhelmed by the honor and responsibility. Now, more than ever, he was aware of his age, and his lack of knowledge and experience. He felt he was overrated, but did not dare say it. His request to turn down the assignment was denied. He recalled a Chinese saying: "Assuming a high position at a young age is not a blessing." For Wen-yi, the saying would become prophecy. It is likely Chiang had rewarded Wen-yi less for the efficient ways he had carried out his various missions than for the loyalty he had displayed from the beginning.

An anxious Wen-yi now faced the new task of providing a political education to 8,000 students in the Academy. The purge had, in large measure, removed 1000 cadets and instructors with Communist leanings, and arrested 400 Communist cadets. My father and his small staff found it strange to be working and living in a building consequently almost emptied of instructors. He now had the responsibility for rebuilding the Whampoa political curriculum and faculty population... but how? He spent many sleepless nights turning the question over in his mind. Finally, with his plan half-formed, he descended upon his first target, nearby Zhongshan University. Wen-yi aggressively recruited faculty and students members. To his delight, each group eagerly accepted the opportunity to be at the prestigious Academy. He asked his new faculty to develop the curriculum and produce political literature and booklets. Luckily, the students and instructors were young, competent, and passionate about succeeding in their assignments. A solid core for the Political Department had been established.

My father gave lectures at several classes and held regular open discussions with the student body. He initiated two magazines and was a regular contributor to Whampoa and Party periodicals. He wrote a book entitled *"Questions on the Chinese Revolution and People's Livelihood."* The book's introduction was written by Dai Chi-tao, scholar and president of Zhongshan University. The book carried the cover signature of Chiang Kai-shek. Wen-yi next opened the Whampoa Bookstore in Guangzhou City. Persistent insecurity drove him to work feverishly to correct what he regarded as his "many shortcomings," although he had earned the respect of the Academy. My father would later say his role in re-establishing the Whampoa Political Department had been one of his truly satisfying accomplishments.

My Mother Bai-jian

Wen-yi's young bride, 16-year-old Bai-jian, had remained in Liling. To fill the void of her absent husband she busied herself taking care of the family elders and caring for the young children. Her status in the village was enhanced by her husband's position and the money he sent home regularly. However, people were also impressed with Bai-jian's intelligence and selflessness.

Wen-yi wrote to Bai-jian regularly. She received the letters eagerly and treasured them. However, she continued not to respond though she knew her husband would be very disappointed. She confided her problem to her mother, who vehemently disagreed with her overly modest perception of herself. Her mother had observed Bai-jian addressing groups of villagers passionately, and eloquently explaining the meaning of Sun Yat-sen's "Three People's Principles" and the aims of the Nationalist Party.

Bai-jian decided to return to the seventh grade, then complete eighth grade in order to hone her writing skills. She became increasingly involved in revolutionary work, organizing groups of youth, peasants, and even elder people to the Nationalist banner. She participated at political meetings, often disguised as a male in order to hear the views expressed.

When my mother received a letter from her husband, now established in Guangzhou, beckoning her to join him, she was ecstatic. She set off on the difficult trip accompanied by her father-in-law and several villagers. The group finally arrived at Whampoa in mid-July 1927. At last, she was reunited with her husband. She stared, finding it hard to believe this dashing, energetic young General before her was the sick, helpless man she had nursed back to health. She laughed and clapped her hands with tears in her eyes. Seeing the tears, Wen-yi struggled to maintain his composure. Chinese custom did not encourage open demonstrations of intimacy. Wen-yi reached for his wife's hand and held it, tightly and awkwardly. His father beamed happily at the couple and promised himself he would make a special offering to Buddha for helping him select this young lady for his son.

The couple settled into comfortable quarters provided by the Academy. Wen-yi and Bai-jian finally had their honeymoon. Bai-jian became pregnant almost immediately. Wen-yi enjoyed the comfort of family life. His circle of friends liked and quickly accepted Bai-jian. My mother wished this would never change. But she knew that would not be.

Chapter 3

Wen-yi and the Bandits

As a result of the country-wide purge of Communists, the left wing of the Nationalists in Wuhan headed by Wang Jing-wei, set out to expel Chiang as the commander-in-chief and from all other positions. In turn, Chiang established the Nationalist government capital at Nanjing.

With the aid of his new German military adviser, Colonel Max Bauer, Chiang Kai-shek established a branch Central Military Academy in the new capital of Nanjing. The Academy would be staffed with many German instructors, emphasizing modern technology and military tactics. Since the Whampoa operation would be transferring to Nanjing, Chiang felt it would be fitting to hold the graduation exercises of the current Whampoa class at the new Central Military Academy. Chiang instructed Wen-yi to lead the cadets to Nanjing for the event to take place on August 15. The cadets were happy to be leaving Whampoa after the grim events of past weeks, when Communist students had been singled out for detention and even execution during the purges at Guangzhou.

My father arrived at Nanjing with my mother and the graduating cadets several days before the ceremonies. As they settled in to wait for the big day, Wen-yi soon became aware that war tensions were building near the capital.

In Wuhan, Wang Jing-wei's situation was bleak. He had great difficulty raising funds, and he had a limited military force. His hoped-for alliance with warlord Feng Yu-xiang had been thwarted by a generous bribe to Feng from Chiang.[1] His only recourse was to unite the Wuhan government with Nanjing on the condition that Chiang step down as the head of government. Chiang, threatened by the forces of warlord Sun Chuang-fong and under pressure to resign by Guangxi leaders Li Zong-ren and Bai Chong-xi,[2] had agreed to do so, though he

33

regarded this merely as a strategic short-term move to secure a longer-term strengthening of power.

One morning a somber Chiang summoned my father to his quarters. He told Wen-yi he would soon be resigning. He urged Wen-yi to return to his post at Whampoa immediately after the graduation ceremony to help maintain order during the current unstable situation. On August 12, Kai-shek publicly announced his decision to resign. He then retreated to his home in Xikou. A pall fell over the cadet group. They felt as though their Leader was abandoning them. Who would now be in charge of assigning their positions after graduation? My father was gravely concerned the Nationalist Party would rupture without Chiang.

The graduation exercises were gloomy. War clouds were gathering and Chiang was gone. But the uncertain future of the cadets ended abruptly with the news that warlord Sun Chuan-fong, encouraged by the unstable political situation in Nanjing, had moved his army to the Yangtze River, threatening Nanjing. The newly graduated 5th class was drafted into units of the Nationalist 1st and 7th Corps as platoon leaders. Wen-yi assisted with the assignments. His duties completed, he and his wife began their journey south to Guangzhou. They saw frenzied activity as military forces deployed to strategic positions in preparation for battle.

On August 25, Sun Chuan-fong's 20,000 troops crossed the Yangtze River and launched an all-out attack on the Nationalist troops. After five days of see-saw battles, a furious counterattack by the Nationalists and Guangxi armies routed the warlord army and sent it in wild retreat across the Yangtze.[3] Casualties on both sides were very high. My father was deeply saddened to learn that half of the graduating cadets had been killed or injured in battle.

Wen-yi's Bandit Roundup - A Dark Comedy

When Wen-yi and Bai-jian returned to Whampoa in September 1927, the Military Academy was in disarray. With

Chiang in exile, dissension among senior officials grew rapidly. The local Nationalist government in Guangzhou was unstable. The future of Whampoa and its remaining cadets was blighted. With Chiang's approval, Whampoa Provost Fang Ding-yin had been reorganizing the entire personnel into the 13th Army Corps, with Fang as corps commander. The corps had room for another division. Since Wen-yi's future was now undefined, he became restless and was tempted to apply for the open position of division commander, a move encouraged by Corps Commander Fang. Wen-yi decided to recruit a sufficient force to complete the division.

He had learned of bandit leaders in the provinces who had shown interest in joining the revolution. Recruiting and converting bandit groups was encouraged by the government. Wen-yi was intrigued by this admittedly chancy opportunity. He had been told by several fellow officers that there were large bandit armies on the border of Hunan and Guangdong provinces. Groups varied in size from dozens to hundreds, and in some cases, several thousand members, organized as armies. Many of these had received training and decent weaponry. When the situation was unfavorable for banditry, they allowed themselves to be recruited into army units, whether government or warlord. It was also not unusual for army deserters or discharged soldiers to join bandit ranks. The larger groups often exercised authority in the locales near their headquarters. Bandits offered protection for money, pillaged villages, and kidnapped wealthy individuals for ransom, with drastic outcomes if payment was not received.

Wen-yi presented his recruitment proposal to General Fang, who readily approved the mission. Wen-yi was promised the new division commander position if he succeeded. He resigned from his job in the Political Department and went forth on his new, dangerous adventure. His anticipation was mixed with a feeling of guilt that he was leaving his pregnant wife and a happy family life again, so soon. He told himself personal feelings must not stand in the way of duty for the Revolution.

Meanwhile, Wen-yi's father had decided to return to Hunan. Wen-yi and Bai-jian converted their savings of $5,000 into gold nuggets, and sewed them into his father's long gown to assure his safety on the road. The money enabled my grandfather to buy several acres of farmland and build a comfortable house in the country. My great-grandparents and the whole family were able to enjoy unaccustomed comfort, thanks to their kind, successful family member. Perhaps this helped my father make peace with his sacrifices.

Prior to his journey my father received promises from friends that they would look after Bai-jian in his absence. Early in November 1927, accompanied by a small team of three armed aides, three thousand dollars, and the promise of more if progress were made, Wen-yi began his expedition filled with a sense of mission. The team took a train north to Shaoguan, then made a two-day trek to Lechang, a border town in Guangdong Province where bandits were active. Shortly after he arrived, Wen-yi learned of a large bandit group in the area, led by Hu Feng-zhang. He had also been told of another large band headed by Xu Han-chen, operating in the province. Each band was said to have over a thousand men, and nearly as many rifles. The bandits occasionally fought each other. Wen-yi sent two aides to the headquarters of the first bandit, Hu, to request a meeting.

The bandit chief asked Wen-yi to meet him at his camp on November 20. Wen-yi and two assistants walked ten miles to the camp, escorted by Hu's rough guides. My father noticed bandits carrying rifles were following them at a distance throughout the trek. On arrival he was greeted by Hu and 200 bandits. The headquarters was arranged like a small fortress in the mountain, surrounded by barriers. The bandit chief was a muscular man in his fifties with hawk-like features. He had a black mustache and intelligent eyes. Hu observed the youthful Wen-yi with a baleful, unwavering stare. His attitude changed, slightly, when he learned of Wen-yi's rank as General. After listening carefully to Wen-yi's proposal, Hu stated he had over 2,000 people, enough to form two regiments. He said his band would join the Nationalist ranks, with several conditions. First, he would be appointed brigade commander. Second, no commitment would be made until he had received funds for uniforms and food as well as an official document regarding his rank.

An excited Wen-yi returned to his lodging late in the afternoon, and sent a report summarizing the outcome of his conversation to the Guangzhou authorities. He requested official acceptance of the conditions and delivery of the funds as quickly as possible. In the meantime he met twice more with Hu, whom he now thought of as "the old hawk," to discuss details of their agreement. Wen-yi felt it would be best to inform him of his plan to visit another gypsy band to the north. The leader clearly was unhappy, but said nothing.

Wen-yi and his aides traveled to Pinshi, a prominent trading town near the border of Hunan and Guangdong Provinces. It was not difficult to learn the location of the camp of Xu Han-chen and his bandit army. Wen-yi sent two aides to establish contact with Xu, and request a meeting. The bandit leader agreed to talk with Wen-yi. Xu turned out to be a younger man, tall, with a narrow, bony frame. He commanded an army of over 2,000 men. Shrewd, piercing eyes gave him the menacing look of a young fox. My father was momentarily amused at his own private names for the two bandit leaders, as the "Old Hawk" and "Young Fox." He and the "Young Fox" developed a rapid rapport. Wen-yi presented the same proposal he had worked out with the "Old Hawk." The young leader's band would be formed into two regiments with the Young Fox as brigade commander in the new Nationalist Army Division. The leader told Wen-yi that, on receipt of initial funding, food supplies, and official status from the Central Government, his brigade would be ready for action by mid-December. An ecstatic Wen-yi wired these favorable results to his superior.

My father suggested the Young Fox move his people to Pinshi. Unfortunately, Wen-yi had not done his homework sufficiently. He was unaware Pinshi was part of the Old Hawk bandits' territory, which they claimed and guarded jealously against any intrusion. The Young Fox was happy to move his men into enemy territory with permission.

Wen-yi had still not received a response or funds from Guangzhou, perhaps because of the prevailing state of disorder. He was forced to buy supplies from the Pinshi trading office with a promissory note for reimbursement by the government. Then, the Old Hawk heard the other bandit group was in his territory. He went into a violent rage. His rival and enemy, in Pinshi, without his permission! Never! This would be a great opportunity to do serious damage to the enemy interlopers. He immediately began preparations to attack the Young Fox bandits. He sent word to the town merchants not to give any supplies to the interlopers. My father instantly noticed the change throughout the village. The trading office refused to provide the promised supplies. The windows and doors of every house and shop were shut and locked. Wen-yi broke out in a sweat. He became aware of the enormity of his blunder.

Pinshi faced the river on one side, with mountains at its back and a narrow street from one end of the village to the other. The Old Hawk could easily encircle the village. There was no escape for the rival group, only death or captivity. When Wen-yi realized the potential disaster, he urged the Young Fox to move his band immediately out of Pinshi to the next town in Hunan. Swift action was automatic for the bandits. They were out of Pinshi by 10:00 p.m. After a two-hour trek the band collected on a mountaintop to await developments in Pinshi.

The Old Hawk's bandits moved silently to surround the dark, quiet village illuminated only by a pale moon. Troops were also placed at both ends of the narrow road through the village. The silence held. Then, suddenly, at 3:00 a.m., heavy gunfire could be heard from the village. The bandits were, unknowingly, shooting at each other. By early morning Wen-yi received a report that the Old Hawk had deployed 1,200 people in the attack on Pinshi, killing over 50 of his own people. Ten villagers also suffered casualties. The Young Fox's troops were unscathed. Wen-yi sent a message to the Old Hawk chastising him for attacking a group that would be part of the same division.

The Young Fox and his band retreated to their headquarters at Linwu, with supplies commandeered from local civilians. The days went by with no messages or funds from Guangzhou. On December 4 the Young Fox and his leaders had a private council of war. They decided they had been deceived. Wen-yi and his men would be executed. Late that afternoon an informant told my father of the decision. Wen-yi decided it was time for him and his team to vanish quietly and without delay. They made their way, mostly by foot, to a town 70 miles from their point of escape, occupied by a Nationalist brigade. Commander Xu Ke-xiang and his 500 troops gave the travelers a cordial welcome. Wen-yi's relief at their escape was overshadowed by his feeling of ineptness and inadequacy in planning and receiving proper assurance of support from headquarters, leading to this tragic, comical outcome.

Guangzhou Uprising

Wen-yi arrived in Guangzhou on December 8, 1927, and suffered another blow. His home was empty. None of the neighbors knew where Bai-jian had gone. Wen-yi walked through the streets of Guangzhou for the entire day looking for her with no success. He had difficulty contacting friends to make inquiries. What he saw were Communist fliers and posters all over the city. People in the stores and on the street were clearly fearful. The signs were ominous and irrefutable. A Communist rebellion was imminent. But he no longer knew the Nationalist people in charge. He could only be a bystander at this time. His immediate alarm and concern was for the safety of his wife. On the afternoon of the 10th, after two frustrating days, he finally ran into his good friend Qu Feng-wu, a political instructor at the Academy. To his amazed joy, Qu told him Bai-jian was now at his home with his wife. Friends had informed Bai-jian the situation in Guangzhou was perilous, especially for senior Nationalist officials like Wen-yi and his family. My mother immediately decided to move to Qu's house, located in a nearby quiet alley. The men hurried to Qu's home. There were rejoicing and expressions of gratitude at the reunion. Signs of an insurrection were now clear. The streets were in turmoil. Any thought of escaping on the afternoon of the 10th was out of the question.

Then, at 3:30 a.m. the following morning, they were awakened by gunshots. They heard heavy firing from the direction of the North Gate. Soon the heavy boom of cannons and sharp rifle fire erupted amid the screams of people. The two couples moved to an upstairs room to observe the battle. Over the next two hours the insurgents launched a furious attack on the Nationalist military warehouse inside the North Gate, removing weapons and ammunition. A small group of Nationalist defenders fought back frantically. The insurgents killed civilians and defenders almost indiscriminately. Houses and buildings were set on fire. The huddled four could hear screaming, crying for help, and pleading for mercy along the street. Factory owners and merchants were placed in chains, and dragged through the street. The two couples climbed to the rooftop and watched as the military warehouse burned. The fire was about two blocks away and spreading. The Qu's wanted to abandon the house. Wen-yi told them it would be safer to stay on the rooftop. They would leave if the fire became an imminent threat. There they remained, alert for danger. Shortly after daybreak, the fire and firing of weapons appeared to diminish.

Heavy firing moved toward the downtown area. The two couples, exhausted, crawled inside and slept fitfully three or four hours. Then Wen-yi climbed back to the rooftop to evaluate the situation. Amidst smoke and burning houses, he saw the red Communist flag with sickle and ax flying atop the

Provincial Capitol Building. The Communists had declared the city was now in the control of the "Guangzhou Soviet Government." However, my father noticed street fighting was still going on; people were waiting for the Nationalist army to arrive. He returned to the three who waited below. He recommended they stay put; the Nationalist Army would surely arrive soon to join with the existing force in the city.

On the evening of December 11, two friends from the downtown area came by to give a brief description of the war zone. Nationalist troops had been attacked at several sites and were still engaged in fierce fighting. There were rumors the central troops of the 4th Army under Hsueh Yueh outside Guangzhou had united with the 5th Corps of Henan and were rushing toward Guangzhou to join the fray. Wen-yi and the others were exultant.

The rumors proved correct. In the morning of December 12th, street fighting became more severe. The Nationalist troops had arrived downtown and were counterattacking. By noon, the Communist red flag over the Capitol building had disappeared. Fighting continued through the day. Finally, the fury abated and the city became quiet with only sporadic gunshots. The Communist uprising had ended in failure. Nationalist forces had moved quickly to suppress the rebellion.

By the morning of the 13th, order was gradually being established in Guangzhou. The Communist 4th Army was retreating in disarray, leaving local insurgents to their own fate. It was a cruel fate. The victors inflicted punishment in kind. Wen-yi ventured out to inspect the devastation and found the Guangzhou he knew turned into a living hell. The streets were littered with human and animal bodies, amidst the debris of destroyed houses. Caravans of 20-30 sanitary carts, each piled with 30-50 corpses, moved silently to disposal pits outside the city. The death toll for the Communist troops was placed at 6,000. Civilian casualties, including workers and Communist sympathizers, were even greater due to savage retribution.

The signs of brutality my father had witnessed on both sides caused him recurring nightmares for a long period of time. He learned he had been in greater peril than he had realized. Interrogation of prisoners disclosed that the Communists were aware Wen-yi had returned to Guangzhou, and had dispatched twenty agents to find and kill him.

The fateful year of 1927 was drawing to a close. This bloody, eventful year, with its countless deaths of participants and citizenry, had brought a series of victories for Chiang, and had rendered the Communists perilously close to extinction.[4] The Nationalists broke off relations with Russia and with the Comintern. The violence had resulted in broad alienation of the masses toward Chiang and his government, largely isolated from the masses.[5]

Chiang was gone, in temporary exile. Wen-yi was now without a formal assignment. He was restless and depressed from the bandit recruitment debacle and the horror of the Guangzhou savagery. His thoughts turned to Shanghai, as did those of other Whampoa colleagues, as a place for much needed "rest and recreation." This was insensitive and inappropriate behavior for a "loving husband" whose wife was in the late stages of her pregnancy; however, this did not deter Wen-yi. He told his wife Bai-jian to remain in Guangzhou. He left for Shanghai as the year ended.

Shanghai had become a magnet for many senior Nationalist officers bent on relaxation. It was the most important cultural and commercial center in Asia. Under the influence of international settlements that dominated the scene, Shanghai offered a heady combination of hedonism with European architecture and flair, side by side with reminders of the ancient past. Wen-yi joined two Whampoa classmates who were in Shanghai to pursue the many pleasures of the town. They were dazzled by the bawdy lifestyle offering entertainment of every variety from gambling, prostitution, and restaurants, to jazz clubs and opium dens. Along the Bund (main drag), was the riverside Peace Hotel on the western bank of the Huangpu

River, with its fancy restaurants. Cabarets featured jazz groups playing Dixieland and "old-style" jazz. The ambiance was reminiscent of Paris, Chicago, or New York. Little wonder that Nationalist officials, my father included, found it difficult to leave this "fairyland" to once again face the realities of war. My father plunged easily into rounds of gambling and womanizing. He found it easy to attract the attention of beautiful women, and considered this an entitlement. He remained in the city for a month. Then, word flew throughout the city that Chiang Kai-shek was back as head of the Nationalist government. Wen-yi's leader was back! It was now the beginning of 1928. Wen-yi hurried back to Nanjing.

Meanwhile, Bai-jian had remained in Guangzhou, restless, alone, and pregnant. She could not help feeling hurt, with a strong sense of abandonment as my father sought his pleasure in Shanghai at this moment of her pregnancy. A belatedly concerned Wen-yi wrote to his wife, urging her to move to the more peaceful Hangzhou and await his return. When she read the letter, she dutifully packed their belongings and traveled by boat from Guangzhou to Shanghai, and then by train to Hangzhou. It was a difficult journey since she was in her eighth month of pregnancy. On arrival in Hangzhou she rented a small place. Physical and mental hardship finally took their toll. She had told herself that, as the daughter of revolution, she could handle all domestic matters alone, without raising concerns to distract her husband. But she could endure the hardship no more. Stifling her resentment and anger, she wrote a polite letter to her husband describing her trip and delicate condition. She told him it was time for him to be at her side.

Chapter 4

Chiang vs. the Warlords and Wen-yi

The year 1928 began on a high note for Chiang. He was back in Nanjing one month after his marriage with Miss Soong Mei-ling. During his exile, the government had appeared rudderless, with many powerful factions in Guangzhou, Nanjing, and North China maneuvering for their own advantages. A strong leader was needed to bring the factions into line. Who but Chiang Kai-shek? The Nationalist Party asked him to reassume his place as commander-in-chief and chairman of the military council. The leftist Wuhan government was now reunited with the Nanjing government under Chiang's leadership. Its leader, Wang Jing-wei, had resigned from his position in December. There were many things for Chiang to attend to. He had to reorganize the government and plan for resumption of the Northern Expedition. He also felt that now was the time to strike hard at the Communists with Borodin gone and the Communist Party in disarray.

However, Chiang was not in a benevolent mood when my father finally reported to him. Wen-yi was immediately subjected to an angry tirade for abandoning his duties to dally in Shanghai. Chiang told Wen-yi he was demoted to lieutenant-colonel, with a substantial downgrade in pay. Wen-yi was assigned as one of six staff assistants who attended to myriad details in planning the next expedition, including logistics, liaison with senior officers in the armies, maintaining records of meetings, and other details. Wen-yi was less dismayed by his demotion than by the nature of the work and the substantial cut in salary. The job was not demanding of either his time or skills.

My father had been in his new job for two weeks when he received a letter from Bai-jian, in Hangzhou. He became alarmed as he read of her delicate physical and mental state. He requested and received a week's leave from his new assignment and hurried to Hangzhou. The day before his arrival, Bai-jian gave birth to a baby boy, but the infant died shortly after birth. The midwife felt the hardships from Bai-jian's travels and exertions in Hangzhou had contributed to the death. When Wen-yi arrived home he found Bai-jian crying inconsolably for her dead child and herself. Wen-yi felt a strong sense of guilt and shame. He told himself this was his doing. If he had come home sooner to take care of her, the baby might have been saved.

It was the Chinese New Year. The young couple sat together, silent, each with tears and their private thoughts. Too soon, it was time for my father to bid my mother farewell, promising they would, very soon, be together again. With a heavy heart he returned to Nanjing.

Chiang's Second Northern Campaign

With Chiang Kai-shek busily engaged with the Second Northern Expedition there was little for Wen-yi and other staff members to do. Restless, my father began to look for other opportunities. During Chiang's exile, one thousand Whampoa cadets of the 6th and 7th Class had deserted turbulent Guangzhou, and were loitering in Shanghai, Nanjing, and Hangzhou with no assignments. Chiang had asked General He Zhong-han to establish a temporary military reception and training camp in Hangzhou to regroup these cadets and train them into battle-ready officers. Zhong-han asked my father to serve as political chief for the camp.[1]

Wen-yi eagerly accepted this opportunity, especially since he knew many of the students. More importantly, it would enable him to be with Bai-jian in Hangzhou. He wrote a letter to Chiang, informing him of He Zhong-han's offer. He asked permission to be re-assigned to duty at Hangzhou. In mid-April 1928, in his usual impetuous manner, Wen-yi decided to leave for Hangzhou without waiting for official permission. He had only been in his current assignment for five weeks, so approval was no certainty. This "impertinence" could well have gotten him into trouble. Fortunately, Kai-shek was deeply involved with the campaign, and quickly gave permission. Wen-yi rented a larger house in Hangzhou and soon rediscovered how much he enjoyed family life with his wife. The setting was ideal at this point in his life. The beautiful West Lake near his home was surrounded by nearby hills ringing with the sound of temple bells. This became for him a spiritual retreat from the turbulence of Nanjing and hedonistic life of Shanghai. He even had time to fish with some of the students or take little boat rides with my now happy mother. For eight months he was able to enjoy his job and his idyllic life.

By the end of 1928, the unification of the government seemed to be in hand. The Nanjing government received prompt international recognition as the sole legitimate government of China. But storm clouds loomed on the horizon. The Northern Expedition had seriously depleted the treasury. Chiang had lost face and gained the anger of the people by allowing Japanese forces to intrude into Shandong Province unchallenged. The Central government had recommended he proceed with plans to reduce the size of the army and to restructure and unify the military under control of the Nanjing government. Chiang moved quickly to downsize his large army into a smaller, better disciplined and trained body along the lines of the German model, with the assistance of Bauer and other German officers. Surplus troops would be used in building up the country's infrastructure.

But Chiang had made a serious mistake. Instead of proceeding slowly and diplomatically, he had moved quickly in demanding compliance by powerful warlord allies, who were not prepared to give up authority or military power to the Nationalist government. One erstwhile ally, Li Zong-ren, acting as head of the Guangxi Political Council, fired the Hunan governor for being too loyal to Chiang Kai-shek. The Nanjing government immediately overruled Li and reinstated the governor.

The Guangxi Clique revolted against Chiang in March 1929. Nationalist 46th corps commander Fang Ding-ying was given the mission of suppressing this rebellion. Wen-yi was appointed political chief of the 46th Corps with the restored rank of major general. My father accepted this post with a mixture of excitement and trepidation. His only prior battle experience had been as a platoon leader in the Eastern Campaign when he was barely graduated from Whampoa Academy. He vacated his position in Hangzhou, bade farewell to his family, and rushed to Nanjing. There he formed a "Political Cadre" of some 20 members from the Central Political Department. The group traveled by boat up the Yangtze River to the corps headquarters in Wuchang. Wen-yi met with Fang Ding-ying, the officers, and the existing political cadres. Commander Fang had been one of Wen-yi's instructors at Whampoa. My father set up the political department, forming a network to gather and analyze enemy intelligence, and helping prepare troops for battle.

The Nationalist Army advanced westward toward the Guangxi Army without opposition. Wen-yi rode a small black horse at the rear of the troop columns, according to military protocol. Commander Fang rode a huge brown mare in front. The trek proceeded without incident, except for a momentary episode in which the corps commander's mare, in heat, began a constant neighing. Wen-yi's horse bolted and galloped crazily through the marching troops toward the mare. When my father's horse was within 2-3 feet of the mare, the commander's guards grabbed at the reins and forced the horse to stop. My father had been holding on with a death clutch.

The Nationalist troops arrived at their destination, ready for battle. However, faced with a superior force bearing down on him, Guangxi leader Li Zong-ren retreated to the safety of his turf. The Nationalist Army returned to Nanjing.

Acting on the recommendations of his German adviser, General Bauer, Chiang pared the 46th Corps down to two Divisions, 10th and 44th. Wen-yi was transferred to the 44th

Division headed by Wan Xuan-wu, who sympathized with warlord Feng Yu-xiang, the "Christian General." My father was not happy. He decided to survey the troops personally. What he found was not encouraging. Wen-yi's 44th Division was made up of a polyglot of regular Nationalists, a large number of converted Communists, and a dismaying number of warlord Feng's old troops who had little familiarity with or interest in revolutionary political issues. To make matters worse, the northern warlord faction and the southern, mostly government troops, regarded each other with disdain. Northerners referred to southerners as "barbarians," while southerners called all northerners "slobs." As Wen-yi made inspection rounds on his little horse, he heard the contemptuous whispers, "Here comes the little barbarian!" He pretended not to hear such remarks since he knew they applied to all troops from the south.

Then, in May 1929, warlord Feng Yu-xiang joined the revolt against Chiang and the Nanjing government with his 300,000 man Northwest Army. Another major western expedition was now imminent. General Fang Ding-ying was placed in command of three divisions including the 44th to meet the threat. My father became increasingly concerned with the ominous undertone of hostility among the northern troops in his division. When he learned his 44th Division would lead the attack, he immediately conveyed his concerns to the corps commander urging the unreliable 44th Division be moved to a less prominent role. His view was considered but rejected. The troops proceeded to west Henan.

When the 44th Division reached their appointed position, the suspect division commander Wan ordered the division to detour toward a small town, Lushan, away from the battle site. Wen-yi's intelligence officers reported that the bulk of the troops in the division would refuse to fight the warlord Feng. My father sent two urgent telegrams to headquarters, reporting that the loyalty of the troops was in doubt and requesting an immediate change in plans. He received no reply.

When the unit arrived at Lushan, Commander Wan and his chief-of-staff called all senior officers and staff to a nearby church hall for a strategy meeting. When everyone had assembled, the group was surrounded by a platoon of armed military guards. All weapons were collected from the officers. The doors were locked and guarded. No communication was allowed. Wen-yi and many of the officers were now captives of mutineers. They remained without communication for three days. Wen-yi felt a deep responsibility for this debacle.

On the fourth day of their captivity, the officers broke out of their prison. The division had vanished. Wen-yi later learned that on the day of their breakout, Nationalist forces had launched an attack on the warlord army at West Henan, forcing Feng's troops to retreat. The captives were now free but did not know where the main force was. The officers had no choice but to find their way back to Wuhan.

A dispirited Wen-yi dreaded the inevitable meeting with Kai-shek. He would request due punishment for being captured, then resign from the military. Wen-yi told himself he would like to resume his education in Japan, or devote himself to his publishing business. He decided first to return to his hometown, Liling, to spend some family time at the new country house.

Early in 1930, Wen-yi and his wife returned to Nanjing. Bai-jian had recently given birth to their second child. The new baby was left in Liling with his grandparents, a common custom in China. Wen-yi was too embarrassed and intimidated to see Chiang, now Generalissimo. However, he was spotted by Chiang Kai-shek one day, and the dreaded moment was at hand. Chiang summoned Wen-yi and inquired where he had been, and why he had not reported in after the West Henan Battle. My father gave Chiang a brief summary of the events and mutiny within the 44th Division. "What does it matter that you reported the possible mutiny of hostile troop factions?" Chiang yelled. "As political chief, it was your responsibility to put down any such actions. It proves you are incompetent!" He berated Wen-yi, enumerating a list of what he perceived to be my father's many faults.

A chastened but equally temperamental Wen-yi retorted, "I was promoted to senior officer beyond my years by you. My military field experience was only in the Eastern Campaign. Since I am too young and inexperienced to handle such military assignments, I would like to go back to school to learn more." Chiang was not used to this kind of talk from a subordinate. He roared, "You are going nowhere, Deng Wen-yi, except where I can keep an eye on you! Why don't you do some real work? Request denied! You'll wait for my orders!"

A week later, Wen-yi was once again demoted to lieutenant colonel! He was assigned as one of Kai-shek's staff secretaries with a drastic reduction in pay from $500 to $170 a month! Wen-yi forced himself to stay calm. He understood why he was being punished. This was not what he wanted. But he also remembered his wife Bai-jian had told him quietly, but firmly, "For once, keep your mouth shut, and do the job. You have already dangerously tried the patience of the Leader."

For the next six months, Wen-yi and Bai-jian had difficulties making ends meet. It was especially hard after living more comfortably as a general for the past three years. Even more degrading, he now had no staff, adjutant, or orderly. He had to do everything for himself.

Whenever Generalissimo attended a meeting or delivered speeches at various sites, Wen-yi, as a staff secretary, was required to be present to produce a record of the event. Staff secretaries had to find room in one of the very few escorting automobiles, competing for space with guards, adjutants, and others. One day, Wen-yi found himself stranded when the escort cars left without him. He was not present to record comments or actions arising from the event. He slipped deeper into Kai-shek's doghouse. Chiang again accused Wen-yi of being lazy and not conscientious. Wen-yi was too proud to mention he could not get a ride.

Little did he know the Leader observed him carefully... One day Chiang abruptly summoned Wen-yi to his office. With no preliminaries he said to Wen-yi, "I want you to be my personal secretary. Do you think you can do the tasks required without causing problems for me or for yourself?" An astounded Wen-yi told his Leader he would do the very best he could. Among his new tasks was to maintain Chiang's schedule, and arrange and record the outcome of his meetings and lectures. He was also responsible for editing and issuing printed documents or news items from Kai-shek's office. He was given two clerks and a scribe to assure that reports were produced in a timely and accurate manner. My father was now a full colonel.

Central Plains War (May-November 1930)

Chiang's recent actions to unify military forces under the Central government caused three enraged warlords, Feng Yu-xiang, Li Zong-ren, and Yan Xu-shan, to form a coalition to oppose him. Yan Xu-shan, commander-in-chief of the powerful coalition, demanded the resignation of Chiang Kai-shek, which was promptly refused. The coalition severed relations with Chiang. Zhang Xue-liang (the Young Marshal) was invited to join the coalition but declined. In February 1930 the warlord coalition army, all former Chiang allies in the Northern Expedition, formed an alliance with Wang Jing-wei and the left wing of the Nationalists. Their armies mounted a strong, coordinated attack on Chiang and his Central Army. Chiang had assembled and deployed an army of 300,000 troops. The battle raged across five provinces, each side experiencing victories and defeats.

Chiang and his staff, including Wen-yi, went to Kaifeng, in Henan Province, to direct the battle against Feng's army, the largest among the warlord coalition. The armies fought a see-saw war of attrition in Henan. Chiang directed operations from aboard an armored train that moved frequently between the battle front and the mobile garrison near the railway station outside Kaifen. Wen-yi was at Chiang's side to render whatever assistance was required.

At one point in the battle, Feng's troops almost captured the Generalissimo during a battlefront inspection. Chiang's mobile garrison around the railway station was well guarded by five trains and a security company encircling the spot where the command armored train rested. The area was considered relatively safe. However, one night in mid-July, rifle fire erupted near the railway station. Alarmed security guards immediately positioned themselves around the armored train. Weapon fire became heavy as the exterior security guards returned fire. Terrified civilians ran aimlessly in and out of the train station. Train whistles screamed signals to clear the way for emergency departure. The place became a scene of noise and confusion. My father was in the third car behind the leading car. He and two aides rushed forward to receive orders.

In the midst of chaos, Chiang emerged from his car without shoes, and calmly ordered the security captain to send two scouts to the firing center, to evaluate the situation. Despite my father's protests, Chiang climbed to the top of the car where he remained for ten minutes trying to gain a sense of the attack. The airport nearby was on fire, but the firing appeared to be receding. The enemy target had been the airport and airplanes. Kai-shek ordered all firing to stop. He directed my father to assemble troops to calm the civilians and to stop any further train movements. Wen-yi's troops moved quickly, restoring civilian order and train movement within an hour. If the enemy had attacked the garrison instead of the airport, the result could have been devastating.

The War of the Central Plains raged from May to November 1930. A turning point in the conflict came when Chiang bribed warlord Zhang Xue-liang to enter the battle as an ally, with payment of ten million yuans and a promise Zhang would control China north of the Yellow River. Zhang's Northeastern Border Defense Army with 400,000 troops then drove the coalition forces out of Beiping and Tianjin, and took control of the Beiping-Wuhan and Tianjin-Pukou railways.[2] Feng and Yan, pinned between Chiang and the Manchurians, surrendered. Yan and Feng were defeated, but they would one day return to play significant roles with the Nationalists against invading Japanese.

Wen-yi did not stay with Chiang to the end of the war. He became ill at the end of July with severe, painful hemorrhoids. The Generalissimo gave him a month sick leave with an unexpected $500 sick pay. Wen-yi was sent to a well-known hospital in Shanghai. Doctors quickly determined the infection was serious. A British surgeon was called to do the necessary surgery. Wen-yi developed pneumonia shortly afterward, and the expected two-week convalescence stretched into almost four weeks. As he prepared to return to duty, he learned Chiang and his retinue had returned to Nanjing. Wen-yi departed for Nanjing.

Chiang had finally emerged victorious, but at a staggering price. Both sides had suffered high casualties, totaling more than 300,000. The Nanjing government was now close to bankruptcy. The troops intended to battle the Communists had been diverted and weakened. The warlord problem was merely stalled. Chiang was able to settle disputes between the Central government and the provincial warlord-governors only by offering the latter bribes or positions in government.

Chapter 5

Chiang and Wen-yi in Exile

Bati Bookstore

My father had always loved books and the publishing business. Back in the spring of 1930, his assignment as one of Chiang's staff secretaries lacked challenge and left him with much idle time. He decided to open a bookstore with printing facilities. He enlisted the aid of several friends with military and cultural backgrounds in raising funds to purchase facilities and printing equipment. Raising the funds was not an easy task, but the founders managed to accumulate over $12,000, issuing stock at $50 per share. Wen-yi and my mother Bai-jian arranged for the use of a building with living quarters. The Bati Bookstore opened as planned. Initial offerings included three new magazines and a series of booklets on military, political, economic, and social issues. My parents also printed and marketed lectures and writings of Chiang Kai-shek, to which my father had easy access. The bookstore did a lively business.

Despite her third pregnancy my mother remained engaged enthusiastically in the bookseller project since she had worked in propaganda activity for the local Nationalist Party in Hunan. Business boomed from the start. But one month later, widespread war erupted between Chiang's forces and several allied warlord armies in the Central Plains of China. The number of military customers dwindled. In order to reduce costs, the store retained only one manager and two clerks. Bai-jian helped out whenever she was needed. She used her household money with no hesitation. My father was in the Central Plains with Chiang and the army, carrying out assignments for the Generalissimo. Nevertheless he managed to remain involved in the business, dealing with publishing and business decisions. When peace was restored the business again enjoyed vigorous growth.

Publishing competitors, resentful of Wen-yi's success, tried to undermine the business by floating rumors the publications had a left-wing flavor. This was quickly dismissed since Wen-yi's rabid anti-Communist position was well known.

A more serious situation arose after Wen-yi's return from the Central Plains. A confidential lecture by Chiang to cadets at the Central Military Academy, two days before New Year's Day 1931, was printed by Wen-yi's paper. Kai-shek sat in his office scanning the newspaper. He noticed the article about his visit to the Academy was extremely detailed. The article included Chiang's reprimand to cadets. It had been a cold and snowy day and the gathering had been outdoors. Some cadets from the south were miserable, suffering from unaccustomed chill. Commandant Chiang, the article said, had chided them, "This weather is not that cold. If you cannot handle this, how will you be able to fight a war in the frigid cold of the Northeast? Your training needs to be stepped up!"

As Chiang read he became livid. He summoned Wen-yi to his office. My father would remember the details of this meeting for a long time. Kai-shek held the article up and furiously demanded, "Why did you release this piece? If the enemy reads about a 'war in the Northeast,' it could be misinterpreted and incite a real war! You must assume full responsibility for this idiocy!"

Wen-yi had no choice but to admit his oversight. "I was negligent in not monitoring the release of the piece. I would not have printed it."

Kai-shek grew even angrier. "You should be concentrating on your job here, without these extraneous distractions. You are making a fortune with your bookstore printing and selling my lectures and papers...exploiting my name. I am of a mind to close down your business!" Kai-shek's face was red with fury.

Chiang's volatile temper had been evident from his early youth in Xikou to his last days in Taiwan. His impulsive, ill-tempered bursts of uncontrolled rage against subordinates and others, with the possible exception of women and visitors, were well known. As Chiang's personal attendant, Wen-yi had many opportunities to observe the volcanic emotions of his leader. He, himself, had been the frequent target of Chiang's wrath. Chen Li-fu, a close friend and former personal secretary of Chiang's, proudly insisted Chiang had never lost his temper with him.[1] This may have been due to the nature of the two aides. Li-fu was more mature, disciplined, and self-contained than the younger Wen-yi. My father had earned Chiang's praise for several original initiatives he had undertaken successfully. But he had also been excoriated and demoted for what, to Chiang, had been foolish, immature actions. My father was also more inclined to argue with his leader when he felt a rebuke was unjustified. This merely served to make Chiang angrier. My mother had several times cautioned her husband to say less and be more restrained in his relationship with his superior. Yet, Wen-yi had also noted that while Chiang was usually quick to criticize and slow to praise, he occasionally showed a softer side, though self-consciously, when trying to make amends for an unjustified tirade against a hapless victim.

At this moment my father was taken aback by the passion of Chiang's outburst. His superior had accused him of making a fortune by printing and selling the leader's lectures and exploiting his name. He was now threatening to close down his publishing business! To his own surprise, Wen-yi heard himself challenging his leader. "A fortune?! What fortune? Have you received more malicious complaints which you believe?" Wen-yi felt he had to vigorously challenge these defamatory accusations in order to discourage them. Heatedly, he added, "I must tell you about my bookstore. I am running it as a means of disseminating important propaganda for you, my teacher. Who else within the party and government propaganda organizations prints your lectures and writings? Only my business prints them in large volume, and provides broad distribution to the troops and the population. We sell these at reasonable prices and expand the operation with the income. Commandant, not only do you not praise me...now you even scold me. If it is your wish, I will not publish your speeches and your other messages from now on!"

My father realized he was on perilous ground, but he could not stop. "As to the matter of profits, my wife and I have taken little money from the store. The editor and few clerks running the store were all trained by me. In hard times, when they have little money to buy rice, I would see that they had sufficient rice for their families. It is simply not true I am making a fortune. Commandant, you should not easily believe petty, malicious reports. You should seek the facts and truth. I cannot possibly accept your suggestions of closing the business. The store was formed with funds from many stock owners. Unless the operation is illegal or corrupt, it cannot be shut down easily."

Having said his lengthy piece, Wen-yi was aghast that he had dared to talk in this manner to his leader. Kai-shek was astounded, and now incensed. He was being lectured to by a subordinate! By Wen-yi! This was brazen insolence! The red in Chiang's face deepened. "You will not lecture me," he thundered. Surprisingly, Chiang did not cut off the discussion. He allowed it to continue, his voice getting steadily louder, as my father became increasingly apprehensive. Stories of Kai-shek's impatience and ill-tempered bursts of rage were legendary. He had once shot a man to death in anger during an argument.

By now my father was very frightened. The Generalissimo was at the edge of exploding. Wen-yi immediately broke off the argument, apologized to Chiang, asked to be excused, and left the office. As he walked past the outer office, he noticed the stricken look on the faces of two staff members. Stunned and hurt, Wen-yi remained at home for two weeks, sulking, yet remorseful. He had not informed anyone, nor sought permission for his absence. No one from Kai-shek's office called. Such action was unthinkable to colleagues who feared the temper of the Generalissimo. Yet, in this curious relationship, Kai-shek chose to ignore my father, where he might have doomed almost anyone else.

Finally, one day, Wen-yi learned Chiang would be speaking at the Sun Yat-sen Mausoleum. He decided to attend, sitting well back in the auditorium. Apparently, during his speech, Kai-shek noticed him in the audience. When the ceremony was over, Kai-shek left the well-wishers surrounding him and walked to where Wen-yi had remained seated. "How are you feeling?" he asked. My father responded that he was not sick.

"If you are not sick, why did you stay away for so long?" He cut off my father's response, saying gently, "Wen-yi, you are very bright, and when you put your mind to it you can do a fine job. But your weakness is laziness. You must reform your behavior and work hard. You will return to headquarters tomorrow morning."

The laziness remark rankled. Chiang had been complaining before that he was doing too much! Fortunately, for once, my father heeded the oft-repeated admonition from my mother, to "think carefully before you say or do anything foolish that may cost you dearly." Wen-yi was back at work the next day, and continued to manage his publishing company. (Later, a major new organization, the Three People's Principles' Lixingshe, acquired the bookstore, and the Bati Bookstore expanded into a chain of stores distributing Nationalist publications in a number of cities, including Nanjing, Hankou, Nanchang, Changsha, and Guiyany.) In his memoirs, Xiao Zuo-lin, a colleague and close friend of my father, wrote that Wen-yi's central publishing house in Nanjing produced and distributed thirty publications, including new and translated works from party members and Kai-shek.[2]

Another Family Tragedy

My mother was back in Nanjing, pregnant and sick, yet she continued to work at the bookstore. She was unable to go to my father in Shanghai to care for him during his recovery from an illness he contracted in the Central Plains War. However, putting to use the writing skills she had improved in school, she wrote to him regularly. Knowing he would be back to Nanjing soon, Bai-jian asked her parents-in-law in Liling to bring her one-year-old son and his wet nurse to join them. The group made preparations for the voyage and traveled through Changsha, Hankuo, and finally by boat on the Yangtze River toward Nanjing. They arrived in the city on the very same day as Wen-yi. The reunion was joyous. The little boy, now slightly more than a year old, screamed "Mama" and "Baba" (Daddy) at the top of his lungs, gibbering excitedly. Viewing his beautiful and energetic son, Wen-yi was happy and moved. The adults exchanged stories of events in the past few months. They had no inkling tragedy was about to strike.

The journey to Nanjing had been made during the extremely hot month of August. The ship had been exceedingly crowded. Unknowingly, the child had been exposed to a flu virus. Now united with his parents, the little boy had laughed and prattled during the day. However, by evening, the baby developed a fever and became fussy, crying constantly. His temperature continued to rise. He became weak. By daybreak, his temperature had risen to well over 100 degrees. A doctor was summoned. The doctor diagnosed the illness as influenza and urged Wen-yi to go to emergency facilities immediately. Wen-yi and his father took the baby to the hospital. The three frightened women burst into tears, and were directed to remain at home. Once in the hospital, the baby's eyes turned dull. Within three hours he was dead despite the efforts of the hospital staff.

My father was numb with grief and disbelief. My grandfather, a devout Buddhist, would not believe the baby had died. It was a rainy and windy day. He carried the little body to the streets, and walked aimlessly chanting and praying in the pouring rain and wind for hours. My father went home to give Bai-jian the heartbreaking news. They cried in each other's arms wordlessly. Finally my father put my mother to bed to rest. In the evening, hearing my grandfather's laments, my mother jumped from her bed and, still dazed from sleep and grief, tumbled down an entire flight of stairs. She was knocked unconscious and her arms and legs were badly injured. Amazingly, the accident did not affect her pregnancy. My father was greatly concerned with my mother's physical condition and emotional anguish. He found a good doctor to attend her and tried his best to console her, with little success.

The baby was placed in a simple coffin and buried in a cemetery in the countryside, attended by Wen-yi, my grandfather, and two clerks from the bookstore. Wen-yi stared, uncomprehendingly. He had enjoyed his lively son for only one day and now he had lost him forever. My father knelt, watching and grieving over the tiny lonely grave.

Turmoil over Chiang's Policy

The year 1931 began badly for Chiang Kai-shek and his loyalists. The Generalissimo faced a number of serious problems. The recent costly War of the Central Plains had placed the government close to financial bankruptcy. Mao Ze-dong had molded several bandit and Communist factions effectively into a major Communist force roaming Hunan, Jiangxi, Fujian, Guangdong, and surrounding provinces. Chiang had launched what would be the first of a series of five "bandit suppression" campaigns against the Communist Army in Jiangxi. The first campaign, December 1930 to January 1931, in Jiangxi, had ended in defeat with heavy loss of men and arms.

There was deep anger within the party and throughout China concerning Chiang's policy to subdue the Communists instead of using the men and resources to oppose the Japanese threat. He had sought to buy time by appeasing the Japanese. The recently defeated warlords Yan Xi-shan and Feng Yu-xiang had been brought into the Nationalist Party and government, albeit reluctantly; they were still restless and sought more influence. Chiang's leftist opponents within the party were maneuvering to usurp his power. In an effort to mollify the edgy warlords, Chiang called a national meeting with the intent of developing a provisional constitution to meet some of the demands of the vanquished warlords. Hu Han-min, chairman of the Legislative Yuan (Department) and a powerful and staunch disciple of Sun Yat-sen, adamantly opposed this action, and resigned from his office in protest. Chiang placed him under house arrest and appointed a new chairman.[3] This was the proverbial last straw. On April 30, 1931, a group of senior party officials broke with Chiang. In the following month they met with Hu Han-min and the liberal party leader, Wang Jing-wei, in Guangzhou. The group proclaimed formation of their own Nationalist government on May 28.

Mukden Incident - The Japanese Invade China

The general population was angry and frustrated at rampant corruption, poverty, and escalation of the civil war. On July 31, 1931, my father followed Chiang on the third "bandit suppression" campaign against the Communists in Jiangxi. The offensive was showing promise of a major victory. However, on September 18, 1931, the Japanese army suddenly initiated an attack on Chinese territory which became known as the Mukden (or 918) Incident. The Japanese blew up the South Manchurian Railway tracks north of Shenyang (Mukden), then accused Chinese troops of sabotage as a justification for continued operations. Japan soon occupied three Chinese northeastern provinces. The Japanese Army encountered little resistance in its conquests. Chiang Kai-shek was preoccupied with the rebel government forming in Guangzhou headed by Hu Han-min, and with his campaign to suppress the multiplying Communists. He was also attempting to pacify a group of unhappy warlords. To buy time, he ordered Zhang Xue-liang and his Manchurian Army to maintain a policy of nonresistance and withdrawal. The country rose up in protest. Demonstrators marched in the streets proclaiming death before surrender. Chiang had to abort his promising campaign against the Communists to return to Nanjing. Wen-yi also followed him back to Nanjing. While my father was away with Chiang in Jiangxi my mother Bai-jian gave birth to a son, Yuan-zhong, her only surviving male child.

Chiang Kai-shek Resigns

Now back in Nanjing, Chiang quickly discovered the city was not a comfortable place for him. The mood of the country was one of deep hostility toward Japan, and resentment against the Nationalist northern commander Zhang Xue-liang for not resisting the Japanese. Widespread protests, led by students and newspapers, clamored for unity of purpose in defending the country against invaders. Students at the Shanghai University organized massive protests against Chiang. They attacked party headquarters, and forced the resignation of the Shanghai mayor, a Kai-shek man. Military guards ringed government buildings in Nanjing and subdued small groups of activists inciting the populace.[4] Kai-shek was left with little choice. In mid-December 1931, he resigned his position as head of the government...but not his influence. He returned to his home in Xikou, taking with him only my father, a telegrapher, and two body guards.

My Parents Stay at Chiang's Ancestral Home

Chiang Kai-shek and his tiny entourage arrived in his hometown of Xikou on December 23, 1931. Since their marriage Kai-shek and his wife Soong Mei-ling stayed at nearby Wen-chang Pavilion, a small villa on the riverfront beside the cemetery of his mother. They celebrated Christmas quietly. Kai-shek had become a Christian as one of the conditions for marrying Mei-ling. Chiang did very little during the first week in Xikou, refusing all attempts by Nanjing to seek his advice on a number of matters.

My father was lodged in Chiang's ancestral home, an imposing residence with 20,000 square feet of floor space surrounded by a 50,000 square foot garden. The structure of the house was traditional Chinese, with an antechamber, back-chamber, two wing-rooms on each side for guests, rooms upstairs, and four verandas. In the front courtyard were three gardens, connected by moon-shaped gates. The front antechamber had a large hall for receptions. A central parlor in the back chamber was used for formal family ceremonies. Each hall boasted a unique plaque, famous paintings, and sculptures. Like many successful men at the time, Chiang Kai-shek had two "official" wives prior to his marriage to Soong Mei-ling. Chiang's first wife, Mme. Mao Fu-mei, had quarters in the west wing. My father was given a guest room toward the front of the house.

Kai-shek's father, an affluent salt merchant, had died when he was seven years old. Chiang was raised by a disciplinarian mother, Mme. Wang Tsai-yu. She arranged a marriage for fourteen-year-old Kai-shek to an illiterate village girl, Mao Fu-mei, five years his senior. Since her son was still very young, the mother forbade any affection or sexual activities between the young couple. Mother-in-law Wang made sure the daughter-in-law knew her position and main role as a helper in the house.

According to Fenby,[5] Fu-mei told Chiang's second wife, Chen Chieh-ji, many years later, "I kept quiet and seldom spoke. More and more I avoided any direct conversation openly with him in the house. That was not easy, however, especially when he asked me questions and expected my answers. The situation went from bad to worse, and Kai-shek soon became impatient with me. I dared not say one word to defend myself, even when he scolded me, for as you know, the villagers in their narrow-mindedness would accuse me of being an un-filial and disobedient daughter-in-law...and you know what that means in an isolated village like ours! The strain gradually caused a split between Kai-shek and me. All I could do was to weep secretly over my utter helplessness, and for a long period I suffered from melancholy."

Soon after his marriage, Chiang left home to pursue an education in Japan and Russia for his future career. On occasional visits home, he would have little to do with Fu-mei. However, Chiang's mother had been told by a fortune teller that a son by Fu-mei would become a great, important man. She therefore commanded her son, threatening suicide, to become intimate with his wife and try for a son. Fu-mei produced a boy, Chiang Ching-kuo, Kai-shek's only son. He would one day become president of the Republic of China in Taiwan. Fu-mei regained status and respect from her husband, but they never again were bedmates. Fu-mei remained celibate and became a devoted Buddhist.[6]

She continued to reside in and manage the main residence efficiently until her death in 1939 during a Japanese bombardment. She was known to be kind and courteous to all visitors.

Thanks to Fu-mei, Wen-yi's daily needs and meals at Chiang's home were seen to, as though he were a family member. After his Spartan existence in the field, he found life during this brief period idyllic. He especially relished the excellent food: meat, fish, and vegetable dishes plus soup for lunch and dinner. They were far better than the spare meals at Chiang's Nanjing residence.

One day in the second week of my father's stay, Chiang invited Wen-yi to accompany him on a picnic outing. The two guards were also brought along. The small group floated down the nearby river on a raft to a large bamboo forest where they would dig for bamboo shoots and have their picnic. Chiang's mood became poetic in this beautiful, serene setting. He turned to my father and said, "Wen-yi, it is best to live life like a bamboo, with a modest, open interior, and strong, disciplined (knotted) exterior. Bamboo has profuse branches and leaves, stays green always, and enjoys a carefree life unaffected by the stormy wind and rain. Bamboo plants unite with one another. Bamboo shoots propagate vigorously to form a forest. Together, they illustrate neatness, beauty, and strength." Wen-yi was amazed and touched by this new side of his leader, and impressed by his words. When he returned to his room, ever the writer, he immediately sought to write down the words Chiang had said, as well as he could remember.

Since they were now sharing the same house, Wen-yi would enjoy an occasional friendly chat with Fu-mei. She was delighted to know Wen-yi and her son Ching-kuo had attended Moscow University together. She told him she missed her son and asked Wen-yi anxiously, "Did Ching-kuo study hard? Was he in good health? Were the living conditions favorable?" My father assured her that her son had always studied hard and was as good as, if not better than, his older peers. He was also healthy, strong, and in good spirits. Most students liked and respected him. Fu-mei smiled happily at this bit of news. My father felt a rush of affection for this gentle woman.

My mother read and reread Wen-yi's letter describing his life in "Shangri-la." In her reply, she wrote wistfully of how wonderful it would be if she could join him. My father urged her to come, provided she could find a good wet nurse to stay home with the baby. My mother was ecstatic! She would be living in Chiang Kai-shek's family home! She quickly found a nurse and hastened to Xikou. A small problem arose. According to local custom, a couple could not live together on the property of another family unless they rented it. Even Chiang's house had to abide by the rules. However, Fu-mei promptly intervened. She was pleased at my mother's visit. She told Wen-yi and Bai-jian to occupy the west wing room. She told my father to write a simple rental agreement and pay rent of one dollar to meet the customs, which he happily did. They now enjoyed extravagant accommodations with wonderful meals served in their room daily.

My parents paid a visit to Fu-mei in her quarters to show their respect and gratitude. She asked kindly, "Are you comfortable here? Are you used to the food and living arrangement?"

Wen-yi answered, "Thank you very much. You are much too kind. We are having such a good time here. Everything is so much better than at home. You are taking such good care of us. We hope we are not imposing too much on you."

"Not at all," she insisted. "I love to have young people here. Have you followed Kai-shek long?" The next half-hour was taken by a summary of my father's experience with Chiang from the early days of Whampoa to the present. My mother then told Fu-mei of her experiences and of raising her children. Fu-mei listened with much interest and asked many questions. She seemed to really enjoy what she called their "youthful enthusiasm."

One day Kai-shek came to the family house for a visit. He sat with my parents and asked my mother many questions about her background and life. At first my father was a bit concerned with how frankly his wife spoke to the Leader. During her service in the propaganda field in Hunan she had developed firm views and had expressed them in discussions with the villagers. My father need not have worried about Kai-shek's reaction. He saw how pleased Kai-shek seemed to be with his exchanges with this passionate but respectful young lady. Chiang asked her to give his regards to her elders at home. He also told her Wen-yi was always diligent and thoughtful in his work. He added it was extraordinary that he should read so voraciously, constantly trying to improve himself. My father was barely able to suppress an expression of amazement and thrill that China's leader should be saying these things to his wife. Wen-yi had become much more used to receiving criticism and satirical comments from the Generalissimo. He later told my mother sheepishly, "I could be pretty inept at times in serving Chiang. He's gotten angry with me, demoted me, praised and promoted me, then made me his personal secretary. He has emphasized my positive qualities to you but has not shared with you his impatience with the foolish things I have done."

This visit to Chiang's home was truly a honeymoon for Bai-jian. She loved to wander past the courtyard to gardens filled with multicolored flowers and honeysuckle which, she heard, had been planted by Chiang's current wife Mei-ling. Wen-yi and Bai-jian explored Xikou and its vicinity. Bai-jian stared at the mountains and hills, the valley rich with flowers and bamboo forests, and old temples. She chattered in excitement and told her husband she had never experienced such a sense of serenity. They saw the village school Chiang had attended as a boy and the new Wu-ling School where Chiang Kai-shek served as president. My mother visited the grave of Kai-shek's mother, Mme. Wang, to pay her respects. At the gravesite Bai-jian tarried for a while, entranced by the panoramic view from the site.

Then suddenly, to Bai-jian's deep disappointment, her idyll with Wen-yi at Xikou was cut short when they received word Wen-yi's grandfather had died. She felt very sad to be leaving, especially for so sad an event. My mother returned to Liling to assist with funeral arrangements.

Kai-shek Resumes Power

While Chiang was in mini-exile in Xikou the Guangzhou faction, led by Wang Jing-wei and Sun Fo (Sun Yat-sen's son), had taken over the reins of government, which was close to bankruptcy. Frantic attempts to raise funds were unsuccessful now that fundraiser T.V. Soong and his influence with Shanghai bankers had departed with Chiang. Bankers refused to lend any more money to Nanjing. Warlords took advantage of the situation and stopped paying taxes. There was little government leaders could do since the military's allegiance was still to Chiang. The Guangzhou faction was left with little choice but to invite Chiang, T.V. Soong, and Kung to join with Wang Jing-wei and his group in leading a coalition government. Near the end of January 1932, Kai-shek returned to Nanjing, preparing once again to take control of the government, with Wang Jing-wei as prime minister.

Chiang officially took over the reins of government in March 1932. He now had the titles of Chairman of the Military Affairs Commission of the Nationalist Government and Chief of the General Staff. Wen-yi was promoted to "escort secretary" of the chairman with increased responsibilities. Chiang asked my father a familiar question, "Wen-yi, do you think you can handle your responsibilities without causing problems for me or for yourself?" Wen-yi answered he would make every effort to do so.

My father observed, with wry amusement, the demeanor of government and military officials assembled to greet the restored leader. When Chiang entered the hall, he was greeted with boisterous applause and shouts of good wishes. However, warm greetings and smiles could not conceal an atmosphere of apprehension. Among the greeters were the very men who, just a few weeks ago, had voted for his resignation. Those who had opposed his policies had not hidden their glee or expressions of "good riddance." My father looked at Chiang's impassive face and wondered what his thoughts might be as he accepted these "warm" expressions of welcome.

While Chiang was preparing himself to resume his role as leader of the government, the Japanese menace continued to increase. In January 1932 the Japanese military had instigated incidents fomenting anti-Japanese sentiment, to justify military action. These warlike acts inflamed the Shanghai natives to a point where an active economic boycott was launched against local Japanese businesses, banks, shops, and goods. Some of the Japanese inhabitants were harassed. Japan used this situation to move Japanese marines into Shanghai "to protect their countrymen." On January 28, a three-month undeclared war was waged in Shanghai, and met with stiff resistance. An armistice agreement was signed on May 5th. Japanese troops began their withdrawal from the city on May 15 and were gone by May 31st. Yet, Chiang still would not be dissuaded from his policy of pacification first, then a united front against Japan.

Chapter 6

A Powerful Force Emerges

While Chiang Kai-shek was temporarily retired in his hometown of Xikou, several of his young Whampoa graduates were busily engaged developing an extensive plan for formation of a new organization that would play a major role in changing the character of Chiang's regime.

Teng Jie, Xiao Zan-you, and He Zhong-han were among the Whampoa Military Academy graduates sent to study in Japan. By 1931 the study group had grown to over 60. These young men were deeply suspicious of Japan's recent actions and intent. Japan had made no secret of its designs on northeastern China as "the Japanese lifeline." Nor did its officials conceal their contempt for the "inept Chinese people" or their ambitions for occupying Manchuria. The Whampoa students in Japan became alarmed as they observed that country's overt actions to create tension and dispute between Korea and China along the Korean-Manchurian border in July 1931. The Chinese student contingent felt a major Japanese invasion was imminent. They selected Teng Jie and Xiao Zan-yu to return home and alert the Nationalist Party officials of the seriousness and danger of the Japanese threat.

Once home, Teng and Xiao were appalled to discover a country deeply divided on China's future course of action. There was no committed preparation against clear signs of an oncoming Japanese invasion. Kai-shek was firmly wed to the idea that an effective response to a Japanese invader could only be accomplished when the Communists were defeated. The country could then give its united strength and support to dealing with outside invaders. It was therefore not surprising that officials listened to the pleas of the two young emissaries with polite disinterest.

A dispirited Teng Jie decided not to return to his studies in Japan. After two weeks of careful thought, he set out to develop a rough plan for a secret political organization, using Whampoa graduates as a cadre source that would mobilize the country politically and militarily around Chiang Kai-shek. Teng Jie now desperately needed the help of influential officials to move his "brain child" toward development of a well-constructed plan that could be presented to Kai-shek. He finally found a strong supporter in Zeng Kuo-qing, then chief secretary of the Military Department of the Nationalist government and a Whampoa first class graduate. Zeng invited ten carefully chosen people to a dinner to unveil the concept and to seek their support and involvement as the core group for the initiative. Everyone present, including my father, was a Whampoa graduate. Wen-yi's presence was undoubtedly due to his position as aide-de-camp to Kai-shek, desire for the presence of a Hunan senior official, and, importantly, Wen-yi's ownership of a successful publishing and bookselling business that offered a powerful means for influencing public and party opinions. After dinner, Teng Jie outlined the goals and structure of the proposed organization. This was followed by a lively discussion of objectives and obstacles to be overcome. The group then unanimously and enthusiastically supported this initiative.

A second and third dinner meeting attended by additional invitees increased the core group to 45. These were drawn entirely from the first six classes of Whampoa Military Academy. General He Zhong-han, one of the three most distinguished of Whampoa graduates, was at the third meeting, which took place just after the September 18, 1931 invasion of northeastern Manchuria by the Japanese. The Japanese action sharply increased the intensity of anti-Japanese sentiment and patriotic emotions of the people.

The group's work was done covertly since Chiang had often expressed disapproval of Whampoa graduates getting involved in political matters. Therefore, it was essential a well-conceived plan be developed prior to presentation to Chiang. A Project

Preparation Committee was formed with Teng Jie as chief secretary, and his wife Chen Qi-kun as assistant secretary. Wen-yi contributed $300 from his Bati Bookstore as seed money for the project. The Preparation Committee rented three rooms on the second floor of a wooden building in Nanjing as an office and meeting place. One member, Kang Ze, moved into a downstairs room as a cover. General Zhong-han's active participation and prestige served to keep preparation work moving at a steady pace.

Zhong-han suggested the name Three People's Principles' Lixingshe (Society of Vigorous Practice) for the new organization. The name was quickly accepted by the group. After four months' hard work, the Project Preparation Committee had developed a detailed blueprint for the Lixingshe, with objectives and strategies for various proposed operations. The proposal was now ready to be presented to Chiang Kai-shek. Teng Jie asked my father, who was in Xikou with Kai-shek, to fill Chiang in on the basic plan and get a reading of Kai-shek's reaction.

When Wen-yi outlined the essence of the Lixingshe plan and its intended objectives, Chiang's instinctive reaction was positive and encouraging. He told Wen-yi he had been thinking along somewhat similar lines. He felt such a quasi-secret organization might be just what he needed to accomplish a number of specific missions. To Teng's delight, Wen-yi told him the Leader would meet with the principals of the plan when he returned to Nanjing.

On January 22, 1932, the day after Kai-shek's return to Nanjing, he met with the principal founders Teng Jie, He Zhong-han, and Kang Ze. My father recorded intimate details of this and further meetings leading to formation of the new Lixingshe organization that would play a key role in the history of the Nationalist Party. Excellent detailed accounts of the founding meetings are given in *Sanminzhuyi Lixingshe Shi*, the authoritative book written by my brother, Deng Yuan-Zhong, based on his discussions with a number of the founders including our father Wen-yi,[1] and in Frederic Wakeman's *Spymaster*.[2]

At the first meeting, Kai-shek listened carefully to the presentations and asked many questions. Finally, he said to the group, "You have grasped the needs of the current crises. This plan is quite appropriate. But you are all still young with limited experience. I am concerned you might not do it properly. Let me lead you all." Because of the potential impact of such an undertaking, Kai-shek suggested it would be prudent to seek the views and counsel of the entire core group.

Teng Jie was asked to formally assemble all charter members for three discussion meetings to be held at Kai-shek's villa next to the Sun Yat-sen Mausoleum beginning at 7:00 p.m. on February 25, 1932. On the first night, 25 members were present. Kai-shek arrived with my father. Chiang sat behind a medium-sized desk, with my father to his right, behind a rectangular coffee table, where he recorded the minutes. A large picture of Sun Yat-sen hung on the wall behind them. Chiang addressed the group, "Our party and nation are in a very difficult position. If you have ideas, please present them freely for us to discuss." Each attendee would be invited to present his views of the current situation, and how to deal with the issues. No formal procedures or time limitations were set. However, according to the usual practice of Whampoa alumni gatherings, those of the earliest class, with highest seniority, spoke first.

He Zhong-han, the eldest of the first class, led off, followed by Xiao Zan-yu, Pan You-quang, and Feng Ti. Kai-shek listened attentively with little interruption. When the meeting ended at 11:00 p.m. Chiang offered no conclusions. He merely said, "Those who did not speak will do so at the next meeting, here, at the same time tomorrow." Then he left with Wen-yi. The ritual was repeated the next evening, again for 4 or 5 hours.

On the third night, speeches continued, concluding with spymaster Dai Li and my father. Teng Jie then gave an impassioned speech meant to inspire his colleagues, but also to impress Chiang. His tone was firm and confident. Finally Kai-shek spoke. He pointedly reminded the group that "quelling internal enemies before expelling external invaders" was a necessity. He emphasized that Japan had been preparing for over 50 years to invade China. He warned that those screaming for war against the Japanese, regardless of current conditions, were not without ulterior motives.

Then, seeking to mollify and encourage his disciples, Kai-shek added ambiguously, "You all have correct views on the status and future of our revolution. You also have appropriate ideas and suggestions to meet the needs. I hope you will utilize the result of these discussions to further develop your final plans. Once the decisions are made, you must work diligently and unselfishly to achieve your goals. You all should vow to be unsung heroes in pursuing your endeavors. You must disregard personal glory and gains and save your country with all your heart and soul. If you would carry out the tasks in such fashion, then you will succeed." [3] To the elation of the group, Kai-shek finally exclaimed, "The organizational procedure and development plan of Lixingshe are all workable. We can have a launching meeting." The Project Preparation Committee proceeded to arrange an initiation event immediately.

The Birth of the Lixingshe

On the morning of the fourth day, the group assembled in the meeting room of Lizhishe (Society of Spirit Encouragement) on Whampoa Road, Nanjing. It was 8:00 a.m. on February 28th. Desks and chairs were arranged in a horseshoe-shape with a seat for Kai-shek at the opening. Chiang spoke for an hour, explaining the significance and agenda for the meeting. Each member was then asked to cast his vote for the leadership positions of the new organization. Teng collected the ballots, sealed them in an envelope, and gave it to Wen-yi for Kai-shek's final decision. Kai-shek then introduced two essay subjects: "A Discussion of Bismarck's Policy of Iron and Blood" and "The Significance of a Cooperative Society." He instructed each attendee to compose an essay on one of the two topics at home and bring it back the next day. Later in Chiang's private office, Wen-yi opened and went through the ballots, adding his personal comments for Chiang.

Next morning, the group returned to the conference room and turned in their essays. Kai-shek entered the classroom accompanied as usual by Wen-yi. When the essays had been collected, Kai-shek began to read each one, making comments, and assigning a grade to each essay. The essays were then returned to their owners. Kai-shek told the group he would make the final assignment of positions based on: 1. the essays; 2. oral presentations during the evening meetings; 3. personal appearance; 4. Whampoa class; 5. experience; and 6. the number of votes each had received from the sealed election.[4]

The group then convened to the auditorium for the swearing-in ceremony before a large photograph of Sun Yat-sen. Each held a written oath on a paper bearing the Kai-shek seal. All raised their right hands and pledged their commitment and fealty to the society and the country. Each stamped his right thumbprint on the oath. The paper texts were collected and solemnly burned. Chiang and the group then held hands in a large circle. Kai-shek declared, "The Three People's Principles' Lixingshe is now officially formed. I will do my best to lead you. From now on you must exert yourselves even harder to unite, strive, and struggle until we achieve our goal. I wish you success." Solemnly, the new officials expressed their loyalty and acceptance of their leader's teachings and direction. The historical and unprecedented meeting ended in excitement and high hopes. On March 1, 1932, Chiang Kai-shek created a top-secret organization which would evolve into a powerful national political force of more than half a million members. Teng Jie was appointed as the first secretary general of the new organization.

As young Whampoa officers, staff, and members began their meetings to discuss and vote on policy and personnel issues, the usually autocratic Chiang, impressed with the enthusiasm of the group, announced his intention to let the group conduct all their business in a democratic manner. Though he would have ultimate veto power, he would only make proposals for his ideas in order to show respect for the authority of the Staff Committee. The group took him at his word. In fact, some of Chiang's proposals were not passed despite face-to-face arguments with their Leader at meetings. Chiang never used his position as chairman to make the final decision. He would only say: "I am twenty years older than you all. I have more experience than you. You people should really listen to me."

On one occasion when founders Teng Jie and Xiao Zan-yu encountered difficulty getting Chiang's final approval on a decision, they sent him a written summary document, with the added note, "The honorable Chiang is temperamental and unpredictable." When they next met, Chiang laughed at them: "You fellows are taking on airs aren't you?" However, later, as the Lixingshe became more aggressive and independent in their actions, Chiang became more uneasy.

Structure and Operations of Lixingshe

The personnel and operations of Lixingshe were mostly secret. The organization was deliberately enshrouded with ambiguity, operating through several "front" organizations. For example, recruitment and training were concealed as formal special government training sessions. Lixingshe intelligence work was performed under a cover of ambiguous names like "Bureau of Investigation and Statistics." Immediate objectives of Lixingshe were to carry out Chiang's strategy of quelling internal enemies, i.e., the warlords and especially the Communists, before dealing with Japanese invaders. The broader goals were to unify China's support, eliminate widespread corruption in the country, and promote a national "renaissance movement" based on Sun Yat-sen's Three People's Principles.

My father continued to play an important role in the operations of Lixingshe despite his other responsibilities. His duties as the Generalissimo's personal secretary had expanded. As Chiang's gatekeeper, Wen-yi must first examine and approve all appointment requests. Through Wen-yi, the secretary general of Lixingshe was able to meet with Kai-shek frequently. When Chiang was away, my father kept him informed of important issues to be dealt with, including those of the Lixingshe. My father had also formed an intelligence group, with Chiang's approval, that collected and analyzed intelligence reports from the Nationalist Party and spymaster Dai Li's intelligence organization for Chiang.

Lixingshe was the flagship organization whose core was made up of 300 carefully selected members to head the organization. The identity of the nuclear group was unknown to outsiders. It was led by the secretary general, appointed by Chiang Kai-shek, and a thirteen-member "Staff Officers' Commission." Wen-yi would later become the 6th secretary general. The Lixingshe founders deliberately set up several layers of front groups, often with overlapping interests and responsibilities. Beyond general missions mentioned above, the core Lixingshe officers sought to establish operations throughout the provinces in areas related to propaganda, intelligence, and police activity.

One of the second-tier cover groups, the Revolutionary Youth Comrades Association (RYCA), sought to mobilize the youth of the country in carrying out the aims of Chiang and the flagship organizations. The core layer within the RYCA included intellectuals, Lixingshe members, and other Whampoa graduates, and government officials. The organization developed provincial offices throughout the country. The scope of its activities was extremely broad, providing a variety of training programs for senior military officers, military academies, and district administrators.

The number of young people applying for membership in the RYCA expanded to the point that RYCA secretary general

Ren Jue-wu decided a third-tier organization was needed to handle the influx of candidates effectively. Requirements for admission to the new entity would be less stringent than for the parent RYCA. In July 1932, Fuxingshe or the Renaissance Society became the third-tier cover group for the Lixingshe. The Lixingshe's influence was soon felt throughout provinces, districts, and counties. However, awkward attempts to maintain secrecy for these organizations resulted in newspapers or the public referring to the Lixingshe by the name of a satellite group such as Fuxingshe, alias Renaissance Society, or the "Blue Shirt Society."

Chinese Cultural Study Society (CCSS)

In December 1933, my father and a small group of carefully selected Kai-shek followers founded yet another organization called the "Chinese Culture Study Society" (CCSS) within the Lixingshe. Working in tandem with elements of the Fuxingshe, it had the important mission of winning the hearts and minds of university students and faculties, as well as other youth groups, to support the aims of Kai-shek and the Nationalist Party. This new organization set out to create extensive mass communications and propaganda channels. Although Kai-shek was nominal head of the society, my father functioned as its operating head on a day-by-day basis. Wen-yi was already established in the publishing business, with broad distribution channels. He had always had an interest in cultural affairs. He agreed to sell his Bati Bookstore to the Lixingshe, adding to their increasing ownership of information sources. In addition to news and propaganda activity, the Cultural Society published an art magazine and a monthly literary magazine. A foundation was established to raise funds to build cultural centers, mobile libraries, and publication/translation systems. Within six months, Wen-yi and his team raised more than one million dollars for these initiatives.

Xiao Zuo-lin, secretary general of CCSS, decided to focus his efforts on Shanghai, since it was the cultural center of the country. He developed allies among the faculty at Shanghai University and sought to recruit student members for the society through visits and campus discussions.

The organization's great success did not sit well with the powerful "CC Clique" led by the influential Chen brothers, Chen Go-fu and Chen Li-fu. The brothers were longtime close friends of Chiang and also members of his inner circle. They regarded the activities of CCSS as an intrusion into their operations. This jealousy was part of an ongoing rivalry between the CC Clique and the Whampoa Clique. The CC Clique now mounted its own effort to wrest the initiative from CCSS. The rivalry was intense. However, CCSS had the advantage of a head start in establishing relationships with the university. The success of the Chen clique initiative was limited.

CC Clique leader Chen Go-fu visited his friend Kai-shek to complain that duplication was causing confusion among the people. CCSS was interfering in an area Kai-shek had agreed was in the CC Clique's domain. This probably was true, since Kai-shek deliberately permitted overlapping activities among factional organizations to maintain a check and balance. Chen Go-fu accused Wen-yi of using CCSS for other personal endeavors. As always, my father was no match for the powerful Chen brothers. Kai-shek was persuaded to dissolve CCSS in July 1934. A disheartened and angry Wen-yi was forced to return the funds he had raised, and arrange for the orderly shutdown of various tasks in progress. The Chinese Culture Study Society had won the battle but lost the war.

The Blue Shirt Society

The use or misuse of the name Blue Shirt Society (BSS) as a synonym for the Lixingshe, or its satellite organizations including the Fuxingshe, has become common with many writers and scholars. Professor Eastman characterized BSS as a fascist organization.[5] However, an opposing view was that Chiang had used the name Blue Shirt as a Chinese template for qualities he admired in Mussolini's Black Shirts in carrying out their assigned missions. These characteristics, such as determination, enthusiasm, discipline, and loyalty, were qualities he felt were needed for the young Whampoa members and leaders of Lixingshe to achieve their objective in re-energizing the party, the country, and the revolution. In other words, Chiang's focus was on the qualities and discipline of the Black Shirts rather than the fascist ideology that was counter to the principles of Sun Yat-sen. However, as Lixingshe expanded it did take on fascist qualities. Maria Hsia Chang and others argued that while BSS displayed some similarities to the Italian Fascist Black Shirts, it also had a large faction who, like Sun Yat-sen, viewed democracy as a long-range goal.[6] At first, the name was applied to foot soldiers and field agents of Lixingshe and its satellite organizations. But the name "Blue Shirt Society" took on a life of its own with the media, the people, and even within the party, overshadowing the true name of the organization. The number of incidents and actions attributed to the Blue Shirts by newspapers and magazines through the years remained lengthy, detailed, and unabated. My brother Deng Yuan-zhong made a persuasive case against the formal existence of a Blue Shirt Society, pointing out that no such name could be found in government organization lists, nor was it ever used by Chiang in reference to the Lixingshe which he led.[7, 8] Neither was it used by my father Wen-yi, who was a founder, theoretician, and later, secretary general of the Lixingshe. But the name persists. As a matter of convenience we will also make use of the name.

Chapter 7

Wen-yi's Intelligence and Strike Force

Wen-yi Heads an Anti-corruption Campaign in Wuhan

In the late spring of 1932 Chiang Kai-shek, chairman of the Military Affairs Commission, was discussing matters he wanted Wen-yi, his executive secretary and chief of aides-de-camp, to attend to for him. They were at the Generalissimo's headquarters at the Nanchang Mobile Garrison. After the day's agenda had been completed, Chiang's tone suddenly turned angry. In his recent visit to Wuhan he was appalled at the sorry state this important city had fallen into. Wuhan was the collective name for the three cities of Hankou, Wuchang, and Hanyang, at the juncture of the Han and Yangtze Rivers in Hubei Province. "The people in Wuhan are dispirited and demoralized by rampant corruption, gambling, prostitution, profiteering, and illicit opium trafficking. It has become an unfortunate reflection of conditions throughout the country. This must not be allowed to go on," said Kai-shek. His motives may not have been entirely pure. As in previous regimes, opium revenues were financing a significant part of the military and government expenditures. Controlling China's illicit narcotics trade would assure a steady source of financial support for the government.[1]

Next he said, "Wen-yi, I have not forgotten your earlier proposal that a special investigative network be established to eliminate corrupt, criminal, and treasonous activities within the military, government, and the civilian population." Chiang then stared at him and said, "I want you to form and lead a task force to clean up all illicit activities in Wuhan. You will have my support in whatever manpower you need." Kai-shek emphasized that Wen-yi would also continue responsibilities as his executive secretary. My father was assigned as chief of the

3rd Investigative Section of the Secretary Department in headquarters for his new responsibility. In his usual manner Chiang was appointing one of his officials to several positions. This mission was not entirely what Wen-yi had proposed to Kai-shek, but it was one element of his plan.

Wuhan had suffered under the repressive control of the Guangxi warlords, and now under the equally repressive rule of the Chen brothers' CC Clique. The city had not recovered from devastating floods in 1931 that drove almost one million peasants into Wuhan to live in squalid conditions during a severe depression. Amid the chaos much of the activity in the city and its underworld came under the control of a powerful gangster leader, Yang Qing-shan. Yang controlled an enormous territory from the middle section of the Yangtze River to Chongqing. He operated a large network of thugs who ran rackets and a remarkable intelligence operation out of hundreds of teahouses, restaurants, gambling houses, and brothels throughout the area.[2] His underworld empire kept equally close tabs on many of the corrupt activities of government officials. Yang had provided intelligence and other services to the powerful CC Clique, bringing profits to the gangster and needed information and actions for the Nationalists.

Of the three cities, Hankou was one of sharp contrasts. It was beautiful along the riverfront Bund, turf of the international community, with its lavish residences, racetrack, tennis courts, bridge parties, and cabarets. To the east, modern streets gave way to narrow streets and alleys lined with wooden shacks and mud houses, where the bulk of the people eked out a meager existence. The merchants had profited richly from an economy provided by the freighters able to berth near the city's Bund, to load and unload cargo. Unfair treaties imposed on China following the "Opium Wars" in the 19th century permitted many nations, including the US, Britain, and various European countries and Japan, to patrol freely Chinese rivers such as the Yangtze to "protect their citizens and their properties." These countries had established concessions in Shanghai and a similar international community along the riverfront Bund in Hankou. British, American, French, Italian, and Japanese gunboats were anchored in the river beside the Bund to protect the properties of their respective countries.

Wen-yi spent several days formulating an action plan. With Chiang's approval, Wen-yi carefully selected seven Blue Shirt members as cadre for the strike force. Among these was the able Qui Kai-ji, a founding Lixingshe member, who would function as Wen-yi's second-in-command. But Kai-shek added another surprise. He had "persuaded" the Hankou gang leader, Yang Qing-shan, to turn over his group in Wuhan to Wen-yi's 3rd Investigative Section in the Wuhan Mobile Garrison during its cleanup mission.[3] This newly added force now gave my father a network of hooligans with an intimate knowledge of underworld activities and useful contacts. Wen-yi recruited additional forces from members of the Blue Shirts. He carefully selected members who had served in political and paramilitary action groups to assure loyalty to Chiang Kai-shek. The 3rd Section was ready for action. The CC Clique was not happy this mission had been given to Wen-yi and the Blue Shirts rather than to its assets in the area. However, Chiang had acted as he often did, assigning overlapping responsibility to different factions to prevent concentration of power by any of them.

Wen-yi and his deputy reviewed targets for action. First they would rout out widespread corruption within the government, police force, and business districts. They would also disrupt Japanese sales of opium and other goods, and eliminate Japanese moles in the Wuhan Garrison Headquarters. On June 15, 1932, the 3rd Section agents began their probe into activities of the Wuhan police. With Wen-yi's new, local intelligence, it was not difficult to identify members known to be accepting graft from merchants and underworld sources in exchange for ignoring illegal trafficking. Dozens of police and high officials were arrested. Two of the most important transgressors were executed as an example. The conduct of the police force improved quickly and dramatically.

Anti-Japanese Activity

Opium use in Hankou had reached alarming levels as supplies of the narcotic from merchants and Japanese, who were seeking to avoid the Special Tax, flooded the market. Narcotics were being refined and converted to morphine within the Japanese Concession, thereby producing capital to supplement the allotment of the Japanese government. Shutting down the opium trade would enable Chiang to monopolize opium traffic along the Yangtze and generate more capital for his military campaigns.[4a] However, Du Yue-sheng and his Green Gang of Shanghai would later remind Chiang of his earlier deal with them: Du would organize and conduct anti-Communist terrorist activity, and in return, Chiang would recognize Du's opium monopoly in the Yangtze Valley. Ties between Chiang's government and the Green Gang had strengthened since the 1927 Shanghai Purge.[4b]

Now, the 3rd Section mounted a broad attack on underworld profiteers, who were smuggling and distributing opium and Japanese goods. The 3rd Section identified a senior government official who was colluding with independent underworld distributors. Interrogation of the official revealed the identity of distributors, opium pushers, and merchants. A mass arrest netted dozens of traffickers. The corrupt senior official was executed and his body paraded through the areas where the goods were being sold. Sales of Japanese opium and other goods dropped from $6 million to $200,000 per month. The Japanese Concession protested it was being harassed by the Chinese 3rd Section unit.

Headquartered within the Japanese compound was a "detective" organization headed by Young Zi-qing. The identity of the detective chief had been kept a secret for several years. Young's agents had been aggressively recruiting local people as distributors and spies for the Japanese. Posing as a purchasing agent for a Riqin Corporation, Chief Young deliberately developed a close friendship with Ye Feng, Commander of Hankuo's Security Garrison Headquarters. Through his new friend Ye, Young managed to plant a mole as a secretary at the garrison headquarters. The 3rd Section learned of the mole and arrested him. During their interrogation, Wen-yi's agents discovered the identity of Young Zi-qing. Young was invited to a business meeting, presumably at the invitation of his friend Commander Ye. A car was sent to bring the unsuspecting Young to the meeting. When the car reached a remote area at the side of the Guangdong Hospital, Young was pulled from the car. He was accused of five major crimes and riddled with bullets on the spot. A list of his crimes was pinned to his body. The list bore the signature, "Traitor Elimination League."[5]

A special force within the 3rd Section had targeted prostitution and gambling operations. Prominent houses and clubs offering these vices were shut down as a warning to the rest. A mysterious "Madam Zhang" became a prime target. She had been operating several private clubs for rich and influential government and military patrons. The clubs' accommodations offered gambling, drugs, and a large selection of women for sexual pleasures. The clubs were also places for gathering important information. These houses had been operating under the protection of local police and a few government officials to shield distinguished clients. One day, Madam Zhang was discovered dead under mysterious circumstances. Her chain of clubs was closed. The message was received by high officials who then shunned this form of entertainment, at least temporarily.

By December 1932, after three months of relentless raids, arrests, and selective executions, Wuhan's crime and corruption were under control, though not eliminated. The success of the investigative strike force surprised and delighted Kai-shek. Wen-yi was startled at his leader's lavish praise. News media in the country carried stories of the successful operation.

They referred to Wen-yi as "one of the Thirteen Grand Guardians of Chiang."

Japanese Gunboat Diplomacy and Wen-yi

The Japanese compound had bitterly complained to its government that activities were being severely impaired by the Chinese 3rd Section unit. In the spring of 1933, under pretense of an inspection tour, a Japanese warship carrying the Royal Prince of Japan and several gunboats arrived at Wuhan. A diplomatic note was dispatched to the governor of Hubei and the mayor of Hankou, insisting on removal of the 3rd Section personnel and termination of its interference with activities of the Japanese and their affiliates. The governor was fearful at prospects of an international incident, particularly involving the future Emperor of Japan. He sent emergency wires to Chiang and Wen-yi who were now both at Nanchang, urging immediate removal of the 3rd Section. Kai-shek was preoccupied with his Communist Suppression Campaign and had no desire to deal with these complaints. However, the danger of an international incident concerned him.

Wen-yi had already received a report of the Japanese threat. He described a possible response to Kai-shek. The 3rd Section had quietly rounded up the Chinese navigators from the Japanese ships at Hankou and had them transported to another location for "relaxation." Navigating the middle and upper Yangtze was treacherous with its dangerous rapids, submerged rocks, strong currents, and depths changing with the seasons. Without local navigators, gunships might get through but warships were at significant risk. The navigators would be returned after the Japanese withdrew the diplomatic note. Kai-shek listened skeptically and directed Wen-yi to go to Wuhan immediately to handle the case personally. It was 3:00 o'clock in the afternoon and raining heavily. My father said he would leave next morning in better weather. Chiang said, "You will leave immediately."

The flight to Wuhan in a fighter plane was bumpy and frightening. The pilot could not find the flooded airport, and was running out of fuel. He was finally forced to make an emergency landing. A shaken Wen-yi had little time to recover from the flight. He met with staff to decide on a mutual face-saving compromise, i.e., if the Japanese called back their diplomatic note and left Wuhan immediately the navigators would be returned, and the 3rd Section force would cease surveillance of the Japanese compound.

Early the next morning the uneasy provincial governor conveyed this compromise to the Japanese flotilla chief. The latter, unsatisfied but also anxious to avoid an "incident," agreed to the governor's proposal. The original navigators were immediately dispatched to the flotilla. The Japanese warships left Wuhan on the third day.

Wen-yi Forms a New Investigative Network.

The 3rd Section's operations were expanded to collect intelligence on corruption and misconduct within the military, particularly within the ranks of middle- and higher-level officers. The 3rd Section agents were embedded into all levels of the army units to monitor suspicious activity and uncover Communist sympathizers.

In one case, a corps commander reported they were under attack by a force of 30,000 Communists and requested permission to retreat. A 3rd Section agent planted in the corps reported the size of the attacking troops at only 3,000. The retreat was denied, and the commander sacked.

The commander of a large unit pursuing a Communist force in Jiangxi Province submitted an optimistic report to Central Headquarters concerning the condition and morale of his army. However, 3rd Section agents supplied a starkly different report. Food and sanitary conditions were poor. Officers were skimming money for the troops, and supplies for the hospitals. Conditions in the field hospitals were unbelievably bad due to inadequate supplies and terrible sanitation conditions.

Mounting death notices from the hospitals were delayed or withheld. Coffins were being reused. Morale of the troops was low. Additional 3rd Section agents were placed in hospitals and among the troops. The commander and several guilty officers were identified and court-martialed. Conditions in the hospital improved markedly. However, motivation among troops and officers remained low. Many complained the Japanese were the enemy, not their Communist countrymen.

In the spring of 1933, as a result of the 3rd Section's success, Wen-yi was appointed chief of the Investigation Department within the "Secretary Department" of the Nanchang Mobile Garrison, which was also Chiang's headquarters. Wen-yi now had more authority, staff members, and official funding. Taking advantage of the 3rd Section's successes, my father reminded Kai-shek of his earlier proposal to establish a network of provincial intelligence action groups to conduct counterespionage and intelligence operations against the Communists and to root out graft and corruption among the military and civilian population. Chiang immediately approved. Wen-yi recruited members from the rapidly expanding Blue Shirts to establish field units in three provinces, Henan, Hubei, and Anhui. These field units reported directly to Wen-yi's central investigation office at Jingtang Lane in Nanchang. Wen-yi now had a broad intelligence network.

Chiang designated Wen-yi's organization to receive, compile, and analyze intelligence reports from two additional intelligence and secret police agencies, the Nationalist Central Bureau of Investigation and Statistics headed by Xu En-zeng, and the Military Affairs Commission's Bureau of Investigation and Statistics headed by Dai Li. Both chiefs, Dai Li in particular, seethed in resentment to be required to submit reports through Wen-yi's organization. Dai Li's secret police organization was growing rapidly and he was already well on his way to becoming the most feared man in China. He envied and coveted a multi-province network. He'd wait and see.

Wen-yi's network had now grown to over one thousand agents. The Intelligence Department continued to receive information from Dai Li's Investigation and Statistic Bureaus, and now, also from the CC Clique. These were used to provide regular briefings to Kai-shek and his military staff. Wen-yi was too absorbed with tasks at hand to concern himself with the rivalry of the powerful heads of the two organizations. He should have been warier.

One day Wen-yi noticed Kai-shek's wife Mei-ling had arrived for a visit. He watched as the couple departed for their walk in the nearby mountains. He suddenly felt pangs of loneliness. He realized how much he had missed his wife, Bai-jian. He felt a sense of guilt they were so often apart. My mother soon received a message to join him at Nanchang. Now it was Wen-yi's turn to take his young wife for a walk in the mountains.

Wen-yi Loses a Secret Document

Early in the summer of 1934 Wen-yi was with Chiang in Lushan, Kuling. The Chiangs had a summer home in the resort area in the Lushan mountains in Jiangxi Province, close to the Yangtze River. Their two-story house, Meilu Villa, was surrounded by trees, with many flowers in the courtyard. Since Wen-yi traveled frequently to Kuling with Kai-shek he had rented a modest house to which he and my mother would go for an occasional brief vacation. Other important officials had homes in the luscious steep hills including Wang Jing-wei and Zhang Xue-liang (the Young Marshal). Chiang had built a large conference center at the edge of the resort where he conducted government and military planning.

Japanese intrusion into Chinese territory that had begun in 1931 was continuing. The fighting was escalating. Chiang's policy of appeasement toward the Japanese intruder to buy time did not prevent him from considering issues to be addressed in the event of a full war. With his advisers he had drawn up a document outlining a broad plan for the transportation of vital logistical assets, if the situation required.

Chiang summoned Wen-yi and handed him a secret document. He explained the document was an extremely sensitive one. Wen-yi was to deliver it to a courier waiting aboard a boat in the Yangtze River. The courier would then carry it to military headquarters in Nanjing. Wen-yi climbed aboard a sedan chair and was carried down the incline by coolies to a car waiting below to take him to the boat. He carefully tucked the document under his seat. The carriers paused at the halfway point called Hero's Cliff. After alighting from the chair he reached for the document. It was not there. His hand frantically swept the area beneath the seat. Incredibly, the article had vanished. Wen-yi broke out in a profuse sweat and became nauseous. It just wasn't possible!

In a panic he enlisted the aid of local police in combing the area. His fear escalated when he thought of the implications of this loss. He offered a reward of $1,000 to the one who found the document. The courier was waiting. Trembling, Wen-yi retraced his route back to the little village atop Lushan. He told himself, if the document should fall into the wrong hands he would have to commit suicide. His one ray of hope was that he had made a copy of the document, as was usual for such important papers. He quickly made still another copy, then returned down the hill. The news was bad. They had not yet found the document.

Moving almost in a trance, Wen-yi climbed into the car that awaited and was driven to the boat, where he handed over his copy to the courier. In the days that followed Wen-yi could not eat or sleep. It would be a catastrophe if the document fell into the hands of a Japanese collaborator. Wen-yi knew his punishment would be severe. Since he led an intelligence agency, how would he be able to explain his negligence? Chiang noticed Wen-yi's state of distraction almost at once. "What is wrong with you, Wen-yi? You look like you are about to die!" he said. My father told him it was just a temporary disturbance.

However, the next day, Chiang saw no change and twice commented on his aide's poor appearance. With good reason! Each day, the news from the police below was negative. The document had not yet been found. Wen-yi would not allow them to stop. Then on the eighth day, incredibly, the chief of police gave Wen-yi the news he had waited so long to hear. The document has been found and is now in the possession of the police chief! Slightly nauseous, but this time, in relief, Wen-yi hurried down to the little village to retrieve the papers.

With a flourish the police chief handed the precious parcel to Wen-yi. "How and where did you find it?" Wen-yi asked, relief sweeping over him like a wave. The chief told him a little boy had been walking along a trail and had spotted the strange paper parcel. He had taken it to his parent who had a small store in the village. The father had given it a quick look, then had tossed it among the firewood. Fortunately, there had been no immediate need for a fire. Police had discovered it during a store by store search for any information. Weak with gratitude, Wen-yi offered the police chief $1,000. "Such an amount is not necessary," said the chief. "$100 each for the policeman and for the child's parent is adequate." My father had aged greatly in one week.

Chapter 8

Disgrace, Vindication

The year 1934 began with great promise for Wen-yi, but would turn into a series of bizarre episodes placing him on an emotional roller coaster. His Investigation Section had expanded into an intelligence and anti-Communist espionage network with branches in three provinces that he ran from the Nanchang/Jiangxi Military Commission Headquarters.

Early in 1933, energized by Chiang's encouragement and acceptance of his proposals, Wen-yi recommended establishment of a special Design Committee, a "think tank" within the Nanchang Mobile Garrison to develop policies and plans for dealing with issues related to Nationalist political and military activity. Committee members would include scholars and industrial and economic experts, some with international experience. This committee would also address issues related to the economy, culture, and society. A pleased Chiang immediately accepted Wen-yi's recommendation. Chiang instructed Wen-yi to prepare a detailed proposal concerning objectives and makeup of the committee. He smilingly warned Wen-yi he would be taking on some additional duties if the committee were formed. He would serve as secretary of the Design Committee, in charge of coordinating committee members and managing results of their meetings.

New Life Movement

For Chiang, the formation of such a committee was timely because he had become increasingly unhappy with the current state of the country. He felt it was in disarray and the people disillusioned by widespread corruption, drug dealing, inflation, and inaction against the Japanese. Chiang felt it was imperative to instill a new sense of purpose and unity within the party and especially among the people. He and his wife Mei-ling had discussed the problem at length and concluded that a national movement was needed to restore Confucian values, including ethics of hard work, proper personal behavior, and hygiene.[1] As Chiang's executive secretary my father soon became aware of the new initiative the Chiangs had been considering. The Generalissimo had warned Wen-yi he would have to stretch himself over the coming weeks. Chiang was now pressing him as secretary of the recently formed Design Committee to also coordinate the actions of a new initiative Chiang would soon discuss with the committee.

Early in January 1934, Kai-shek met with the committee and spoke at length about the sad state into which the people had fallen. Undisciplined, intemperate behavior and bad social habits could not be allowed to continue if the country were to be united and freed from dangerous predators. He had discussed these problems with Mei-ling and listened to her views. He now wanted to share with the committee a broad outline of what he wished to accomplish, with the committee's assistance. He charged the group with the task of designing a framework and plans for launching a countrywide campaign to accomplish the desired goals. Simply stated, Kai-shek wanted a national conformity to his views and wishes.

The committee set to work at a frenzied pace. Their effort was led by the governor of Jiangxi Province, Xiong Shi-hui, who was also chief of staff at Nanchang Headquarters. The task took the name "New Life Movement." Within a week, my father had prepared the first draft that was sent to Kai-shek. Chiang personally edited the draft and returned it with numerous comments and suggestions. Five drafts followed in rapid succession. Kai-shek was now satisfied. An official "Special Staff Organization" was established at the beginning of February to set the Movement into motion on a wide scale. My father was assigned as this organization's secretary, with a modest monthly budget of $1,000.

The New Life Movement was officially launched at a mass meeting on February 19, 1934 by Governor Xiong Shi-hui at Nanchang City Park. My father reported that 10,000 people were expected. Three times that number showed up. The speeches outlined in broad terms the nature of the "rules" all citizens should strive to adopt. The crowd reaction was loud and enthusiastic.

At first, the seemingly benign rules stressing courteous behavior, cleanup of homes and streets, avoiding opium sales and use, and improved public health and hygiene measures received a favorable, even enthusiastic response by the people, particularly university students. The peasantry generally ignored the movement. My father was elated at the affirmative response in urban areas as the movement built up steam. He felt, perhaps naively, that he had made a positive contribution to people's welfare. However, the initial supportive reception waned as over-zealous groups, including the Blue Shirts, using fascist measures, began to issue long lists of do's and don'ts intruding into the most personal actions of individuals. Women were told how they must and must not dress, wear their hair, or act. Gowns were to be ankle-length; no tight clothes; hair combed back; no curls; no walking arm-in-arm; and no mixed bathing. Soon confusion was followed by scorn. The movement which had started with great hope and fanfare gradually dwindled, though Kai-shek continued to place a happy face on it.

Yet, despite this well-intentioned social engineering gone bad, the country was in the midst of what would later be known as the Nanjing Decade (1927-1937) or the Golden Ten Years, during which substantial progress was being made on a broad front. It was an era of reform and reconstruction that saw rapid expansion in agriculture, industry, business, banking, and democratic elections. In 1934, the Legislative Yuan was at work drafting a constitution for the Republic of China.

The Nanchang Airfield Affair
Meanwhile, an event had been unfolding that would later shatter my father's position and relationship with Chiang Kai-shek. The incident would thereafter be known as the

93

"Nanchang Airfield Affair." It began with a mysterious fire that broke out at the airport serving as a training base for the Nationalist air force. The blaze spread throughout the entire airfield, destroying barracks, hangars, and planes. A furious Chiang Kai-shek fired the aviation commissioner, Xu Pei-gen, and his staff. He ordered Wen-yi and his Intelligence Section to conduct an investigation of the cause of fire. During the probe, Wen-yi's investigators were told by workers at the field that an airplane was being cleaned with solvent when sparks from a nearby source ignited the solvent. There was a sudden burst of flames from the hot surfaces of the aircraft. The flames spread to other planes, and eventually to buildings and hangars. Investigators examined surviving documents and reported they could find no evidence of criminal activity. Sensing an opportunity to usurp Blue Shirt power, rivals Chen Li-fu and Yang Yong-tai circulated a rumor that the airport commandant Xu Pei-gen had deliberately set the fire to cover evidence of embezzlement activity, prior to a pending audit. They further suggested Deng Wen-yi had colluded with fellow Blue Shirt Xu Pei-gen in the cover-up. Shanghai newspapers printed these rumors and accused Wen-yi of collusion and taking a bribe of $200,000. There were loud demands for another investigation.

Wily Yang Yong-tai quickly recommended Dai Li be appointed to re-investigate. The fox was now in the hen house. Dai Li had long coveted Wen-yi's powerful 6th Intelligence Department. This situation presented an opportunity not to be missed. A brief background is needed to understand the reason for Dai Li's strong desire to get control of my father's organization. Kai-shek had given Dai Li permission to expand police and intelligence activities of his Special Services Division (SSD) to balance the powerful CC Clique headed by Chen Li-fu and his brother Go-fu. The two secret services developed an uneasy cooperation. Chen Li-fu disliked Dai Li and his often ruthless and terrorist methods. Dai Li was aware of this but moved ahead with his plans, undeterred. However, what Dai Li seriously lacked was an intelligence network like Wen-yi's, with broad, established contacts and influence with the military and civilian police throughout three provinces.

Wakeman says Dai Li's investigation placed the blame for the airfield fire cover-up directly on Wen-yi. An enraged and disappointed Kai-shek immediately relieved Wen-yi of all his important posts. Dai Li was there to pick up the pieces.[2] He took over my father's powerful Investigation Section and combined it with his own. Manpower at his command suddenly increased from 145 to 1722 following the airfield incident, and his empire had now spread to a number of cities and provincial districts.[3]

My father wrote the following account of the outcome[4]: *Commandant Chiang sent me a telegram to wait for him at Lushan (the mountain resort area where the Chiangs had a lovely home and my parents a rented cottage). I immediately left for Lushan. Commandant was angry. He did not want to discuss the facts of the incident. He asked me why I would accept such bribes. Uncertain whether he was serious or testing me, I laughed and said, "Why would I destroy my integrity for a mere $200,000? I do not need any money."*

"You do not need any money, but you can give money to your friends!" Chiang said.

Disbelieving, I replied, "Do you not, by now, know me better than that? It is ridiculous to accuse me of graft and accepting bribes. Please, send a truly independent group to find out the facts. And please do not punish Xu Pei-gen. If the facts prove my report inaccurate, that I am indeed corrupt, I am willing to pay with my life. I will ask you to punish me first, then the leader of the Aviation Group."

The Generalissimo appeared to calm down somewhat. He said, "Wen-yi, you are my student, my subordinate. How can you treat me and this situation with such a mocking and callous attitude?"

Soberly I answered, "Commandant, this case was clearly a deliberate plot to frame a high-level staff member and create trouble for him. Yet, you would believe it and want to punish me right away. I should cry and plead. But I cannot cry. So I can only laugh. Please forgive me. Please allow the time to do a thorough investigation. I am the suspect. You can place me in prison or I will stay in Lushan waiting for the re-investigation result. I will not escape."

"I will send people to investigate," said Generalissimo.

I went to my living quarters at the office building, packed my essential things, and walked away to my own home in Lushan, waiting for further orders.

This was my most disrespectful reaction to the Generalissimo in ten years. It was also my way to demonstrate my integrity and to refute the devious, anti-revolutionary plot. It temporarily concluded my close association with Chiang of the past ten years. Two months later, the re-investigation determined that I did nothing wrong, that the report I had submitted was correct. Commissioner Xu Pei-gen was exonerated.

The Aftermath

One day, Kai-shek summoned Wen-yi to his office. A somewhat subdued Chiang gently informed my fatherthat the results of the completed investigation had supported his conclusion. Wen-yi had been vindicated. My father felt a rush of conflicting emotions...enormous relief, elation, and a strong anger. His superior had rushed to judgment despite their close working relationship. My father was recalling words Chiang often liked to state...words Wen-yi had even published and knew by heart. "Misuse of one's position to serve private ends is corrupt...on the other hand, we must be responsible for preventing our subordinates from being penalized by groups or individuals maligning them as they try to do their jobs." Wen-yi wondered why his hero was quicker in leaping to the first part of his mandate than to the second part. He was tempted but did not dare remind the Generalissimo of his words.

Kai-shek, by now familiar with Wen-yi's temperament, noted his struggle to maintain composure. It was my father's

30th birthday. From his desk drawer Chiang pulled a personally drawn calligraphy containing words of good wishes for a bright future, and presented it to his subordinate. Chiang then said he was appointing my father acting secretary general of the powerful Lixingshe Society, pending the return of Liu Jian-qun, who was on sick leave. It was a memorable birthday for my father. He left the meeting in a daze, no longer feeling despair, but joy at his exoneration, and, yes, anger toward Kai-shek, excitement over his new appointment, and a pleasant surprise at the show of embarrassment on the part of his Leader!

Later, wryly commenting on the plots and intrigues that he had suffered, Wen-yi said, "I guess I am, after all, an amateur. I just don't do this (covert) kind of work very well." Of Dai Li, (for whom my father had mixed feelings - admiration for his drive and resourcefulness, and repulsion for his crude, merciless character) he added, "If we want to have a Himmler, then we only have Dai Li, who has the capacity for that."[5] Known as Chiang Kai-shek's most trusted protector, Dai Li would often be compared to Himmler by colleagues and foreigners who dealt with him. He would also become the most feared man in China. Of his own propaganda activity, Wen-yi jokingly referred to himself as a sort of Goebbels without claws.

At the end of 1934, the Nationalist government presented Wen-yi with the "award of excellence" medal. Typically, my father said, "I can never forget the bounty and kindness of my Commandant."

Wen-yi is Appointed Chinese Military Attaché in Moscow

In 1935, when Liu Jian-qun resumed his office as secretary general of the Lixingshe, Chiang, perhaps still penitent from unjustly punishing Wen-yi in the airfield fire incident, and to demonstrate confidence in his young aide, informed Wen-yi he was being appointed to the post of chief military attaché in the Chinese Embassy in Moscow. Head Military Attaché in Moscow! He left the meeting in a daze. Wen-yi spent two weeks celebrating the New Year with family, relatives, and friends. Their two sons and a daughter were living with Wen-yi's parents in Liling since Wen-yi and Bai-jian were frequently required to move between Nanjing, Wuhan, and Nanchang. The children were ecstatic to see both their Baba and Mama. Wen-yi was assured by his parents that his wife and children would be properly cared for while he was away. He was to concentrate only on his job.

Wen-yi Visits an Old Enemy Warlord
Before leaving for Moscow, Wen-yi took a quick trip to see old friends and officials in the provinces, seeking any knowledge and wisdom that might better prepare him for his new assignment. In Changsha, Wen-yi had dinner with General Hu Zong-nan, a friend and distinguished Whampoa first class graduate, with whom he discussed major national and world events. Wen-yi spent three days in Wuhan and enjoyed several farewell parties with many old colleagues and friends. In Beijing, he enlisted the aid of a high official to arrange an introduction and invitation to visit Wu Pei-fu, the powerful, learned leader of the northern warlords. Wu and his army had fought many battles against Nationalist troops. He had managed to rule over three northeastern provinces. He also knew of my father. Wu Pei-fu, known as the "Philosopher General," wrote poetry and did calligraphy. He was a dedicated drinker of brandy and an admirer of George Washington. It is not surprising the literary Deng Wen-yi and Wu spent two afternoons conversing about many subjects. Their exchanges were frank and flowed easily. Wen-yi asked many questions and received straightforward answers.

My father asked Wu what would eventually become of the Japanese intrusion into Manchuria. Wu answered by telling an ancient story with the moral that evil engagements always lead to self-ruin. Wu was confident the Japanese invasion of China should not last over ten years. But there were still many problems in the world.

Wen-yi then asked, "Who could rule China successfully?"

Wu, smiling: "You are probably asking me about Chiang Kai-shek. Chiang is a great leader and a blessing for China. Does it surprise you to hear this?"

Wen-yi: "If so, then why is the revolution and unification of China still in shambles?"

Wu: "It is always such that one wave hardly ceases than another wave starts."

Wen-yi persisted. "After all, it has been 20 years since Chiang pursued the revolution with Sun Yat-sen, and ten years since the formation of Whampoa."

Wu: "The world now is complicated and Chiang lacks truly talented assistants to help him."

Wen-yi: "But we are a democracy now. There is the Nationalist party to help Chiang."

Wu: "Yes, they are there. But allow me to ask, who among the Nationalists have the competence to help Chiang. Until such talents emerge, Chiang will continue to run into trouble."

Wen-yi: "I have told you of my new assignment. What are the factors that I must pay attention to as a young diplomat in Russia?"

Wu answered with the words of Confucius. "Speak reliably, behave respectably. It would work even in a barbarous country."

They had both enjoyed their amiable conversations. It was difficult now for my father to see Wu as the old and constant enemy. Wu presented Wen-yi with one of his own paintings of bamboo upon his departure. As he left, Wen-yi was reminded of the Chinese proverb, "One evening's talk with a wise man is superior to ten years' study of books."

Chapter 9

Wen-yi, Military Attaché in Russia

When it was time to depart, Wen-yi did so with a heavy heart and a sense of guilt. He had faithfully sent money home for his parents and siblings. Yet, he felt regret he had not spent much time with his parents and children. He also had mixed feelings about his qualifications to carry out his assignment as chief military attaché in the Russian embassy, in addition to coordinating activities of all military attachés in Europe. The international situation was complicated and unstable. There was an anti-Communist alliance of Germany, Italy, and Japan. China's urgent need was to obtain a military alliance with Russia against Japan. Russia and Japan, however, appeared to have an unwritten non-aggression pact with each other. Germany and Russia were contemplating a non-aggression agreement. These alliances were not in China's interests. It all pointed to a difficult Chinese diplomacy with Russia and the whole of Europe.

Wen-yi was also aware of the significant role he had played as a student at Sun Yat-sen University in Moscow ten years before. Having been selected by the Comintern to return to China with other Communist students to participate in a Communist revolution, he had become a mole, unearthed the plot, and played an important role in thwarting the attempted Communist uprising. Wen-yi had later written an anti-Communist article that was posted at the Academy. Would the Russians seek retribution or show hostility toward him? He also faced language, staffing, and personnel problems. He would have to deal with these immediate issues.

Wen-yi and three aides boarded the same Soviet ocean liner, the "Northerner," that had conveyed him from Russia eight years ago. The Trans-Siberian train made the 5,600 mile trip to Moscow in eleven days. The first class compartment helped to make the trip smoother and more comfortable. When they arrived in Moscow they immediately faced a housing problem. The Chinese embassy could provide only one room as office and residence for the chief military attaché. Wen-yi decided he would not stay at the embassy. His three assistants, however, stayed in the cramped quarters. Wen-yi found temporary lodgings at a hotel while he arranged rental of one entire floor consisting of seven rooms with two living rooms in a building near downtown. It served comfortably as attaché offices and living quarters. Because of the scarcity of rental properties my father signed a lease requiring him to pay $10,000 in advance. His colleagues disapproved of such unnecessary extravagance. Wen-yi responded that savings could be made in other areas. After all, he now had a generous expense account. With the living situation settled, he began a program of frequent travel in Russia to better understand the country.

He was amazed at how much Moscow had changed from the city he had known ten years earlier. There was now an impressive marble-lined subway system. A magnificent park with outdoor amusement facilities was now spread in an area close to the Moscow River, and featured prominent signs and slogans such as "Overtake America" and "Surpass America." During his first month in Moscow, Wen-yi was also busy getting acquainted with members of the diplomatic community, an oasis for foreigners in the cold and unfriendly police state. Wen-yi found himself at a disadvantage due to his limited knowledge of the Russian language. Unfortunately, his interpreters were not allowed at social events. Diplomats had their own supplies of good liquor, cigars, and cigarettes and often supplied them lavishly at the frequent parties to stave off boredom and frustration in this drab country. Wen-yi's susceptibility to headaches from smoke and his limited tolerance of alcohol presented another problem during endless well wishing toasts. Fortunately, he became flushed and silent rather than loud and offensive under the influence of liquor.

At one such event he was approached by two Japanese diplomats. One of them smiled and said, "Well, Colonel Deng! The last that I heard, you were a Major General. Now you are here representing your country as a Colonel. How could that be?!"

Ignoring the taunt Wen-yi replied, "The responsibility I have here is of greater concern to me than the rank with which I do it. Is that not as it should be?" The embarrassed diplomat hurriedly agreed it was a worthy spirit and quickly moved away. These events were not the highlights of my father's diplomatic career.

Wen-yi had made some progress with the ladies. With his good looks, position, money, a car, and an apartment, it was easy for him to make discreet conquests. Once, this almost got him into trouble when he employed a pretty female tutor. Although he had several interpreters to accompany him in discharging his daily duties, he felt it was imperative to receive concentrated tutoring in the Russian language. He hired a woman who gave him two-hour Russian language lessons each day. Wen-yi enjoyed banter with his attractive tutor; however, he was not happy with her incessant cigarette smoking that filled the room with a stale odor and smoke. He asked her whether all women in Moscow smoked. She answered casually that over seventy percent of the women smoked.

"Cigarettes are quite expensive and women's wages are limited. How do they manage it?" Wen-yi asked.

"That's why I tutor Russian," replied the tutor.

"There cannot be sufficient demand for women Russian tutors," observed Wen-yi.

"Then she would just take on boyfriends," commented the young woman meaningfully.[1]

Wen-yi's first instinct was to take advantage of the opening she had given him; however, he quickly dismissed this temptation with the realization she might possibly, even probably, be a government employee sent to monitor any information that could be gleaned when she was with him.

One day, Wen-yi received an invitation to join other diplomats and Russian officials, as guests of Josef Stalin, in reviewing the spectacular annual May Day parade and ceremonies. On an overcast morning, as the sun tried to break through misty rain, my father took his place with other foreign diplomats in the reviewing stand decked with red bunting, past which would march endless waves of military units and workers. Music blared from guard towers as parade units marched past Stalin and senior Soviet officials. Wen-yi stood in full military attire, with medals, decorations, and even his saber. On certain occasions, such as this, he would be in full military regalia in the morning, change into a suit for the afternoon event, then don a tuxedo with tails for social gatherings in the evening. At such times, Wen-yi could not help but think of his simple lifestyle in remote Liling.

Several weeks later, Wen-yi received an invitation to attend the July Nazi rally in Nuremberg intended to demonstrate the might of the German people, and strengthen the image of Adolf Hitler as Germany's savior. Wen-yi and two friends fluent in German sat in the section for diplomats, facing tens of thousands of people, including Nazi members, and youth guard groups. Hitler arrived amidst thunderous applause, hails, and military band music. He spoke powerfully for 20 minutes, ranting about the evil of Jews, Christians, and especially the dangers of Soviet Bolshevism. Like the USSR May Day parade, Third Reich organizations including the Wehrmacht, SS, Labor Service, Hitler Youth, and others, paraded before Hitler and his senior staff.

Wen-yi Meets a Soviet Hero from his Whampoa Days

In the early spring of 1936 Wen-yi met with now Soviet Marshal Blucher. General Vassili K. Blucher had called himself Galen in China from 1924 to 1927 while he served as Chiang Kai-shek's Soviet military adviser. He had helped Chiang form the Whampoa Military Academy and the National

Revolutionary Army. Galen had planned the successful preemptive Eastern Expedition strike against warlord Chen Jiong-ming as well as the Northern Expedition which solidified Chiang's position and the Nationalist Party in China. Wen-yi had been a newly graduated officer of Whampoa when he was assigned to his first combat duty as a platoon leader during the Eastern Expedition. His admiration for Galen had remained unwavering through the years. Wen-yi was thrilled now to be conversing with this great man from the narrower gulf between their standings. Blucher, of course, would not have known Wen-yi in those early days. However, he appeared genuinely delighted to meet Wen-yi, especially when he learned of Wen-yi's close working relationship with Chiang. The two men had a long conversation on many issues.

Displaying a slight air of superiority, Blucher told Wen-yi he was made a marshal of the Soviet Union in 1935. He had recently been designated commander of the Far East Front against the Japanese. Blucher was generous in his praise of the Chinese troops he had helped to lead. Surprisingly, he expressed much admiration for the Generalissimo. Blucher said that the poorly equipped, poorly supplied, and even poorly fed and clothed Chinese soldiers would fight anywhere and fight bravely with little complaint. "The Russian Red Army," he explained, "must have leather shoes, good coffee, and sound retirement plans." However, he was quite critical of the Nationalist party and government's overt neglect of the people and their livelihood.[2]

Little did both men know as they chatted comfortably, that the great terror of 1937-1938 and purge of the Red Army command which Stalin initiated in 1937 would claim Blucher during the next year. In July 1938 Blucher was suddenly dismissed from his post and arrested on Stalin's order. He was imprisoned without a trial and tortured to death when he refused to sign a false indictment. However, his standing with the people remained high.[3] Even Hitler, commenting on Stalin's wave of terror, said, "Stalin is probably sick in the brain. His bloody regime cannot otherwise be explained."4

Moscow - the Comintern

Wen-yi was instructed to assess the political climate of Soviet Russia's "Communist International" (Comintern) toward China. Chiang suspected the Soviets were playing a balancing game with Japan and China. Georgi Dimitrov, Comintern head of China Affairs, and Wang Ming, head of the Chinese Communist Party delegation to the Comintern, had just issued a declaration urging the Nationalists and the Chinese Communist Party (CCP) to discontinue their civil war and adopt a united front policy against Japan. For Russia, a China united against Japan would reduce the risk of a Japanese attack on Russian territory. However, the Soviets did not want to antagonize Japan by forming an overt alliance with Kai-shek, nor even to appear to be mediating a unification of Nationalists and Communists. Stalin also wanted to avert any Sino-Japanese alliance placing China's great natural resources at the disposition of Japan. Therefore, Stalin needed to appear open to the possibility of an alliance with Kai-shek.

Wen-yi and the Comintern

Wen-yi had returned to China in November 1935 to report to Kai-shek what he had learned of Russia's views on a cessation of the Nationalist-CCP civil war, and its concerns about Japan. Comintern agent Pan Han-nian had suggested to Wen-yi in Moscow that my father contact Chen Go-fu, a member of Kai-shek's innermost circle, regarding possible talks leading to an agreement between the two countries. A memoir by Go-fu's brother Chen Li-fu confirms this overture did occur. Wen-yi met with Chiang Kai-shek for one and a half hours, presenting a "political situation" report for Europe and Russia. Kai-shek was delighted Wen-yi's findings supported his thinking, and instructed him to present the information to the chief of the Executive Branch, Wang Jing-wei, and to the

Foreign Affairs Department and Nationalist Party officials. The Generalissimo also asked Wen-yi to take a few days to rest. Wen-yi ruefully said to my mother, "What a pleasant change to be receiving our leader's praise and kindness instead of a boot in the backside!"

Chiang had decided to put his own diplomatic initiative into play. His ultimate objective was to obtain a military alliance with the Soviets in the event of full war with Japan. He knew the Soviet Union wanted a unified China to engage the Japanese troops in a protracted war, thereby tying up a major portion of Japan's military assets. Chiang intended to use this as his bargaining chip in negotiations with the Soviets. The Russians similarly understood Chiang's interest in seeking negotiations with their country. Chiang's diplomacy would be conducted at two levels. At one level there would be discussions with the Comintern on the subject of unification of Chinese Communists and Nationalists against Japan. Chiang instructed my father to return to Moscow to arrange a meeting with the prominent Chinese Communist Wang Ming, now a member of the Comintern. Wang had been, at one point, Mao Ze-dong's closest rival for leadership of their party. Wen-yi was to sound him out regarding the basis for any future negotiations between the Nationalists and Chinese Communists. Chiang wanted the talks to take place in Moscow, not Nanjing. However, Kai-shek did not disclose the entire strategy to Wen-yi. He also instructed his chief negotiator Chen Li-fu to go secretly to Moscow and try to negotiate a mutual military assistance alliance with Stalin. Wen-yi's discussions were to provide an incentive for Stalin's receptivity to Li-fu's proposal.

Wen-yi told my mother Bai-jian that he wanted her to accompany him to Moscow. She was thrilled. To travel to another world, and to be with her husband!! However, fate once again dealt a cruel blow. She discovered she was pregnant, again. She decided to abort the pregnancy. The procedure went poorly, and she became very ill. A saddened Wen-yi had little choice but to proceed to Moscow alone. Bai-jian slowly recovered. To ease her pain and disappointment (and his own sense of guilt) my father encouraged my mother to use their savings to have a new home built in Nanjing. Bai-jian threw herself into the task with energy. The house would be modest, but conveniently located near the Mausoleum Park area, not far from many of the palatial homes, including Kai-shek's villa.

Wen-yi arrived in Moscow on January 3, 1936. He immediately requested a meeting with Wang Ming, according to Kai-shek's instructions. The Comintern Committee discussed the request and decided to send its representative Pan Han-nian to visit Wen-yi, to set the stage for an official meeting with Wang Ming. My father was quite familiar with Wang's background, including his rivalry with Mao Ze-dong. Wang's support of Marxism and earlier Comintern policies had dominated the strategy of the Communist Central Committee. For the past four years Wang had been living in Moscow as director of the CCP delegation to the Comintern. He was highly regarded within the Comintern and had been elected executive commissioner and member of the Praesidium.

On January 17 Wang Ming and Wen-yi sat silently staring at each other across the table, each seeking to form some initial impressions. Wen-yi saw a self-assured, youthful man of haughty demeanor gained from his years as a CCP leader. This man was an intellectual and a devoted follower of Stalin, Marx, and Lenin. On his part, Wang looked skeptically at the lean, young man trying to maintain a calm posture, but displaying a bit of uneasiness belying his confident exterior. He asked my father, "Are you sure you have the authority of Chiang Kai-shek to have these discussions with me?" My father assured him Kai-shek had specifically instructed him to do so. "You seem young to be placed in such a position," Wang Ming said. In fact, each was born in the same year. Both had attended the Sun Yat-sen University in Moscow at the same time. Wang had quickly risen to become leader of the Communist student faction. In his current position Wang wielded considerable influence within both the Comintern and the CCP.

Wang began by pointing out the Soviet Union had not seen anything to indicate the Nationalists truly wanted to fight the Japanese. "What facts have you to assure us that the Nationalist government will fight?" he asked. "There is no solid evidence that you are ready to commit against the Japanese." Wen-yi began to enumerate actions by the Nationalists showing they were indeed seriously preparing for such an eventuality. Wang brushed the comments aside with the observation that the Nationalists were still killing Communists and suppressing an anti-Japanese movement in China. Despite his protests and examples to the contrary, Wen-yi was having difficulty allaying Wang's doubts regarding Kai-shek's intentions. Finally, after hours of discussion, Wang Ming suggested Wen-yi telegraph Kai-shek to ask if he would allow a CCP Comintern negotiator to come to Nanjing and continue discussion. Wen-yi assured Wang there would be no problem, and added, "Give me a couple of days to get back to you. Meanwhile, why don't you arrange for a visa?"

When Kai-shek received Wen-yi's telegram informing him of his actions with Wang Ming, the Generalissimo exploded. This was precisely what Kai-shek did not want at this point. Wen-yi had moved too fast. He sent Wen-yi a scathing wire asking him, "Are you on drugs?" He instructed my father to tell Wang immediately that there would be no meeting in Nanjing at this time. The wire further instructed Wen-yi to join Chen Li-fu in Berlin for consultation. My father was completely mystified and stunned. He thought he had succeeded in moving things forward by arranging the Nanjing meeting, even if he may have exceeded his authority. However, Chiang had chosen not to reveal the entire strategy to Wen-yi.

My father was now in an extremely awkward position. His meeting with Wang Ming on January 23 went badly. An embarrassed Wen-yi informed the Comintern agent that the trip to China could not proceed. Wang Ming was furious. "This is very bad," he said. He had informed the Comintern that Kai-shek was moving in their direction. This was to be his major coup. Now it was evaporating. Wang upbraided my father, accusing him of lying just to collect information...that he never had Kai-shek's authority to conduct any preliminary negotiations. Wen-yi protested he had not misled Wang. Final negotiations were merely being postponed. The 30-year-old Wang retorted he should have known that a young, 30-year-old military attaché would not be empowered to represent Kai-shek in a binding way. Downcast and bewildered, Wen-yi prepared to travel to Berlin to join Chen Li-fu.

Chen Li-fu's Mission Aborted

While Wen-yi was negotiating with Wang Ming, Chiang's trusted agent, Chen Li-fu, was proceeding under secrecy to Moscow to meet with Stalin and senior officials. Secrecy was a must for the Soviets who were concerned with repercussions from Japan, and even Nazi Germany, if they learned of the meeting. Chen traveled incognito, with a false passport. When he arrived in Berlin, he found a telegram from Chiang ordering him to stay in Berlin until he received further instructions. However, to avoid staying too long in one place, Chen traveled from one country to another in Europe awaiting new instructions. Finally, he received word the timing was unfavorable. Japan had learned of Chen Li-fu's mission. The Soviets feared this information might provoke a hostile action by Japan against the USSR.[5] Chiang ordered Chen to return home. Negotiations would be pursued by a different venue. Chen took a circuitous route back, visiting additional countries. When Wen-yi arrived in Berlin, he learned Chen had left the city. In his memoirs, Wen-yi stated his position in Moscow was now untenable. In order to end this awkward situation, Kai-shek ordered Wen-yi to go on a "fact-finding" tour to several European countries and the United States, similar to what Chen Li-fu had been doing.

Chiang had to alter his strategy. He now instructed Chen Li-fu to arrange a meeting in Nanjing with the Soviet ambassador to China. Their talks took place in 1936. Chen pressed

Ambassador Dimitri Bogomoloff to sign a "mutual assistance" (i.e. military alliance) accord with China, as a deterrent to Japan. The Soviets insisted such an alliance was too risky. It could result in a German-Japanese alliance against the Soviet Union.[6] Chiang had to settle for a safer mutual non-aggression pact, far short of a military alliance. However, he felt it might, at least, deter the Soviets from aiding the CCP in their civil war. The Sino-Soviet non-aggression treaty was signed on August 21, 1937 in Nanjing by Foreign Minister Wang Chung-hui.[7]

Chapter 10

A Kidnapped Generalissimo, a Disgraced Rescuer

In early August 1936, Deng Wen-yi had returned to Nanjing from the last leg of his multi-nation tour, including the United States, as directed by Chiang. The Generalissimo was not in the city. My father was currently between assignments. A group of Fuxingshe Blue Shirt officials was preparing to travel to Guangzhou to help head off another uprising against the Nationalist government by the powerful warlords of the Guangxi Clique. Clique leaders were mobilizing for resistance against Japan and pressuring Chiang to shift his priorities to Japan. The Fuxingshe group invited Wen-yi to join them for their meeting with Chiang. On the third day Chiang Kai-shek arrived in Guangzhou. Next morning he summoned the group including my father to meet with him. Wen-yi dressed hastily to avoid being late. He was well aware of Chiang's insistence on proper attire for officials. He apologized to the Leader for his dress and was relieved when Kai-shek good-naturedly dismissed the issue. Chiang wanted to decide on the best means to defuse the simmering uprising. When the meeting was over Chiang asked Wen-yi to remain a few minutes. Kai-shek instructed him to proceed to Nanjing and wait there for his return.

Following the strategy developed during the meeting with his subordinates, Chiang managed to avert the imminent Guangxi uprising by ordering deployment of a Nationalist force and threatening the Guangxi leaders with bombings. Chiang added a 'carrot' with an offer of monthly payments to the Guangxi Clique. However, the truce was a fragile one.

Within the week Chiang was back in Nanjing, and summoned Wen-yi to his office. The initial conversation ranged from my father's recent tour to some specific problems related to activities of the Lixingshe. The Blue Shirt organization was now actively engaged in propaganda, cultural affairs, and police and intelligence activities. Finally, Kai-shek brought up his reason for this meeting. He explained that the secretary general of Lixingshe and Fuxingshe, Liu Jian-qun, would remain in Guangdong to coordinate military and political activity in the aftermath of the recent incident. Therefore, he could not continue in his present capacity as secretary general of the two large organizations. Chiang turned to Wen-yi and said, "You will assume the position of the secretary general." My father was overwhelmed. Two years earlier he had served in that position on a temporary basis during Liu Jian-qun's illness. He now stammered his thanks to Chiang for his confidence, adding he wasn't sure he could do the job properly. Chiang assured him he would not be making the appointment if he did not believe he would do well in that position. Bolstered by his Leader's trust, my father accepted the responsibility, secretly hoping it might be an interim appointment.

Turmoil at Xian and Nanjing
Wen-yi had no sooner settled into his new position than an event unfolded that shook the country to its core. This now famous event has been told in many ways, by many historians and writers. On December 8, 1937, Chiang Kai-shek had traveled to the outskirts of Xian, capital of Shaanxi Province, with his personal bodyguards and 20 military escorts. He planned to prod his two reluctant senior officers, General Zhang Xue-liang (the "Young Marshal"), who commanded the Northeastern Army, and General Yang Hu-cheng, pacification commissioner of Shaanxi Province, to mount a more vigorous campaign than they had done and bring the battle with Communist forces north of Xian to a successful conclusion. The Generalissimo later insisted he had been made aware of his personal danger by a noted journalist, Chang Chi-luan, who had been in Xian. He told Kai-shek there was widespread unrest among the troops [1] and angry demonstrations by

students and townspeople in the capital, demanding an end to civil war and unification against the Japanese threat. Nevertheless, Kai-shek and his retinue proceeded with his mission to Xian. Then, suddenly and incredibly, the Generalissimo discovered his two recalcitrant subordinates had taken control of the situation. He was now their captive.

Several versions have been offered concerning the role and motivation of Zhang Xue-liang in arranging Kai-shek's capture. Chang and Halliday suggest there was a secret plan to kill Kai-shek so that Xue-liang might take control of the entire country.[2] In Fenby's persuasive account, Young Marshal Zhang, fearing loss of his command and desirous of ending the civil war, had been communicating with the Communists, including Zhou En-lai, on the need for a united front against the Japanese.[3] Yang Hu-cheng also had ties with the Communist Party. His wife was a member of the CCP and had married Yang in January 1928 with the approval of the party.[4]

Kai-shek's harrowing experience began on the morning of December 12, 1936. His diary notes are informative but self-serving. He had been doing his usual morning exercises when the sounds of gunfire erupted outside his quarters. Chiang's headquarters was being attacked by troops led by a young Colonel Sun, acting without orders from the two generals. Several senior officers were killed. Kai-shek's bodyguards were putting up a fierce resistance. Two soldiers were sent to help Kai-shek escape through a window to the nearby mountain. A bruised, cold, and tired Chiang was eventually discovered hiding in a cave, and was taken by car to Xian where the two rebel generals, Young Marshal Zhang and Yang, awaited him at Yang's headquarters. The Generalissimo berated the two and told them he had nothing to discuss with his subordinates. Zhang tried to persuade Kai-shek to find common ground with the Communists on a united front defense of the country against Japan. A furious Kai-shek remained obstinate and defiant, referring to the incident as mutiny and Zhang as a rebel. Zhang insisted his actions were revolutionary, not mutinous.[5]

The first impulse of the CCP, particularly Mao Ze-dong, had been to put Kai-shek on public trial and have him executed. However, Stalin neither wanted nor would allow such an action. Two urgent telegrams to a furious Mao from Stalin strongly urged the CCP to work for Chiang's release.[6] Stalin felt Zhang Xue-liang had neither power nor talent to lead any united front initiative. Kai-shek was the only one with the prestige and power to lead a united campaign against the Japanese (which was in Soviet Russia's strategic interests). Mao reluctantly saw the logic of Russia's position and took satisfaction in Chiang's humiliation.

Wen-yi Acts Unilaterally

Wen-yi, now secretary general of the Lixingshe and Fuxingshe, received a wire at 4:00 p.m. on the first day, from Blue Shirt members in Xian informing him of the developing situation, but with little detail. In Xian the Lixingshe office and its members had been dealt a devastating blow by the forces of Zhang and Yang, resulting in arrest or execution. Information was slow, sporadic and unreliable. My father worked frantically through the rest of the day, seeking any additional information and thinking of possible actions the Lixingshe might take to free their Leader. He feared the possibility, however slim, that the Communists, with Russian help, would remove Kai-shek to Xinjiang or Russia by air. To my father it seemed no one in authority was taking any action. Most of the Central and some provincial government and military officials were in Xian for a military meeting and under house arrest. He decided to take the initiative. In his memoirs Wen-yi states, "Timing was critical. I took the initiative, however inappropriately, and sent two urgent telegrams over my signature as the Secretary General of the Lixingshe. One wire went to Division Commander Wang Yao-wu asking him to deploy his troops to join with the Commander of the 13th Division near Xian. The second wire went to the 28th Division Commander, Dong Ji, asking him to immediately take control of the strategic Tong Pass near Xian and to await developments."[7] Wen-yi, once again, had knowingly exceeded his authority. He had taken action faster than the Nanjing government. This time he would pay dearly for his actions, however well-intentioned they may have been.

Meanwhile, news of Kai-shek's abduction spread wildly through Nanjing and the rest of the country. The Central Executive Committee of the government in Nanjing met in heated discussion regarding what actions were to be taken. The welfare of the whole country could not be disregarded.

At 8:00 p.m. that evening Wen-yi held an emergency meeting with senior Lixingshe and Fuxingshe officials, including He Zhong-han and Dai Li, to review the action he had taken and decide what further steps must be taken to save the life of their leader. General He and my father called for the mobilization of Blue Shirt members around the country. A statement issued by 176 young generals denounced Young Marshal Zhang Xue-liang.

However, Wen-yi's action had caused a split within the Lixingshe. Co-founders Teng Ji and Kang Ze refused to attend the emergency meeting. They insisted such policies and decisions should be made by the Central Executive Committee, not the Lixingshe or its secretary general.[8] Meanwhile at the Central Executive Committee war minister He Ying-qin strongly urged a military assault on Xian, while a smaller group recommended negotiation to free Chiang. The Government Committee was enraged by the action taken by Wen-yi and the Lixingshe. Their anger was not with the strategy but the manner in which the Lixingshe had taken preemptive action without authority of the Central government. A lone Lixingshe agent left the government meeting to inform Wen-yi's meeting of the direction of discussion at the Executive Committee meeting.

Early on Sunday, December 13, Mme. Chiang arrived in Nanjing, and found the Central Executive Committee in tumult. On learning of the Lixingshe's action, Mme Chiang Kai-shek and H.H. Kung, Kai-shek's brother-in-law, who was now acting premier, requested a meeting with Wen-yi to hear what the Lixingshe intended by the actions it had taken. When my father explained his actions were precautionary, Mme. Kai-shek, somewhat reassured, again made clear she strongly favored a solution by peaceful negotiations. Then she added, "If peaceful means fail, then it is not too late to use force."[9] He Zhong-han later strongly supported War Minister General He Ying-qin, over Mme. Chiang's objection, in urging Central Government officials to attack and bomb Xian.

The next thirteen days in Xian and Nanjing were scenes of chaos and confusion. Kai-shek remained aloof in his headquarters, while his mediators sought to find ways to obtain his release. On December 22, Mme. Chiang flew to Xian with a group that included Dai Li. By now, Nationalist forces had arrived and surrounded Xian. A meeting was arranged between Mme. Chiang and senior Communist leader Zhou En-lai. The discussions were productive. Kai-shek agreed to meet with Zhou. Their meeting on Christmas Eve produced a verbal agreement that the two sides would unite in a common action against the Japanese aggressor. Fellow conspirator General Yang was against sending Chiang back to Nanjing, for fear that he might end up as the sacrificial goat. An offer of a generous sum of money, a guarantee of safety for Yang and his officers, and a vacation in Europe bought his agreement. However, Chiang would harbor deep resentment against Yang for years, with eventual fatal consequences.[10a,10b]

Kai-shek and his party were taken to the airport where a plane was idling, ready to leave. Taking what he may have felt was his least dangerous option, the Young Marshal insisted on accompanying Kai-shek back to Nanjing, saying his place as a soldier was to ensure that the Leader arrived safely. Kai-shek was pleased by this gesture since Zhang, now a prisoner, had accepted the blame for the Xian Incident, and provided a measure of face-saving for Chiang Kai-shek. They arrived in Nanjing on December 26th to a tumultuous reception which, Chiang later admitted, he received with gratitude and shame. He told the jubilant crowd it was his personal shame that he had not properly taught his subordinates to foresee and prepare for such unexpected contingencies. Though Zhang would remain in comfortable house arrest for many years, he had become a heroic figure to the people for bringing about the united front they had long been asking for. Wen-yi writes that when he heard Kai-shek had arrived safely in Nanjing, he was "overjoyed, mixed with a sense of relief and pride that he had played a significant role in bringing about his leader's return."[11] He would not have been so jubilant if he had known what was in store for the Lixingshe and himself as a result of their actions.

Post Xian Repercussions

For several weeks following the conclusion of the Xian Incident, rumors and disputes continued among government factions concerning roles played by officials in Nanjing. There has been much confusion and many contradictory accounts regarding the punitive force sent to Xian during Chiang's captivity. The motives of Wen-yi and those of He Zhong-han and War Minister He Yin-qin were questioned. Chiang was made aware of the actions of the Blue Shirts as well as the decision of the Central Government in Nanjing led by He Ying-qin to bomb Xian and launch a punitive force. Chiang was not surprised He Ying-qin and He Zhong-han had been accused of conspiracy. He had been aware both men had shown strong ambitions to rise in the party and the government. Wakeman observes that Chiang had been suspicious of Zhong-han's efforts to use his position as head of the Fuxingshe and his prominent position in the Whampoa Clique to promote his political influence in the party and government.[12] He Zhong-han had little choice but to "resign" his position as head of the

Fuxingshe, which Chiang immediately accepted. Zhong-han was sent to Europe on an exploration tour. Again, this was a routine method for Kai-shek to dismiss high-level military and administrative personnel, equivalent to exile.

He Ying-qin particularly had earned the permanent enmity of Mei-ling, Chiang's wife, for the way he had dismissed her appeal to the Central Government official to use negotiations. Ying-qin, a senior and influential official, had vehemently opposed her plea as "a woman pleading for the life of her husband." She would thereafter refer to him as "an old fool" and in even more unflattering ways. She undoubtedly conveyed her feelings to Chiang. Laura Tyson Li writes Mei-ling was so outraged at the treatment she received by Nanjing during her husband's captivity that she wrote a 26-page account of her encounters with officials. Although she did not publish the essay, Chiang undoubtedly read it.[13]

Chiang was furious at the Lixingshe for what he now regarded as their unauthorized military actions in Xian. He demonstrated his displeasure with the arrest or removal from their positions of a number of Blue Shirt members. Chiang gave orders to shut down *China Daily*, the main newspaper of the Lixingshe. Ironically, in his own account of the Xian incident, Chiang wrote, perhaps as a fanciful afterthought, how pleased he had been to hear that troops and planes were active in the Xian area. He added, "The news bears out the strong determination of the Central Government to suppress the rebellion. I was very glad."[14]

However, Chiang seems to have dismissed the possibility that Wen-yi had acted for any selfish reasons. In their long roller coaster relationship Wen-yi had been steadfast in his loyalty and had worked closely with Chiang in a number of capacities throughout recent years. He had never shown great political ambitions or wile. Xu You-wei and P. Billingsley, in their re-investigation of the Lixingshe's role in the Xian Incident, state that motives "veered between absolute loyalty, as represented by Deng Wen-yi, Chiang's former personal secretary, and the calculating response of those more politically ambitious like Generals He Ying-qin and He Zhong-han."[15] Chiang was angry that Wen-yi had overstepped his authority in deploying troops to standby positions, without authorization from the Central government. This was an act of insubordination that threatened the governance of the Central government and of Kai-shek himself. It was another example of the Lixingshe's tendency to take independent action. Chiang did not immediately ask Wen-yi to resign. Instead, he instructed Wen-yi to quietly consult and plan with Chen Li-fu to set up procedures for restructuring the Lixingshe. Two meetings were held with Chiang over the following weeks to discuss their progress.

Then suddenly, in late February 1937, a furious Kai-shek summoned Wen-yi to his office. He immediately began to berate his subordinate over reports of his "corrupt conduct" during the Xian Incident. A thunderstruck Wen-yi could hardly speak. "What have I done to merit your anger?" he stammered.

The answer astounded him. "You have taken advantage of the Xian situation by misusing 200,000 dollars of Fuxingshe funds," Chiang shouted. He said he had received a report from the Intelligence Department accusing Wen-yi of corruption on two counts. First, that he had misused the Lixingshe reserve fund in support of punitive action during the Incident, and also enriched himself. Secondly, the report accused Wen-yi of using his generous salary and budget as military attaché in Moscow to build a large house in Nanjing.

A flabbergasted Wen-yi tried to explain the Lixingshe funds had been used in the preparation and deployment of dozens of Blue Shirt members throughout the provinces to rally and maintain stability in the country, in support for Chiang during the Xian Incident. His modest house in Nanjing had been planned and work started before his assignment as military attaché, and was done with savings they had put aside for this purpose. Ironically, as a Lixingshe party theoretician, Wen-yi had helped write rules of ethical behavior for the Lixingshe. The rules required members of the Lixingshe to register their personal property. Any increase in future holdings would have to be accounted for by their regular salaries, subject to spot check. Embezzlement in excess of 200 yuans could be punishable by prison and 500 yuans by death. Many wily senior officials managed to enrich themselves while evading discovery and punishment. Wen-yi had neither guile nor stomach to take such risks.

Wen-yi told Kai-shek this was not the first time rivals and enemies of the Lixingshe had conspired to gain advantages by maligning the organization and him. Kai-shek was in no mood to listen. Chiang refused my father's plea for an investigation to determine whether the charges were valid or malicious. Instead he angrily informed Wen-yi he was relieved of all duties and titles. His position as Lixingshe chief would be taken by Zheng Jie-min, a Dai Li intelligence agent! Dai Li again! The issue was settled! Wen-yi stared at his leader in disbelief. It was all he could do to hold his anger in check. He was overcome with a sense of unreality and despair. His positions, reputation, and friendship with his Leader were in shambles because of vicious slander Chiang had chosen to believe. Kai-shek had again acted viscerally just as he had, incorrectly, in the Nanchang Airfieldnightmare. Completely dejected, Wen-yi also resigned from his position as deputy chief staff officer of Central Headquarters of the New Life Movement.

Hong Fu-jin, a senior military man who had worked closely with Wen-yi, observed around this time that Chiang would become upset and furious whenever Wen-yi's name arose. None of his influential good friends could help him. Nobody dared to face Chiang and speak for Deng Wen-yi. The Generalissimo moved ahead to dissolve the Lixingshe and Fuxingshe, i.e., the Blue Shirt Society.

My father remained at home, disgraced, with no job. He resented that Kai-shek had so readily accepted those vicious allegations, especially since Chiang was aware of the dirty games rivals played within the Nationalist as well as the

Communist Party, garnering advantage by planting false "intelligence" of corruption against high Nationalist officials, using internal contacts and newspapers' "tips." He wondered when these recurring nightmares would end.

The answer came quickly and horribly. In April of 1937, a bandit gang, perhaps having heard about the accusations leveled at Wen-yi and his "new-found riches," kidnapped his father from his home in Liling, Hunan and took him to their mountain camp in Wansai, in Jiangxi Province. Government officials and their families were prime targets of bandit groups, since it was assumed they would be more likely to pay ransom for the return of the captives. The bandits demanded a ransom of ten thousand dollars for Wen-yi's father. My father hurried to Liling to do what he could to obtain his father's release. Three relatives were sent to Jiangxi to establish contact with the kidnappers while my father frantically tried to raise the ransom. He had difficulty raising the full amount. When the news reached the governor at Changsha he offered to provide the needed ransom money.

It was too late. In June, two of the three relatives returned from Jiangxi with the grisly news they had found the kidnappers' camp, and in nearby woods they had discovered Wen-yi's father's mutilated body which had been chopped nine times. The remains were placed in a wooden box in a peasant's home awaiting my father's instructions.

When my father learned of this terrible ending, he collapsed. He remained inconsolable for days. In a fury he asked the military in the region to search for the kidnappers and kill them. One thousand citizens in Liling attended the funeral to honor their respected neighbor. Two weeks later the Jiangxi provincial troops reported the kidnappers had been found and killed.

Still grieving, Wen-yi received a letter from his close friend Xiao Zan-yu, now Kai- shek's personal secretary. The letter mentioned that during a senior staff meeting the Generalissimo had commented it saddened him to think that Wen-yi, one of the very few people who had not sought to acquire riches in the positions he had held over the years, should ultimately succumb to temptation. He added reproachfully that Wen-yi had built himself a fine big house, a sign of corruption. Chiang speculated Wen-yi had "succumbed" during his appointment as military attaché in Moscow.

It was true that, for his entire career, my father had displayed an "easy-come easy-go" attitude toward money. He readily spent government money for a "rest-and-relaxation" week in Shanghai. As a military attaché with a generous budget, he had spent money with careless indifference. When air tickets to another country were not available he would simply charter a flight. On his return to Nanjing from his multi-country "fact-finding" tour, he presented the wives of four colleagues each with a diamond ring. Unused traveler's checks were thrown into a drawer rather than being returned to the government. Yet, in accord with the Lixingshe warning against accumulating personal wealth other than by salary, his personal wealth had remained modest. It was up to my mother to take care of house expenses and save a small sum each month from his salary.

American vs Chinese Views of Corruption

Writer John Booth sat in the office of the US ambassador to China, Dr. John Leighton Stuart, former Protestant Minister, discussing Chinese morality and corruption. Stuart offered an unusually insightful analysis of corruption and moral standards in China compared to those of the US.

He told John Booth, "What we in the US regard as corruption is often entirely moral by Chinese standards. A public official often helps himself to public funds because he feels disloyal to his family not to share some of his benefits with his family who had toiled to help him to become a successful government official. If he does not return their kindness and sacrifice, he would be unmoral. He is fulfilling his highest duty to his family."[16] Apparently my father had made a distinction between this kind of corruption with family and friends and the immoral corruption of bankers and financial schemers like the Soongs and the Kungs, who amassed huge fortunes with their corrupt practices.

Wen-yi's spirit was at a low point. He wrote a long letter to his friend Xiao Zan-yu, again explaining the Fuxingshe funds in question were expended deploying dozens of Lixingshe agents throughout the provinces to reduce the possibility of mischief and to rally support for Kai-shek. Not so much as a dollar had he taken. My father's letter pointed out that his "fine big house" was a small six-room building on a leased lot his wife had built, at a mere $3000 from their savings, while he served in Moscow. (However, in view of his history of loose handling of money, it seems probable he may have sent some funds home to aid the original building budget.) As for enriching himself, his letter went on to say he had been unable to raise the $10,000 ransom demand. As a result, the impatient bandits had hacked his father to death. Did Kai-shek really think he would not pay the ransom if he had had the money? Xiao Zan-yu remembered the kindness of my mother and father during his illness. He showed the letter to the Generalissimo, adding that Wen-yi was incapable of the corruption with which he had been charged. Zan-yu later told my father that Kai-shek put on his glasses, read the letter slowly, without comment, then sighed. Yet, despite the logic of Wen-yi's self-defense, doubts remained. As the years progressed Kai-shek would continue to rebuke, demote, and promote Wen-yi, but the older brother-younger brother relationship would never be quite the same.

Wen-yi thought, how ironic...that his quick and decisive action to protect his Leader had ultimately caused his own downfall and had contributed to dissolution of the Lixingshe. Yet, contrarily, for the remainder of his life my father would insist that his actions during the Xian crisis were among the most important and satisfying in his experience, notwithstanding the consequences.

One month later Chiang delivered a Good Friday message to the country, referring to the Xian Incident, urging that sinners who repent should always be allowed to start life anew.[17] But he had, once again, forgotten his wife's admonition about treating subordinates fairly. Mei-ling said to husband Kai-shek, "Your temper is no good. You never patiently explain things to your subordinates. Also you never listen to their opinions. I'm much worried because of all this."[18]

Chapter 11

Amid the Horror a Bundle of Joy

Chiang Kai-shek was back in Nanjing from captivity in Xian. His agreement to unite his forces with those of the Communists to fight Japanese invaders had created a surge of nationalism throughout the country, boosting Chiang Kai-shek's reputation as it had not been for a long time. War tensions had risen. Japan now faced the threat of a united China, with possible help from Soviet Russia.

Chiang Kai-shek moved quickly to abolish the powerful Fuxingshe and Lixingshe. This was one of the conditions of the unification agreement insisted on by the Communists. However, Chiang had already decided to terminate the organization in its present form. He had grown increasingly uneasy with the Blue Shirts' tendency to engage in independent action without consulting Central authority. Its unilateral action during Chiang's captivity was the last straw. At this point Chiang also decided to neutralize the incessant factional fighting among the powerful Whampoa Clique, the Chen brother's CC Clique, and Dai Li's secret police. The CC Clique and Blue Shirts Society were dissolved. This was a heart-wrenching blow to my father, as one of the original founders of the latter group.

On March 29, 1938 Chiang established a new organization, "Three People's Principles' Youth Corps," which he hoped would revitalize the party. Many members of the dissolved society and cliques joined the new Youth Corps. In May, senior officials and members of the Blue Shirt Society gathered in Wuhan at a final conference to mark its cessation. All believed abandonment of the secret organizations would lead to the eventual failure of the Nationalist Party in China. Within a year, factional struggles were rampant within the Youth Corps.

On July 7, 1937, Japanese troops, on pretext of a field exercise, entered and occupied the city of Wanping near

Beiping. This action, known as the Marco Polo Bridge Incident, marked the beginning of China's "War of Resistance" against the Japanese intruders. By late July, the Japanese had seized Tianjin. Neither country would ever be the same. The Japanese, with a better trained and equipped army, began a rapid drive south, intent on taking over the major cities of China in three months.[1]

In August the Japanese struck in full force at Shanghai. On August 13, 1937, Chiang Kai-shek committed to Shanghai half a million troops, including 80,000 German-trained troops and some of his best generals. He hoped a formidable resistance might deter Japanese aggression. The battle raged through August, September, and October. The Chinese troops fought well, forcing Japan to send formidable reinforcements and hundreds of planes and warships. The Chinese troops finally retreated, many heading for Nanjing. The Shanghai Battle had been costly, with casualties of 300,000. The ruined city had lost 70 percent of its industrial capability.

Party officials asked Wen-yi to visit the provincial headquarters in the country to assess their state of readiness and make recommendations on how each province could best prepare to deal with the invader. Wen-yi did not feel he could refuse. The mayor of Qingdao, a famous northern resort city, was grateful for Wen-yi's assistance and asked him to stay for a day or two and enjoy the city. Wen-yi swam and lay on the beautiful beach. However, he was restless. When he heard about the outbreak of the August 13 Shanghai Battle, he quickly concluded his task and hurried back to Nanjing.

In Nanjing, Wen-yi observed troops and military vehicles scurrying in every direction. War in Shanghai was raging with no end in sight. Now, air raid sirens sounded and scores of Japanese bombers appeared to attack military transportation activity. Wen-yi knew it would be only a matter of time before Japan attacked Nanjing. Bai-jian was about to have a baby (me). No safe hospital could be found in Nanjing. The government and major factories were being dismantled and moved to Wuhan, the new site of government. Art treasures were packed and shipped. The civilian population was fleeing the city in droves. My mother packed household articles, and with four children and her mother, sought temporary safety in Wuhu, a city on the southeast bank of the Yangtze River, 50 miles from Nanjing.

My mother was admitted to the Wuhu General Hospital, located on a hill with a panoramic view of Wuhu and the Yangtze for miles in each direction. With Shanghai enveloped in total war, Bai-jian's and Wen-yi's newest daughter was born. The situation was so chaotic and perilous, there was no immediate opportunity to officially record my birth and name; I was simply called Tiny Sister. After my birth Bai-jian was forced to take her large family and flee to our hometown of Liling in October 1937. I was barely three weeks old. My father remained in Nanjing.

Kai-shek was also in Nanjing, but he had decided not to lead the defense against an inevitable assault on the city. On December 8, Kai-shek and Madam Chiang flew out of Nanjing. My father left at the same time. Kai-shek had ordered an army of 100,000 troops to defend the city against the rapidly advancing Japanese. General Tang En-bo was now in command of Chinese forces. My uncle Deng Wen-shi, commander of the 4th Infantry Regiment, moved into the city. His troops had fought well and bravely in the Shanghai Battle. However, the bulk of the troops in Nanjing lacked training, equipment, and organization. They were no match for the well-trained, seasoned troops from Japan. There was no support from the air force. Recognizing his impossible position, General Tang requested but was denied permission to retreat. Later, however, when the situation had turned dire, Chiang did order him to retreat. Amid the chaos it became every man for himself. Tang escaped without arranging a formal surrender.

It took only four days for the Japanese to capture Nanjing.[2] What followed has since been described in such terms as the "Asian holocaust of World War II," "genocide in the 20th century," and "the darkest side of human history." "The Rape of Nanjing" is an apt title. Sadistic Japanese soldiers conducted a seven-week rampage of massacre, rape, looting, and arson. Over 170,000 troops and 350,000 noncombatants were killed. The number of women brutally raped has been estimated at 20,000 to 80,000.[3] This atrocity has left its mark on the Chinese people to this day. After Nanjing, the Japanese moved across the North China plain and along the Yangtze westward, occupying major cities and railway lines in eastern and central China.

Chinese unity in the War of Resistance against Japan was hampered by the self-interest of the Communists (CCP) and to a lesser degree the Nationalists, each looking beyond the current war to conserve men and equipment for the ultimate internal struggle for supremacy. Each pursued a separate strategy. The Nationalists would engage the Japanese in major battles while the Communists would resort primarily to guerilla warfare. Japan's drive into the northern provinces moved quickly. By the summer of 1938, Japanese troops were approaching Wuhan. Southeast China was in peril. The Nationalist government was soon forced to move its capital again from Wuhan to Chongqing, a mountainous city further up the Yangtze River. On October 25, 1938, Japan seized Wuhan.

When the Shanghai Battle started, He Zong-han was called back from Europe to resume his position as chief of the Political Indoctrination Department in the General Military Affairs Commission. Zhong-han appointed Wen-yi as the chief committee member of a group conducting anti-Japanese propaganda and intelligence in Wuhan. The committee, however, was soon disbanded.

Wen-yi's second job in Wuhan was as chief political instructor of the Wartime Cadres Regiment and assistant director of its political department with the rank of major general. The newly-formed regiment was recruiting young cadets and cadres for training. Training and propaganda work were quite familiar to Wen-yi. With his broad contacts, he quickly recruited over 150 full- and part-time instructors, and established a political training program for the 5,000 patriotic young cadres.

In 1938, He Zhong-han and a group of senior officers recommended Wen-yi for the position of chief of the Political Department in the Chengdu Central Military Academy since he was eminently qualified. In August 1938, a reluctant Kai-shek appointed Wen-yi to this position with the rank of major general.

My mother was in Liling without Wen-yi. With Japanese invaders approaching, she gathered the family of ten and moved to the safety of Guiyang, an inland city south of Chongqing.

Wen-yi Moves to Chengdu Military Academy

As a result of Japanese military activity in the Wuhan area, a decision was made to form a new, expanded Central Military Academy in Chengdu. The Academy would become the principal training center for the country, uniting Communist and Nationalist cadets from all regional military schools.[4] At the end of August 1938 my father, the newly appointed political chief of the Central Military Academy, flew from Hankou to Chongqing to take charge of cadets lodged in the city. By the spring of 1939, Wen-yi and the Chonqing contingent were settled in the now completed Chengdu facilities, prepared to handle a large increase in cadets and instructors.

Chengdu, located in southwest China, is the capital of Sichuan, one of the large provinces, about the size of Brazil. The climate in Chengdu is subtropical and incessantly humid. Chengdu's history dates back over 2300 years. (Actually it is much older. In 1985, an ancient building complex was discovered by the west city gate, identified as a palace of the Shang Dynasty, built 3600 years ago!) The city had broad main streets with many narrow, unpaved side streets where the poor lived in dilapidated huts. Central streets like East Great Street were lined with stores and shops displaying their merchandise in attractive fashion. The many teahouses in Chengdu, estimated at 600-1000, with as many toilets nearby, [5] were constant sources for rumors and impromptu entertainers.[6] Teahouses were also an attraction for cadets, although frequenting them was not encouraged. For the young cadets weary of the Spartan surroundings and discipline of the Military Academy, the bohemian atmosphere represented a refreshing change.

Wen-yi had just gotten settled when he received a letter from wife Bai-jian on September 11. He read the letter carefully once, then a second time. *"You have just started a new job, and there are surely numerous tasks to be addressed. However, there is no need to rush through everything at once. You only have so much energy. If you demand too much, you will turn people against you. You should proceed in an orderly fashion, and tasks need not be tackled all at once at your whim. If you talk too long, you are bound to slip and give your foes issues to attack. Even though your words are good as gold, you would still make people jealous and resentful. It is best to keep a low profile. Do not act at will as you have done before; it will lead to your downfall. In your current circumstance, you can neither display your shortcomings, nor your strengths. It will be a fiasco otherwise. Try hard to be brief whenever you give a speech. You must be responsible for what you say and do! Think things through before you act. Stay calm. You should rest at least 2-3 hours during the day each day. You know, if you force your way through things, something will go wrong. Several of your earlier failures were because you did too much and said too much. I hope you will always remember these lessons vividly and correct yourself accordingly. Your temperament tends to be rash or impetuous, and not very considered or meticulous. To correct such a shortcoming, all you need is to pause more, do more thinking, and spend more time on the important issues. Work on the most important points. Then you can do nothing wrong!"* Wen-yi was, once again, surprised at his wife's wisdom. He considered her words among the best advice he had ever received. However, Wen-yi was Wen-yi.

The Academy attendance numbered seven thousand including instructors and cadets of the 13th, 14th, and 15th classes. Shortly after his arrival Wen-yi noticed an abundance of Communist literature and booklets, and a sparse collection of material from the Nationalist Party. The Chinese Communist Party had aggressively infiltrated the Academy. Wen-yi decided to discourage the activity of CCP students involved in pro-Communist propaganda and recruitment of non-Communist candidates.

During a September weekly meeting, some cadets protested loudly during the provost's speech, demanding more clothing and travel money for the graduating class. When their demand was rejected, the ringleaders shouted slogans to incite a riot. Wen-yi took notice of the leaders and trouble makers, then went to the podium. Bai-jian's good advice was forgotten. He gave a two-hour lecture on military and political events of the war, and shamed the cadets for making unreasonable demands while China was struggling for survival. Later, several cadet informers secretly visited Wen-yi and identified the activist Communist members. As a result, eight students were charged as instigators of riots and disruptions. They were arrested and court-martialed. Wen-yi then proceeded to coordinate a broad effort by the staff to print a set of Whampoa-published booklets and a *National Military Daily* newspaper.

In the fall of 1939, Chiang arrived at the Military Academy to participate in the graduation ceremony of the 15th class. Chiang's anger with Wen-yi was still evident. Chiang walked in an inspection ritual on the parade grounds with Wen-yi following behind, as befitted his position at the Academy. Suddenly Chiang turned and said, "You follow me everywhere. Does it make you feel good? I can't stand your face and demeanor. Get out of my sight!" This outburst was delivered in front of all the cadets, instructors, and guests. Wen-yi struggled to maintain his poise. The minute the ceremony was over, he rushed home overcome with shame and rage. Two Academy colleagues came to visit that evening. They saw his hurt and shame. Wen-yi shouted angrily, "I was treated worse than a bastard; what could be the meaning of such a life?"

One of his colleagues said, "He hates and loves you very deeply. Eventually he will change his current state of mind." These words were prophetic. The next day, Wen-yi came to the Academy to work as usual, his manner completely impassive. The Academy now had over 10,000 cadets and staff, and constituted a formidable force. Wen-yi was pleased with the improved cohesion of the cadet corps. They were becoming battle-ready.

A mobile garrison was formed in Chengdu for the Military Affairs Commission to handle the military and political affairs of Sichuan and Xikang Provinces. Wen-yi was appointed chief of the political department of the garrison as a concurrent position. His responsibility had now expanded to include political education as well as political work with troops in the two provinces. Wen-yi was pleased with this appointment, but the elation would soon be gone.

Chapter 12

Goodbye Mother, Now I Am a Weed

My mother, Bai-jian, had been tending the large family household in Guiyang. She decided it was time for the family to be together with Wen-yi in Chengdu. She was pregnant again, but she managed the difficult journey without complaint. Once the family was settled in Chengdu, she participated in a number of local activities in support of the war. Under the direction of Madame Chiang Kai-shek, Bai-jian engaged in fund-raising, visiting wounded soldiers and families of soldiers, and coordinating Military Academy community affairs for staff families. She remained active in all her duties into late pregnancy. In August 1939 Bai-jian developed a sore throat and spells of coughing. She had always been healthy and strong, and had simply ignored such minor discomforts. The air raids on Chengdu had suddenly increased. She was forced to move the family to the safety of the countryside. During these strenuous activities, she became ill. A doctor diagnosed her illness as tuberculosis. Bai-jian refused medications, fearing the medicine might harm the fetus. Her illness progressed. In the middle of October she was taken to the hospital. She remained there several weeks, continuing to refuse all medications. She delivered a baby boy on November 5th, 1939.

Ten days later, a worried Wen-yi hovered anxiously over her bed. Her mind was clear as she looked at her husband. She was grateful he was with her. She had done much thinking, and felt an urgent need to discuss with him things that had to be done, that she would never get to do. As she began to share her thoughts, my father suddenly became frightened. Shortly after midnight Wen-yi returned home from his vigil at the hospital. He was still stunned by the many things she had said to him. He was afraid these might be her last words. Sleep was impossible. To assuage his own misery he found a pen and paper, and began to write all he could remember of her words.

She had told him, "I have tried never to do a bad thing in my life, and have always willingly sacrificed myself for the family. But I don't think I can survive this hurdle. I had to place my baby's well-being before my own. I must share some of my concerns with you now. Your father's grave site is not fully finished. You must send 100 silver dollars home to have it finished. I haven't seen your mother for two days. I feel bad that I cannot be with her to serve her. My own mother is approaching 60. She has shared many hardships with me over the past ten years, and I have been inadequate in comforting her. Everyone respects her when I am there. I hope they will continue to respect her when I am gone. Please do not inform her of my condition. We must spare her from the fright and pain."

She had gently held his hand and said, "Wen-yi, we have been married for fifteen years, and we have always gotten along well, through good times and ones of stress. Recently, you have been especially sweet and considerate. I am so unwilling to leave you. I can only blame myself that I may not have the joy of growing old with you. You must take good care of yourself and continue your important work for the country and the family.

"I need to talk about our children. Yuan-zhong and his younger brother are doing well and study hard. I am sure their two grandmothers will take good care of them. Big Sis (Yuan-pin) and Tiny Sis (Yuan-yu, me) are fine. I do feel terrible about Second Sis (Yuan-Ai). She has sores on her feet and I did not have them treated well. Please take good care of her for me. And, above all, you must make a special effort to raise our new baby. I don't know how he is doing now. I long to see him.

"My friends and the wives of your close friends in particular have been very nice to me. Please give my regards to every one of them. Other than my mother, I have no other concerns. I know that you will take care of everything. I have not much time left. With all my heart, I still wish I would not die. But I know that may not be possible. I hope you will not be too sad.

You must take good care of yourself." My father sat in a chair and bowed his head in his arms and wept.

My mother passed away at 10:00 a.m. the next morning. In her fifteen-year marriage to Wen-yi, she had borne eight children. The newborn baby died one month after her passing. Only four of her eight children survived into adulthood.

Wen-yi was overcome with grief. He felt a deep sense of guilt for placing his career first and not being with Bai-jian when she needed him to be there. Despite his considerable writing skills, he found he was unable to express his feelings adequately. My father received 80 letters of condolence, including poems, and couplets. He asked several of their dear friends to write a brief recollection of Bai-jian as she crossed their lives. He would collect them into an album for her children which would serve as a testimonial bouquet to honor her. Two letters from among their closest friends are particularly touching.

Bai- jian, with love, from Xiao Zan-yu:

(A close friend and Whampoa graduate, he had studied in Moscow with Wen-yi, had risen to the rank of general, and worked closely with Chiang Kai-shek.)

On November 15th 1939, Li Bai-jian, wife of my friend Wen-yi, passed away in Chengdu. When I saw the notice in the newspaper, I immediately sent Wen-yi my condolence and asked for details. My brother informed me that Wen-yi had decided not to send out an obituary notice. My brother sent a large wreath in my behalf. He also told me of the baby boy that was born ten days before her death. Finally Wen-yi's letter arrived. He indicated that the funeral was on November 20th with the coffin stored in a temple to be shipped to their hometown, Liling, at the high tide next spring. He asked me to send a eulogy for a memorial album he was assembling for their children and grandchildren. Alas! How can I possibly not do so! Bai-jian was a very special woman in my eyes!

I first met Bai-jian in Nanjing in the fall of 1927 when I followed Wen-yi back from Russia. She looked girlish but unusually graceful. In the spring of 1929, I stayed at Bai-jian's place on my way to Japan. One day we talked about marriage and man/woman relationships in China. Bai-jian expressed the view that those men who were unfaithful or had multiple wives were despicable; however, their wives were partially to blame, since their lack of independence and self-esteem encouraged such behavior. She would never place herself in such a demeaning circumstance. She added that she pitied those women who lacked an independent spirit or self-respect. This was a surprising point of view, not often heard from women. I noted that her opinions were shrewd, well considered, and given calmly, with assurance. I began to view her with awe and respect. This, then, was my initial impression of Bai-jian.

She impressed me even more profoundly and earned a place in my heart until this day during the three months I stayed in her home. After the Japanese army initiated the Mukden Incident on September 18, 1931, I left Japan and came back to Nanjing. I was hospitalized with a bad case of typhoid fever. Bai-jian was asked by Wen-yi to take me to her home to recuperate. Although Wen-yi and I had been close friends, I had not known Bai-jian well. Wen-yi was often not at home. I was in a great dilemma concerning my friend's kind offer. However, with no family or other close friends in Nanjing, I did not have much choice, and accepted the offer reluctantly but gratefully.

One of Bai-jian's daily pleasures was playing Mah-jongg with her friends. When I arrived at her home, Bai-jian noticed that I did not know the game, and needed a quiet environment. She suggested to her friends that it would be best not to have the games at her house for a while. There was no Mah-jongg game in her house during my entire stay. Her family ate together, in typical Chinese fashion, and shared their favorite spicy Hunan dishes. Bai-jian observed that these

SHADOWS IN THE LOTUS POOL

were not my favorite. As she learned which foods I liked, the standard family fare gradually changed and the spicy dishes were no more.

Friendship is the most valuable thing in the world. Wen-yi had always been generous and gregarious. Bai-jian understood and respected that. She had a warm and kind nature. She treated me sincerely, affectionately, and properly. I was, and am, grateful and touched to this day.

We stayed in touch, on and off, during the following years. Every time we got together, we were as joyous as a family. Whenever she wrote to me, she would sign "your sister Bai-jian" and address me as "Master Xiao." When I wrote to her, I also called myself "Master Xiao."

Last June, Wen-yi came to Chongqing from Chengdu, bearing a letter from Bai-jian. She said she had just finished the entire book series of Su Man-shu, a famous Chinese author who tried to become a Buddhist monk. She said that Man-shu and I were very alike, etc. I laughed and put her letter aside with a warm feeling. Bai-jian had often teased me that I would become a Buddhist monk one day. She probably meant that I preferred a quiet and simple lifestyle as a loner. We often wrote Bai-jian group letters as a fun game. Everybody including Generals Xuan Shou-jian and He Zhong-han would write a paragraph with diverse messages mixed with humor. There were various participants. Wen-yi, (Liu) Yong-yao and I were the willing "designated chief writers." Although Bai-jian was unusually smart, enlightened, gracious, and serious, she could be quite humorous too. Her friends were all enchanted by her warm and gracious presence. Due to our close friendship with Wen-yi, my wife and I naturally became very close friends with Bai-jian.

This year I had permission from Generalissimo Chiang to take one year off to study. After I came to Leshan Mountain in August, I wrote Bai-jian about my current isolated living condition, that although I was not keen to imitate Man-shu, I was, however, becoming him. I asked her to fulfill her promise *and to bring Wen-yi for a visit to Emeishan with my wife and me. She answered that she and Wen-yi would definitely come. Due to the hectic schedule of Wen-yi, the trip never materialized. Soon I got word of her sickness. Who would ever have imagined that an illness in her life's prime would lead to her demise?*

Now Bai-jian has left us forever. And we have not even reached our middle age. This was not just Wen-yi's misfortune. This was the worst adversity for anyone. A philosopher would know fate and accept fate. What else can we do but to accept?

Tribute to Sister Deng Li Bai-jian, Yuan Shou-qian:

(A Whampoa alumnus; highly regarded by Wen-yi and military colleagues.)

Sister Deng Li Bai-jian passed away this past winter. Wen-yi has sent me her life story that he wrote, including her last words. His pain and grief exuded from his every sentence so that I could not finish reading it. Mourning for the deceased and thinking of my old friend leave me a sorrow that will stay with me for a long, long time.

I have often considered that caring for the elders, serving one's husband, raising the children, and managing the household are fine virtues for an able woman...but not enough to distinguish her as extraordinary. I have seen, heard, and now read of Sister Deng's many virtues. Her one most rare and precious merit was rising from being a good friend in her private chamber into a courtier offering sage, forthright guidance and admonition to her husband with regard to his work environment. Sister Deng usually observed all quietly. When Wen-yi was potentially in real trouble, she would often advise him earnestly and sincerely. She would even present him with pros and cons and debate with him continuously until he saw the light. Her succinct vision and explicit opinions are acknowledged clearly in Wen-yi's writing. Alas, courtiers and friends who offer forthright admonition are hard to come by even in history, not to mention in a private chamber! As for Sister Deng, I am full of admiration and respect. Now her brilliant light has faded forever.

On the first anniversary of Bai-jian's death, my father wrote a testament to his late wife for the last time.

In Memory of Madame Bai-jian, Deng Wen-yi:

It has been a year since Bai-jian passed away. Her image appears frequently before me. I am often listless and disheartened in the middle of the night. I have seen her in my dream as if her spirit persisted. For the first anniversary of her death, I printed this album as a memento for the children. I also want to pass along to her the happenings in the past year.

My dear Bai-jian:

Most of the items you instructed me to carry out have been done. However, it shames me to acknowledge that the baby was not well cared for, as I had no choice but to leave for Xian. The baby died within a month. The other children are healthy and in school. I will try my best to bring up them into useful members of the country. Your mother has been extremely sad and misses you badly. She has lost some weight but is healthy. She has made a great effort in taking care of the children for me. I am pleased to tell you that my mother and siblings are all doing well.

I am getting stronger physically as well as spiritually. But I still have too many jobs and am overloaded with heavy responsibilities. In my distress, I often become tiresome, and I neglect my work and friends. With the encouragement of the family and the recommendation of good friends, I have recently become engaged to Miss Shen Wen-ying. Miss Shen is gentle and kind-hearted, good in serving the old and the young, and able to attend to the family business. She will try to follow your footsteps to help my career and family. I believe you would understand and not blame me. I hope and trust that you will not think me insensitive or selfish.

Your good friends have all sent their condolences. Many of them broke down crying over the sad news. Some did not believe...they said you could not die, you will not die. You will always be alive to them though you are gone. It was moving to witness such deep and genuine friendship. You earned their devotion when you were alive, and you are not forgotten now that you have passed away. Some have missed you dearly, and blamed me harshly. I am ashamed and will do my best to improve so I will not waste your deep love and nurture of the past fifteen years.

In the past year, European warfare has expanded. The Chinese war against Japan is prolonged. This could be an opportunity for China to catch up. Perhaps in ten or twenty years, there will be a peaceful Asia. Since you were concerned about saving the country, I hope you are encouraged to hear this.

You took such good care of me in all aspects, and made my life rich and radiant. Without you I feel like I am missing both my hands. Daily chaos depresses me, and I find no pleasure in life. During the past year I have found myself passive and pessimistic, in shadows. They say I am garrulous, but I lack the skill of knowing people, and there are few friends who really know me. The saddest part of life is not that I am concerned that people do not know me, but rather, that I do not know people. In these current difficult times, friends seem not as trustworthy and families don't get along. When you were here, everything seemed to work smoothly; without you, everything is falling apart.. I am deeply disturbed at how different things are. I seek friends carefully and am anxiously selecting a wife. I can only tell my sorrow and misery to you, my deceased wife, and no one else. I hope in the other world, Bai-jian, you will continue to help and guide me. I am grateful for the abundance of articles from all the friends and teachers. I hope our children, grandchildren, and descendants will value this remembrance. You will always be in our hearts.

I was a two-year old toddler when Bai-jian died, unaware my whole world had suddenly turned upside-down, and that I had become an unwanted child. As I read accounts of my mother's sacrifices for her children and her deathbed concerns for her husband and her family, it was difficult to stop the tears for a mother I never had the opportunity to know.

Chapter 13

Reprimand, Promotion, and a New Wife

After my mother died, Wen-yi plunged into his dual work as political chief of the Central Military Academy and the mobile garrison in Chengdu. The Academy had expanded to over 10,000 cadets. The Sichuan Garrison had seven regiments. In the spring of 1940, Chengdu encountered a food shortage due to a severe drought. Trouble began to spring up around the city. Groups of students burned storage barns and looted the foodstuff. Outlaws and gangs intercepted and robbed incoming shipments of food. Communist instigators took advantage of the unrest to incite and recruit the people to their cause. Communist leaders arrived in Chengdu to supervise a "famine riot" scheduled for March.

The mobile garrison assembled a task force to maintain surveillance on this tense situation. As political head of the garrison, Wen-yi was a key member of the task force, which soon established a blacklist of possible instigators. Wen-yi held a series of emergency meetings with key task force members, including the Sichuan Nationalist Party chief, Huang Ji-lu. The group agreed on a plan to arrest the primary instigators prior to the riot. Wen-yi would coordinate and supervise the action.

During the next three days nearly 400 suspected instigators were quietly arrested. Two high-level Communists confessed to the plot. The riot attempt was foiled. Suspects were held for slightly over one week, then released. Twenty Communists ringleaders were flown to Chongqing for trial. Huang Ji-lu went to Chongqing to fill in Chiang Kai-shek on the details and outcome of the action, reserving the lion's share of credit to himself. Chiang complimented Huang and commented: "From now on, that area of Sichuan should be calm and safe for awhile." Wen-yi remained the unsung hero. However he felt gratified he finally had something to show for his three years in "the great rear" during wartime.

Still grieving over his wife's death, and facing the task of managing a large household, he grew more harsh in his treatment of cadets and faculty. Complaints about Wen-yi increased. In the fall of 1940 Chiang Kai-shek, as Commandant of the Central Military Academy, spent several days at the Academy for general inspection and personnel appraisals. He heard the complaints about Wen-yi from several sources. With a fierce scowl, Chiang severely criticized Wen-yi, "Why is it that you can never change your bad habits! You always grab power and mind other people's business. You just don't pay any attention to what I've said to you. Everything here in Chengdu seems to be in fine order except the reports of your power grabbing and getting into other people's business. This is most annoying and it bothers me!"

Dumbfounded, Wen-yi stuttered, "Commandant, this can't be true. Mine is a staff position. I have no sole authority over any person or dollar. How can I possibly grab any power? I could be blamed for assuming responsibilities for too many jobs that are piled on me. That is far from power grabbing."

"Talking back is another bad habit of yours! No matter! You should pay more attention to getting along with people."

Wen-yi decided he had no choice but to accept the blame without comment. However, the reprimand from his Leader was painful and caused him almost a week of sleepless nights. A senior Academy officer commented: "Deng Wen-yi is really having some tough luck. He gets scolded by the Commandant repeatedly. It is such a shame."

Wen-yi took seriously the recommendation to focus on "getting along with people." My father had always been gregarious, and also a spendthrift and womanizer. But now, he felt the need for the stability of married life. As an eligible bachelor and highly placed official, he was constantly sought by willing women and eager matchmakers, almost from the moment of my mother's death. Dalliance was one thing, but he knew he had to choose a wife carefully. He consulted with family members, friends, and colleagues about the problem. He even prepared a list of qualities he would like in a woman... one who would please him and help with his family.

Among the recipients of Wen-yi's largesse when he was chief military attaché in Moscow with a generous budget, was a poor scholar named Wang Shao-chen. Wang, now head of the Economics Department in Sichuan University, heard of Wen-yi's plight. He sought out Wen-yi and told him: "In my department there is a new graduate who is already regarded as the beauty queen of Sichuan University. She is also highly intelligent and still available; however, she may be unwilling to marry a widower with many children."

"She sounds like a jewel," Wen-yi said. "Could you introduce her to me and let me decide how to proceed?" He was intrigued by the general description of the young graduate: beautiful and educated. It was a challenge! He could hardly wait to meet her. He had always been very work-oriented and was well cared for by the loving wife he had lost. He felt any domestic problem could be worked out. He brightened considerably at the possibility. Their meeting was quickly arranged.

Her name was Shen Wen-ying, and she was born in 1917 in Wuxiang, Sichuan, a salt-producing county in south-central China. Her father was a thrifty, shrewd, and well-to-do salt producer who had five daughters. As a second child with a strong-willed elder sister, Wen-ying had learned to be tenacious in her efforts to hold her own against such a sibling. Wen-ying's parents were strict and protective of their daughters. They had prospered during the Resistance against the Japanese War when the demand for Sichuan salt rose dramatically, after the Japanese occupied the coastal area and cut off the source of sea salt. Although Sichuan men were generally short, the entire Shen family was tall and good-looking. Since Wen-ying's father had no sons, he was determined to give the two older girls the best education available, so they could later help to take care of the family. Wen-ying was ten years old when she and her sister were sent to Chongqing for their schooling. The journey through the countryside was unsafe because of marauding bandits. The father hired guards with excellent martial skills to escort the girls to their destination.

The sisters lived in their uncle's house in Chongqing until they were old enough to attend boarding school. The large and more cultured city fascinated Wen-ying. She particularly admired her uncle's exquisite paintings. The uncle, an accomplished artist, was enchanted by his ten-year-old niece and gave her painting lessons. Chinese watercolor painting became Wen-ying's life-long hobby. Her uncle even framed and displayed one of her paintings.

The two girls were the first from Wuxiang County to enter college. Wen-ying's older sister studied accounting and later became a successful accountant in the Communist regime. Wen-ying entered Sichuan University in 1936 and majored in economics. The school soon absorbed several other universities forced to flee from the occupied territories. The atmosphere on campus turned very political and tension increased. Communists, radicals, and political activists were constantly busy on the campus with aggressive recruiting programs. As a result students watched each other closely and suspiciously.

Wen-ying had developed into an unusually beautiful young woman, and received much admiring attention from male students at the University. She ignored the girls, who envied her and disliked her self-absorbed vanity. She placed the attentive young men into two categories, political zealots and rich playboys, both groups with indefinite future goals. She cared for neither. The end of the 1930s was an exciting time in China, but Wen-ying did not involve herself with any of the student movements. Therefore, she had few close friends. She began to worry about her future after graduation from the University.

When Chairman Wang introduced her to my father, an important general and handsome, she was immediately taken by him. The now 23-year-old woman was enchanted by this charming, dashing general who was thirteen years older. His status as a recent widower assured he did not have an old-fashioned wife hidden somewhere, as was the common practice in China at the time. He offered the possibility of a future, proper marriage. The fact that he had five young children did not faze her.

After a whirlwind courtship, they were married on November 24, 1940, barely one year after the death of my mother Bai-jian. They had a Western-style wedding ceremony. Wen-ying wore a veil and a fashionable white gown with a full train. My aunt Bi-xia served as her bridesmaid in a long white dress. There were two flower girls. My father, the groom, was in resplendent military attire with an exquisite saber. Huang Ji-lu, the Sichuan Nationalist Party chief, served as his best man. Five hundred guests attended. Chiang Kai-shek sent a personally produced calligraphy: "Yi Shi Yi Jia" or "Wishing you a happy and harmonious family."

Wen-yi's family turned out to be an entirely new experience for the bride. Bai-jian had loved and been adored by both my maternal and paternal families. They now had expectations of how a loving daughter-in-law would comport herself with her elders. However, Wen-ying had been raised in an affluent family where emotions were calmer and the daughters were accustomed to being served rather than serving. Therefore, Wen-ying was not prepared for the large, loud new family she had just inherited. She suddenly felt threatened and dismayed. She soon learned that Wen-yi's mother Ho and Bai-jian's mother Pan had taken in Wen-yi's five motherless children between them. She was disconcerted to learn that Pan, rather than Wen-yi's mother, had been the long-time money-keeper for Wen-yi during his marriage to Bai-jian. This had been a source of bitterness for mother-in-law Ho. It often flared into open clashes. Now, both mothers-in-law were trying to establish their positions with the new wife.

Wen-ying tried to appear cool on the surface but could hardly conceal her apprehension toward the large family and simmering rivalry. She felt slightly more at ease with her new mother-in-law, Ho, who was kinder, more easygoing, and closer to my father. In contrast to Ho's old-fashioned and gentle demeanor, Pan was far sharper and more outgoing. She even socialized with some of my father's friends. Ho's advantage was not lost on my maternal grandmother Pan. She arranged a quiet lunch with Wen-ying during which she disclosed, in great detail, how Ho had arranged a tryst between her relative, Aunt May, and Wen-yi, hoping to gain additional influence with him. This information so shocked Wen-ying that she rushed to the bathroom and vomited. She prayed this might just be petty gossip. It could not possibly be true!

When Wen-ying was alone with her new husband she confronted him with what she had learned. Another shock awaited her. Wen-yi blandly told her the account was true...it was no big deal. His comment was devastating. A sense of insecurity enveloped Wen-ying that would persist for the rest of their marriage. She vowed to keep as distant as possible from Wen-yi's families, starting immediately.

Wen-ying pressed my father to retrieve from his mother-in-law the money and other valuables in Grandma Pan's charge so that she, Wen-ying, could manage them. However, this was not easily done. My father encountered resistance, and succeeded in getting only some of the assets for his new wife. Wen-ying was very unhappy with the situation, and vowed to accumulate as much money as she could, on her own, from the very beginning of the marriage.

The old family members, accustomed to my father's generous and easygoing first wife, were bewildered and chagrined with the young, conceited beauty from Sichuan. Wen-ying discouraged any attempts to bond with them. She was, after all, beautiful and well-educated. Therefore, she was a superior person, wasn't she? She wanted no part of the Deng clan. She implored her new husband to move the big family away to give them some privacy and space. Wen-yi persuaded Grandmother Ho to take a grandson and two older granddaughters to the home in Hunan. My oldest brother

Yuan-zhong and I would move with Grandmother Pan to our country house in Chengdu.

Finally Wen-ying was alone with my father in their city house near the Chengdu Military Academy. My father's friends and their wives viewed the scattering of the children with disapproval. Wen-ying was isolated socially, a situation she favored. Like my mother, Wen-ying became pregnant immediately and continuously after she was married. She, however, had a purpose. She wanted to build her own dynasty. My father continued to be embarrassed when wives of his friends chided him for acceding to his new wife's insistence that the children from his first marriage be split up to live with relatives. He was also feeling the financial pinch of now having to support three family households.

While Wen-ying was busy building a new life for herself, Wen-yi did not stay idle. He felt re-assured by Kai-shek's calligraphy wedding gift, which is usually sent by the relatives or close friends of the betrothed couple. Encouraged by a new sense of affinity from Chiang, Wen-yi wrote a letter to Kai-shek and one to the Political Department of the Military Affairs Commission stating that he had done and learned all he could in the "great rear" over the past three years. He now felt compelled to work closer to the battlefield. The letter must have surprised or impressed Chiang. In the spring of 1941, three months after he remarried, Wen-yi was promoted from major general to lieutenant general and assigned as political chief of the Third Military Territory covering five provinces in the South-East.

Chapter 14

WWII, Wen-yi in the 3rd War Zone

When Wen-yi received his official orders he quickly packed and left for Shangrao, in Jiangxi Province, headquarters of the 3rd War Zone to which he was assigned. He now wore his new gold collar patch with two gold triangles and red edging for his new rank. He allowed himself to indulge in the romantic notion he would be meeting the enemy face to face, and making a direct contribution to the safety of his country. He was reluctant to leave his beautiful, young wife. However, he discovered to his surprise and relief that Wen-ying preferred to stay home, to read and paint. Wen-ying remained in the house in the city, insisting she would receive better medical care there. She gave birth to her first baby girl in the fall of 1941.

Wen-yi knew his appointment reflected the importance Chiang Kai-shek placed on political and propaganda activity within the military. Chiang repeatedly remarked, "Propaganda is more important than battle. Attacking the heart is superior to attacking a city." He insisted his earlier victories over the Communists were due 70% to political work and 30% to military effort, with propaganda as the most important political element. These were the areas where Wen-yi hoped he could make his greatest contributions. It was a big comfort to him to think that Chiang, after their recent confrontations, had seen fit to give him this appointment and rank.

The Chinese Military Affairs Commission had divided the country into nine War Zones. Each War Zone was responsible for any military action required within provinces assigned to the zone. Wen-yi's 3rd War Zone, commanded by General Gu Zhu-tong, was the largest Military Area, covering five provinces. General Gu was a longtime supporter and close adviser to Chiang. Since Gu and Wen-yi had been members of the Whampoa Clique, the commander welcomed him as a trusted member of his staff and promised full support.

After an arduous trip Wen-yi finally arrived at Shangrao in northeast Jiangxi Province. This city was important because of its strategic location on the Zhejiang-Jiangxi railway line that linked Nanchang, 120 miles to the west, and Hangzhou, capital of Zhejiang Province, to the east. Shangrao bordered the provinces of Zhejiang, Fujian and Anhui.

Wen-yi's expectations and illusions began to deteriorate almost immediately. The central military headquarters was located at a primitive and obscure site. The offices and living quarters of the Political Department consisted of a number of shabby cottages rented from civilians. After the relative luxury of the "great rear" it was difficult adjusting to the new and unfamiliar environment that would now be his military home.

The war with Japan had settled into a stalemate throughout all the provinces. Large frontal battles had given way to guerilla war by Communist troops, and skirmishes in the interior where the invader was more vulnerable to attack or sabotage. The ranks of the Japanese army had been thinned by the necessity to maintain control of cities and other captured coastal areas of East China. It was difficult for them to move troops and armor to respond nimbly to guerrilla attacks. Meanwhile, both Nationalists and Communists sought ways to preserve as much of their forces as possible.

Wen-yi soon discovered this assignment would not be what he had hoped. He quickly sensed a strong antipathy within the ranks for any political officer intent on political indoctrination and improving the resolve of the military. Wen-yi had experienced some hostility at the Chengdu Military Academy but had attributed it to a natural resentment from Communists cadets. At Shangrao he moved quickly to develop a political training course and identify candidates for intensive training, to form a cadre of qualified political officers for duty at regimental and company levels. It was even more difficult finding and training propagandists willing to work in the villages throughout the provinces to strengthen the support of the population. The civilian population had become increasingly disillusioned with the Nationalist Party. More importantly, civilians were too absorbed with survival under terrible conditions to pay heed to the propaganda of political specialists. The rift between the people and the solders had widened alarmingly. There was an innate fear of predator groups, because warlord and bandit armies descended on villages and farms and commandeered food and possessions. The feelings of the countryside were no less kind toward the government's tax collectors and landlords who kept most of the crop the peasants had sown.

Wen-yi finally had to admit that many of the senior officers in the army, perhaps including himself, were appointed based on their loyalty to the Generalissimo rather than their abilities. Many field officers either lacked the ability or the encouragement to improvise or set strategy based on situations they were confronting. Wen-yi had several times seen his recommendations denied or ignored. He wistfully remembered earlier times when he was closer to Chiang, and how he was able to persuade the Leader to take specific actions that were carried out promptly and successfully.

Wen-yi now had to deal with discontented soldiers who were underpaid, hungry, and surly. They tended to behave badly, and caused hatred among the civilian population when they helped themselves to the meager food and supplies of the local people. Words and slogans from the propagandist had little chance of assuaging the deep-seated fears and suspicions of the peasantry. Attempts to recruit local young men to fill the depleted ranks of the armies met stiff resistance from the angry population, who needed young men to till the fields. Young men barricaded or hid themselves to avoid being taken into the military.

Shortly after his arrival, Wen-yi found many of his responsibilities for the 3rd War Zone were being carried out for Jiangxi Province by Chiang's son Ching-kuo, as assistant director to the governor of the province. Though Wen-yi's responsibility extended to five provinces, Ching-kuo's influence was greater due to his status as heir-apparent to his father's position as head of the Republic of China. Chiang Ching-kuo had undertaken the task of directing the recruitment and political training of the Three People's Principles' Youth Corps, and the political indoctrination of the military for his assigned province of Jiangxi. In 1937, Chiang Kai-shek had become disillusioned with the Nationalist Party which, he felt, was corrupt and ineffectual. The members had become dejected, with little enthusiasm.[1] The Generalissimo had pinned his hopes on the Three People's Principles' Youth Corps to inspire the regime with a renewed idealism and energy. However, after 1939, the corps lost its primacy over the Nationalist Party. A tighter rein was placed on the organization by Chiang. Its role was scaled back to recruitment and indoctrination of the nation's youth. Nevertheless, Ching-kuo's personal interest in the Youth Corps as part of his power base remained strong. The corps grew rapidly from 1,034 members in 1938 to over 500,000 by 1943.[2] Wen-yi had similar responsibilities for the entire five-province 3rd War Zone, including the Youth Corps; however, he had no such ambitions and was content to work cooperatively with Ching-kuo.

In the summer of 1941, Wen-yi conducted a Youth Corps summer camp program for 400 men and women (in two-to-one ratio), mostly college students and young government workers, in Shangrao. Wen-yi functioned as the camp commandant. The students were given simple khaki cotton uniforms with slip-on fabric shoes. Camp life was Spartan but lively and colorful. The daily schedule included a half-day of political training, and a half-day for cultural and extracurricular activities. Evening sessions included political discussions or debates on current event or topics of interest to the cadets. The weekend program consisted of military exercises, swimming, hiking, and mountain climbing activities. Wen-yi was eager to learn the thoughts of these young men and women on how best to reach the people to strengthen their support for the government. Wen-yi arranged to spend much time with the group during the

40 days. He participated in many of the activities and all of the evening discussions. He had at least two individual conversations with each student.

Wen-yi particularly looked forward to the evening sessions. These were a revelation to him. The corps had been successful in increasing educational opportunities for inland communities.[3] The group now proposed to Wen-yi that cultural offerings should be provided to the villagers and the military people as relief from the daily dismal conditions, privations imposed by the non-ending war. Work groups were assigned to develop their thought and action plans. Almost overnight, the *Front Line* newspaper produced by the War Zone was expanded to include cultural items, cartoons, news releases, and special features.

Wen-yi Inherits an Internment Camp

My father had been given the unwanted task of overseeing the internment camp at Shangrao holding 3,000 Communist prisoners from General Gu's battle with the new Fourth Army.[4] The Shangrao prison staff included members of the Youth Corps, military personnel, and political specialists. The prisoners were given lectures, reading materials, and constant propaganda to re-educate them to the Nationalist ideology. Those who were judged to have been successfully indoctrinated (or had skillfully pretended to be) were given freedom to do menial tasks or to make some money by producing articles for use. Others were kept under observation for signs of "progress." Closer scrutiny was given to a smaller group of "troublemakers" who were inclined to encourage revolt. There was also a holding cage for 20 Japanese soldiers who were awaiting transfer to an interrogation center.

Pearl Harbor and the New US-China Alliance

Suddenly, on December 7, 1941, the Japanese air force delivered an unexpected, crippling bombardment of the US fleet at Pearl Harbor. The US declared war on Japan. On the following day China formally declared war on Japan, Germany, and Italy. The complexion of the war with Japan had changed radically. China was no longer alone in its struggle. The US alliance with China also served America's strategic interest. China would continue to keep a substantial part of the Japanese army, equipment, and air power tied down in their War of Resistance. It would also provide airbases for US air attacks on Japan and its supply lines. On January 3, 1942 the Allied countries jointly appointed Chiang Kai-shek as the allied chief in the China War Zone. These developments electrified and brought renewed hope to all of China.

The Japanese Attack the 3rd War Zone

On April 18, 1942, the US undertook a bold, risky move to boost American morale after a string of Japanese victories. It launched, for the first time ever, sixteen B-25 Mitchell bombers, each with a five-man crew from the carrier USS Hornet, for an unprecedented and daring bombing attack on Tokyo, Nagoya, and Yokohama, causing many fires in the cities. However, returning from the mission, the planes ran out of fuel. The crews were forced to bail out or crash-land in the Chinese provinces of Zhejiang and Jiangxi. Sixty-four airmen parachuted into the area around Zhejiang. Most were rescued, carried to safety, given shelter, and nursed back to health by the Chinese civilians. Eight airmen were picked up by Japanese patrols. Three of the men were publicly executed, and the remaining imprisoned for the duration of the war. The unexpected raid stunned the Japanese people and its leaders with the sudden recognition that the US air force could now attack Japanese shipping in the South China Sea, cutting off the supply of oil and other vital materials.[5]

In June, a force of 53 Japanese battalions (100,000 troops) launched a pincer campaign in the 3rd War Zone. The main objective was to destroy airfields to deprive the Americans of bases for future air strikes against Japan, and to destroy food sources. Its second objective was to punish the Chinese people for rescuing and sheltering the US airmen who had bombed their homeland. Japanese troops moving from the east targeted strategically located Shangrao. In the face of the threat of a major military attack by the Japanese, a decision was made to move the 3ʳᵈ War Zone Headquarters at Shangrao to Fujian Province. Headquarters and the internment camp were dismantled and the retreat begun to a more secure zone in southern Jiangxi and northern Fujian Province. The prisoners were escorted by a heavily armed military detail, in the intense summer heat. All but 500 of the prisoners were allowed to walk unconfined.

Wen-yi and two of his aides were last to leave, having remained to observe the progress of the Japanese force. They watched as their base at Shangrao was shelled by Japanese artillery, causing fire and ruin. The small group hurried away in their car to join the main body. As they crossed a pontoon bridge they were spotted by two Japanese planes. A quick strafing run missed the car, which immediately headed for a wooded area to hide. On the fourth day a Communist guerrilla force who had been following the retreat mounted a successful breakout strike prearranged with some of the Communist war prisoners. Many of the interned prisoners were quickly recaptured by the troops. The relocation move took two weeks.

The Japanese Atrocities

As the Japanese army retreated it unleashed a campaign of biological warfare across East China. Retreating invaders deliberately placed lethal pathogens, including plague, typhoid, cholera, and anthrax, in the food and wells in villages in dozens of counties, as punishment to those who had assisted the American airmen, and to render the area unusable for airbases.⁶ Behind this horror was mastermind General Shiro Ishii, a microbiology expert who commanded Unit 731 located in Manchuria in northeastern China. Planes from his unit circled villages known to have harbored Doolittle's fliers, spraying mists of plague, cholera, and other pathogens from the tail section onto the villages and rice fields. Within two weeks villagers were dying horrible deaths. Widespread outbreak of diseases followed in Zhejiang, especially in the area of Jinhua and Xiayi in Jiangxi. In three months an estimated 250,000 civilians and soldiers had died from the pathogens, more than the combined death toll of Hiroshima and Nagasaki.[7]

As the Chinese engaged in their planned withdrawal to a safe zone Wen-yi was instructed to plan and assemble a sizable military and provincial political force to guide many thousands of civilians with their portable belongings to safety zones, following the general route of the troops. Wen-yi reconnoitered the exit roads past Quzhou and Jinhua in a car with his staff. There were many logistical problems to be solved to meet the needs of the huge civilian population. He remained in close contact with Commander Gu to secure food and medical assistance for the civilian followers. During the two weeks of military withdrawal, nearly one million civilians, old and young, walked nearly 200 miles from central Zhejiang toward the boarder of Zhejiang and Jiangxi to reach safe zones.

My father reestablished the political army headquarters in Fujian. He felt the internment camp had outlived its usefulness. The required manpower and money could be used in better ways. He recommended to General Gu that the camp be closed. Gu agreed and formed a committee to analyze the attitude and behavior of the remaining interned prisoners during their almost three-year captivity. Those most familiar with the prisoners placed them into two groups. The largest group contained the least rebellious. These would be given a choice of joining the Nationalists or "escaping." A small group who were judged to be the hardcore chronic troublemakers who had not responded to the three-year reform program would always be a threat. These would be executed. This decision affected Wen-yi more than his fellow military officers who were more battle-hardened than he. Two weeks later the camp was shut down.

Wen-yi Visits a Troubled University

Wen-yi learned that Communist student agitators at Xiamen University in Fujian were causing considerable disruption. He decided to visit the University, which had been temporarily relocated from Xiamen to the safety of mountainous Yangting in western Fujian. The university president received Wen-yi coolly. He reluctantly agreed to give Wen-yi 15 minutes to address the student body at the regular morning assembly. My father began a quick, terse analysis of the harrowing events in Jiangxi and Zhejiang and internationally. The meeting was allowed to go on for 90 minutes. The young audience asked that the talk and discussion be continued in the afternoon. Taking his cue from the student body, the now cordial university president invited Wen-yi to have lunch with him and some faculty members and to resume the assembly after the lunch period. In the afternoon session Wen-yi was careful to avoid partisan comments, but talked of the country's challenges against the Japanese and China's place in the international community. A week later he received a letter of thanks from the university president expressing his appreciation for Wen-yi's calming talk and discussion with the students. The student body agreed to a moratorium on their clashes and to unite against the Japanese.

Meanwhile in Chongqing, a brooding Chiang, desperate for a better quality military, again decided to place his trust in the nation's youth. He raised the inspiring slogan, "An inch of blood for an inch of country, a hundred thousand youths for a hundred thousand troops," and enlisted thousands of college, high school, and high quality youth. The well-trained youth would form the core of the new Youth Army, and would provide a new energy and loyalty to the Nationalists. The Generalissimo recalled his son Chiang Ching-kuo from his job in Jiangxi to be director of studies at the new cadets' school in Chongqing, with the Generalissimo as nominal president. He also ordered Wen-yi to Chongqing in the winter of 1943, to serve as the chief member of the planning committee to develop a political training curriculum for the new Central Cadre Academy. The Academy would have a university structure with a graduate school (Research Division) for university graduates and an undergraduate school (Special Training Division) for high school graduates. My father was also assigned as chief instructor at the undergraduate school and instructor in the graduate school.[8] Local professors were pressed into service to teach a variety of academic subjects. Of the 7,000 applicants, 300 students were selected for the rigorous first one-year curriculum of the graduate school, and 400 for the undergraduate school. These were to be candidates for future top jobs in the government.[9]

Happily, our family was reunited with Wen-yi in Chongqing. I left Chengdu to join the family. We lived in a house along the Yangtze River within the Central Cadres Academy grounds. Finally, Wen-yi was able to live with his family again. But he was heavily involved with his work and had little time to see much of his three little squabbling daughters. Meanwhile my brother remained in Chengdu and my two elder sisters in Liling, Hunan.

Wen-yi enjoyed teaching, though the instructors found it difficult to cover the entire military-political curriculum crammed into an accelerated three-month term. Wen-yi and the rest of the teaching staff spent almost all of their time with students. After two semesters Wen-yi's duties with the Youth Corps were completed. He officially resigned from all his current affiliations including the 3rd War Zone. He was appointed bureau chief in the Central Political Department for the Nationwide Military Political Works. His responsibility was now considerably increased and so was the complexity of the job. However, it was free of the multiple jobs he had been dealing with in the past. This would quickly prove to be a mistake.

Chapter 15

A Weed in the Wind

A Chinese proverb says a child with a mother is a jewel and a child without a mother is a weed. When I was two years old, my mother died, and I became a weed. My new stepmother Wen-ying was living in the city of Chengdu and planning to join my father in Jiangxi. My Big Brother Yuan-zhong and I were with our Grandmother Pan in our country house in the suburb of Chengdu. Our house was located in an exclusive suburban enclave, built by the government for high-ranking officers, to provide some protection from Japanese air raids. It was a large, elevated one-story house with a long, wide porch across the entire front. The property included detached quarters for guards and kitchen staff. The house was encircled by a lovely garden, and protected by a tall surrounding wall. A fig tree in the backyard provided a constant supply of delicious fruit during the season. Outside the wall was a large apple orchard.

Grandma Pan soon realized she would be alone with no steady income, no support, and a troublesome little girl on her hands. She needed to reduce her expenses. My wet nurse was the first one to be dismissed. Two maids followed. Big Brother, as the eldest son, was my father's favorite and adored by Grandma. She sent him to the best boarding school in the city. Soon only Grandma and I remained in the large country house. We still had a cook and two male servants who had no place to go. She decided to rent out the guard house, and later, part of the main house for income. She also became a vegetarian and turned to the Buddhist religion for comfort.

Grandma was not interested in me, another girl. It did not help that I was a bit of an imp, and at times, even unruly, a consequence of improper caring and discipline. Grandma constantly complained about the heartaches I caused her. She ignored me as much as she could and wished, I was sure, that I would disappear.

I was left to fend for myself, grateful for any occasional kindness that came my way. Once, when Grandma had to be away, she locked the doors of the main house and left me in the "care" of the men servants. I was three years old. I had to share the bed of one of the servants and was molested. Fortunately I was too young to fully comprehend this horror. Eventually, all the servants were gone and there was only a local, part-time helper. Now, when Grandma had to be away, she locked me in a room. The window of the room was too high for me to climb out. I was enraged and exhausted with crying and screaming. I often ended up loudly singing songs I made up, denigrating my grandmother.

We were in the midst of the bitter Sino-Japanese War, and China was struggling for its survival. Children and adults were dying throughout the land. Peaceful Chengdu seemed like heaven under the circumstances. At age 4 or 5, I often roamed about the beautiful countryside, usually with some neighborhood children. The land was fertile and we feasted on tomatoes, peas, broad beans, and anything edible. We amused ourselves by collecting silk worms. We picked leaves from mulberry bushes to feed our personal collections of worms kept in shoe boxes. We competed in finding the choicest silk worms based on the size and color of the worms and cocoons. The lovely pink cocoons were the most desirable.

My young friends and I decided to steal apples from the trees in the orchard next door. Since I was the smallest one, I was boosted to the top of the wall to do the picking. I was busy choosing and picking the ripe apples when the angry owner descended on us. Everybody dispersed. I was left alone on top of the wall, too afraid to jump down. The neighbor helped me down roughly, and confronted my grandmother with the loot and the looter. Grandma gave me a whipping.

At the age of four I attended kindergarten. I had to walk past a large flock of geese gathered along a creek. One or two cantankerous geese would always stiffen their long necks, raise their feathers, spread their wings, and chase after me. Each day

I approached the area cautiously, then ran as fast as I could, praying I would not stumble.

The restrictive classroom atmosphere was hard on me. I was restless and bored. Most of the pupils were from good families and well cared for. Nobody wanted to be friendly with an untidy little girl. Without tap water and proper facilities, bathing me was troublesome for Grandma. Once, when I had developed a rash due to the heat, the part-time maid bathed me with a pink water containing potassium permanganate, a primitive disinfectant.

When I was six, Uncle Wen-can, my father's cousin, came to borrow money. Of course Grandma was not going to give him any. She made me sleep with him at night, and again I was molested. I was helpless, enraged, and miserable. I hated this uncle and Grandma. The experience placed a greater distance between Grandma Pan and me.

One day, my stepmother Wen-ying made one of her rare visits, accompanied by her sister. I watched as they peeled and ate one juicy pear after another. Pears were rare and special. Though I stared, licking my lips, they did not offer me so much as a sliver. In fact, they never even looked at me. For Wen-ying, her six-year-old stepdaughter simply did not exist.

As did many children, I developed a bloated belly due to a serious case of tapeworms. There was no one to take me to the doctor or provide the needed medicine. One day the tenant of our main house spread some mysterious medicinal plant roots over the back patio to dry under the sun. They looked edible and I helped myself to a handful. The result was miraculous. I eliminated all the tapeworms from my system. I felt invincible. I had cured myself of the parasite, an award for being adventurous in eating all kinds of strange things.

I often listened to the adults as they conversed. I felt it would be wonderful to be able to use some elegant-sounding words. I found myself trying to imitate their language. When I casually told a tenant in our guardhouse that he was being "preposterous," he smiled and said to his companion, "Who would believe that a little girl could use words like that!" The unaccustomed compliment and kindness made me feel warm and proud.

Big brother Yuan-zhong, seven years older than I, was a happy part of my childhood, and I longed for his visits from school. Grandma and I usually ate simple vegetarian food in small portions. I was always hungry and craved meat. Only when Big Brother came home would Grandma prepare meats and plenty of food. My brother often allowed me to join him as he played with his neighborhood friends. I felt proud to be seen with him. One night he and his friends took me to a school play. As we walked home, I was delighted to see a clear moon in the creek as we crossed the little stone bridge. I noticed the bright moon always remained directly over my head. I asked my brother why the moon always seemed to follow us. He quickly changed the subject.

My brother occasionally allowed me to go with him to the market. I watched as he played the dangerous sugar-cane cutting game. For a small amount of money, he would take his turn, standing on a stool, wielding a sharp cleaver, hacking at a tall, fat, and free-standing sugar cane. It was scary yet thrilling to see the shining cleaver coming down with such speed. The hacker kept whatever piece he could chop from the cane. We shared the pieces from his prize. But the best moment for me was when he bought me a large, steaming sweet-bun. As I bit into it, hot spiced sugar and fat would squirt and drip down my face and hands. It was heavenly!

Such happy moments, however, were few. Big Brother did not come home often. Alas, when I later tried to tell Big Brother of those happy times and how much they had meant to me, he did not even recall that I had been in the Chengdu country house.

I seemed to be constantly hungry. One day, as I was playing on the street, one of Grandma's friends asked me to take her gift of four boiled eggs and four rice pastries to Grandma for the coming May festival. The temptation was too strong. I feasted on the treasured goods during the day, and said nothing about it to Grandma. On the May festival day, some relatives and her friend were coming. I was sure her friend would mention the eggs and pastries. I was in serious trouble. I knew the issue would come up after the company departed. I remained outdoors in the street as long as I could. Finally near dusk, I came home. Full of apprehension, I walked back and forth in the garden along the front porch, and dared not enter the house. Aunt Bi-xia, my father's youngest sister who was the most kind to her motherless nieces, was sitting on the porch with the other visitors. When they saw me they beckoned me to come in. But I was worrying about a possible whipping. I continued walking back and forth trying to decide what to do. I heard Aunt Bi-xia say, "Look at the pathetic little thing! This is so sad." She called out, "This is Aunt, Tiny Sis! Come on in! Everything will be all right!" My poor Grandma! I had no idea that the sympathy of the relatives caused her more embarrassment than the anger about the eggs and pastries.

Grandma came from a humble background. She had noted my independence and, yes, spunk, and used this as her excuse for letting me fend for myself... to grow up on my own. I would have preferred that she showed more caring and understanding. On the other hand, she never asked me to do any house chores or to wait on her. She placed me into school as early as possible. She had taken away the opportunity for her only daughter Bai-jian, my mother, to attend school so that she could help out around the house and in the field. Bai-jian had to wait until she was much older to resume her education.

Eventually, I became too much for Grandma. She informed my father and stepmother, now in Chongqing, in no uncertain terms, that she was returning me to them. She would find somebody to take me to Chongqing. Within days she found an acquaintance who would be traveling to that city. She packed my bag and sent for the man who would escort me. As I prepared to leave, my grandmother sat with me and said in a kindly voice, "I cannot take care of you any longer. You must be more obedient to your stepmother than you have been with me. You must control your high spirit. Do you understand?"

I nodded, then burst into tears. Clearly uncomfortable, Grandma patted my hair awkwardly and said, "Go now."

I was apprehensive about leaving Chengdu where I had lived six of my seven years. Chongqing was 200 miles east of Chengdu. Travel was slow due to the war. The bus made an overnight stop on the way. My temporary custodian was a lean, small man. During supper, he hinted to me we could have fun in bed. The glitter in his eyes frightened me. When we went to the room, I felt homesick for Chengdu, fearful of the unknown ahead, and petrified what this man was going to do to me. I started to cry loudly and miserably. My crying dampened his ardor. He said he had children of his own and he would not touch me. Tears saved me. The next day I was delivered to my father's house. I was seven years old. My life in Chengdu was over. I arrived in Chongqing, the war capital of China, in the winter of 1944.

Following Japan's massacre and occupation of Nanjing in 1937, the government was forced to move to Wuhan, and later to Chongqing which became the official provisional capital for the Nationalist Government from 1938 to 1946. The Japanese onslaught forced the Nationalist government to dismantle and move factories and equipment to the new wartime capital. With these came hordes of migrants, students, and universities, transforming the inland port into China's political, industrial, economical, and cultural center. The constant and heavy bombardment of Chongqing by the Japanese air force was alleviated only by mountains and almost perpetual fog.

Compared to Nanjing and Chengdu, Chongqing appeared almost primitive, built on steep slopes overlooking the confluence of two major rivers. Crude streets were laid out haphazardly. Local transportation consisted mainly of walking through muddy roads, climbing a series of stairways to get from the lower to upper levels of the city, or hiring sedan chairs or rickshaws. Little was done to improve the infrastructure or ambiance of the city, except for government buildings and grounds.

Freshly arrived in Chongqing, I was relieved to find my father had arranged a jeep and driver to wait for me at the bus station. This cheer, however, was short-lived. Our upward journey took us to Renaissance Ridge, a government housing complex for high-ranking officers. We passed an entrance heavily guarded by soldiers carrying big guns, and approached a dark forest along a lonely road with no signs of life. I felt many eyes watching from behind trees. I grew uneasy and apprehensive. "What if my stepmother does not want me? If I misbehave again, would the soldiers punish me?" I held onto my seat tightly. As the jeep moved along the seemingly endless winding road, my panic increased. I began to tremble and became nauseous. Suddenly, I was blinded by brilliant lights. I could see open earth and sky...and there, perched on the edge of a high cliff, my father's house. From the jeep, I stared into the vast space below, where two large rivers converged and intersected the city of Chongqing. But my exhilaration was momentary. There was no one outside to greet me. My worst fears were confirmed. The mistress of the spectacular house was not interested in my arrival. My father was away on assignment.

At 27, my stepmother Wen-ying felt burdened with raising two daughters of her own and being heavily pregnant with a third. She had always been intimidated by my father's large family, including my mother's relatives. She was not happy to see me, a reminder of my mother. I had borne the negligence of my grandmother in Chengdu. Now I could see the obvious resentment from my stepmother. I was afraid of her.

My stepmother carried her resentment to the dining table, pointedly keeping the better quality foods from me. I was very conscious of her scowling glances as we ate. I dared not reach for the meat and vegetable dishes. My bowl contained plain rice, with a hint of vegetable. My father was rarely home and was unaware of this mistreatment. He had always been self-centered and was now preoccupied with improving his unstable relationship with Chiang Kai-shek. Wen-yi spent most of his time at government headquarters or traveling. As always, he treated his daughters with a sort of benevolent neglect. My half-sisters, at least, enjoyed the affection of their mother. At one of his few appearances at the dinner table, my father remarked on my "preference" for rice. "You are picky about what you eat," he said. "You should eat more meat and vegetables. It is your sisters who should eat more rice." My eyes welled up, but I did not dare to complain.

I enrolled in a grade school for the children of officers. I was immediately an outcast because of my shabby clothes and awkward behavior. The girls were busily engaged in knitting projects. I looked on with envy. I did not have an allowance and received no encouragement at home for such frivolous things. I found two sturdy old incense sticks and asked the girls for end-pieces of yarn they discarded. One girl even gave me a generous amount. I tied the pieces together and began happily to knit a long scarf. The task gave me a sense of accomplishment. Then, the girl who gave me the large amount of yarn demanded it be returned. I had to unravel the entire project. My pent-up misery overflowed into a prolonged period of crying. My stepmother's sister who was staying with us at the time was curious and asked me what was wrong. Tearfully, I told her. She sniffed, adding, "What is the fuss? Just go and buy some." She was not aware I had no money, nor did she offer to help me.

My classmates had come to Chongqing from various parts of the country. Most conversed in cultured Mandarin. We were often required to recite verses from books during class. One day, after I had completed my recitation, the teacher asked the class, "Does everybody notice that Deng Yuan-yu converses in Sichuan dialog only, but recites in perfect Mandarin?" A compliment! I treasured that moment for the entire day.

My father's youngest sister, Aunt Bi-xia, attended college in Chongqing and visited us sometimes. On my day off from school, she occasionally took me to her dormitory and sometimes would allow me to remain overnight with her. These were among the few happy times of my stay in Chongqing. She bought delicious hot, spicy Sichuan dishes which we happily shared. We rode a three-piece-chair or "slippery poles" containing a piece of wood for seat, a piece for the back, and a piece for the feet roped between two long bamboo poles, shouldered by two carriers. This was a common method of transportation in the hilly city. I was thrilled and scared as the carriers ran up and down the very steep mountain paths like goats galloping in a great hurry.

I confess, I was mischievous even with my favorite young aunt. She loved to tell her friends of the day she had left me alone in her dormitory while she attended classes. When she returned to the room, she stared at my face, now completely covered with her lipstick, rouge, and eye make-up. I felt sheepish, but joyful at her howls of laughter. I cherished this young woman. She remained the only person who always remembered me and showed me constant kindness and affection during that period of my life, something I had not received from my grandmother, my brother, or my stepmother, and only sparingly from my father Wen-yi.

In September 1945 the exciting word spread throughout the city: the Japanese had surrendered to the Allies!! Aunt Bi-xia took me to town to see the victory parade. The streets were packed with people and jeeps, amid euphoria and continuous bursts from firecrackers. This was the first time I had seen so many foreigners. Many stood erect in their slow-moving jeeps, laughing and flashing the victory signs with both hands. We all laughed and waved back happily. The foreigners seemed happy and friendly, though they all looked the same to me.

During these months, I had grown substantially. My clothes became worn and tight. My young aunt was outraged at the poor quality and condition of my clothes. She complained loudly to my father and demanded money to buy proper clothing and shoes for me. Of course my father complied, which infuriated my stepmother. Her attitude toward me became even chillier. Then, one morning, I finally rebelled openly against my stepmother, over an egg. At breakfast, there was often a platter of fried "pocket eggs" for the whole family, except me. Eggs were special during those days. The cook and servants were aware of my stepmother's slight. In a defiant mood, I helped myself to an egg as everybody sat for breakfast. The startled maid tried to stop me. I snapped at her, "My father's money paid for all these; why can't I have one!" The table froze at this outburst. My stepmother's face turned white with anger and astonishment. She ordered me to leave the room. Word spread quickly among the servants and family. This was a first! Little Yuan-yu was the only one among the siblings who had dared to defy her stepmother! My stepmother was already frustrated with the birth of yet a third, to her, worthless baby daughter. My defiance was the last straw! She complained bitterly to my father that she was overburdened and could not handle such a "rebellious child." She persisted with her complaints and threats until my father promised to find another solution.

I was shunted from one family to another as a temporary measure. I stayed with several of my father's friends with children. They noted that I was always either fighting with the children or leading them into mischievous pursuits. One by one, they returned me to my father. I was then sent to a young couple with no children. I stayed with the Lins for several weeks. In their close living quarters, it was difficult not to see the blood in the bathroom where Auntie Lin used the toilet. I was amazed at the woman's lack of alarm, not yet aware of the normal monthly occurrence for young women. When my brother came to visit me and the young family, I loudly and excitedly related to him how "Auntie Lin was sick and passed a lot of blood in the bathroom the other day." Mrs. Lin and my brother were very embarrassed. I was soon returned to my father and stepmother, again!

My stepmother became alarmed at the prospect of having to raise me. The following weekend, my father and stepmother were chatting in the large covered patio facing the dazzling open valley below. I played quietly on the veranda nearby trying to overhear their conversation. I heard my stepmother's loud lament and ultimatum to my father. "You see? Nobody can handle her. She is driving everyone crazy here. She has to go. I don't care where or how!!" Shockingly, I heard my father reply: "All right, I will send her away."

I cried myself to sleep that night. What will become of me?

My father was much troubled by this problem. He finally thought of his brother Deng Wen-shi who had often jokingly teased Wen-yi to give him a couple of his daughters. Wen-yi wrote a letter to Wen-shi explaining Wen-ying just could not handle all these children and asking whether he would consider adopting me.

Uncle Wen-shi was born in 1906 in Liling, Hunan, two years after my father. He was a graduate of the fourth class at Whampoa Military Academy in 1926. While my father worked closely with Chiang Kai-shek and the Nationalist Regime as a senior staff officer, my uncle was an army field officer. He saw his first action as a platoon leader during the Northern Expedition against the warlords in the north. In 1936, now a lieutenant colonel, he participated in the rescue mission during Generalissimo Chiang Kai-shek's captivity, known as the Xian Incident. The following year, he commanded a regiment that fought valiantly in the famous Shanghai Battle against the Japanese. He was also in the one-week unsuccessful battle against Japanese invaders, resulting in the Nanjing massacre. He was forced to retreat with 1,000 troops from Nanjing. Wen-shi had seen action in many battles during the long Sino-Japanese war, and was promoted to major general in 1942. My uncle was commander of the 65th Regiment, 205th Division of the Youth Corps[1] in 1945.

Wen-shi was delighted to receive my father's offer. He discussed the matter with his wife Ke-ming, who was childless. They had adopted a boy, Yuan-cheng, now seven years old. They both thought it would be nice to have a little girl about the same age to play together. Wen-shi wrote back and accepted

Wen-yi's offer gladly. Several of his officers in training in Chongqing would accompany me on their trip back to Shaoguan.

My fate was settled and I was about to be handed off, once again, to another household in a strange place. Since I was still in the family, my father felt the arrangement would not change my relationship with him. Upon my departure, Wen-yi told me in a kind voice, "Yuan-yu, you will have a long journey. Your uncle and aunt do not have a daughter. They will take you into their family. You should call them Baba (Dad) and Mama. Try to be good and to please them!" I started to cry quietly. My father watched. He seemed sad and even a bit upset.

I was eight years old. I left my father's spectacular house by the same route by which I had arrived a year before. Nobody came to see me leave or to say goodbye.

Chapter 16

Taiwan - Shangri La on the Island of Sadness

As I began my journey eastward to join my uncle and his family I felt miserable and afraid, with no idea of what lay ahead. The colonel assigned to escort me to my new destiny, however, was gentle and kind. We left Chongqing with two other officers in a jeep. Everybody was friendly and reassuring, and we had nice food all the time. I soon relaxed and was curious about everything along the way. It was a long trip that took several days. I was very tired when we finally reached Uncle Wen-shi's 65th Regiment, 205th Division of the Youth Corps in Shaoguan, Guangdong Province in southeastern China. It was evening, and I could hardly keep my eyes open. However, I remembered to address my uncle "Baba" as I had been told. Wen-shi seemed pleased to be called by that name.

I noticed he was much darker-skinned than my father. He had large black eyes with short hair. He told his adjutant, "It is too late to leave the regiment now. Yuan-yu can sleep with me tonight." My uncle normally stayed with the troops at the regiment. The colonel, my traveling companion, commented, "That might not be a good idea, Regimental Commander. I am afraid she has lice in her hair."

I slept on a cot at the regiment. The next morning, I was sent to my aunt Ke-ming in the family quarters located four or five miles from the post. The property was well sheltered from Japanese air raids during the war. As I approached my aunt's house, the door opened immediately. Before me was Aunt Ke-ming, tall, serious, stylishly dressed, and highly excited at my arrival. My cousin Yuan-cheng, their adopted son, was considerably less enthusiastic. A group of military wives had gathered to view the new daughter of the regimental commander. Their welcoming smiles were soon replaced by much muttering among the group. The new arrival needed a bath, badly! A tub of hot water was brought into the large room. My aunt removed my knitted sweater top and pants. The ladies gasped. I wore not a stitch of underwear. I felt ashamed at their expressions of horror. Before long, my hair was scrubbed and the lice removed. My dingy clothes were replaced with much better quality garments, including new underwear.

Despite this promising start, I soon encountered problems in my new life. Yuan-cheng, one year younger than me, had been spoiled by much attention and resented my intrusion. Almost immediately, he began to taunt me. "Leave, go away, we don't want you here!" he yelled at me repeatedly. I cried. I felt trapped and fearful. Where could I go? What would become of me? I blamed myself. I felt bad and worthless. That was why nobody wanted or loved me. I soon found Yuan-cheng was equally disrespectful with the servants. He had already acquired the title of "obnoxious terror" among them. Yuan-cheng would pinch and kick me quietly for no reason. When I fought back openly and loudly, my aunt Ke-ming immediately took his side and chided me for picking on him. It was inconceivable to her that her darling boy would instigate any fights. My promising beginning was quickly turning into another nightmare. I soon discovered that, despite the happy front she had displayed with the military wives earlier, Ke-ming would not be a solace for me. I was simply a new headache for her.

However, she faced a more serious problem. My uncle was rarely home. Several friends kept informing her of his numerous extramarital indiscretions. She was powerless to deal with her dilemma. I recalled an incident I had witnessed earlier in Chongqing. A young woman arrived at my father's house one day, crying, screaming, and causing a huge commotion. She identified herself as a mistress of Wen-shi when he was quartered in Chongqing. He had abandoned her when he relocated to Guangdong. The woman had been expelled from her family for the shame she had brought them. She was destitute and demanded compensation. She was finally given a small amount of money and turned away by the servants.

I began to understand why Ke-ming was unhappy, unstable, and irritable. Her demeanor was one of an intensely frustrated and ill-tempered woman, insecure with her status. We attended a reception for Wen-shi's vice commander and his pretty young concubine. The vice commander's wife, much older than her husband and frumpy, was busy serving as hostess with a brave, forced smile. I saw Ke-ming's expression as she reacted to the wife's barely concealed misery. It was a reminder of her predicament. Ke-ming's inability to bear children added to her insecurity. Unfortunately for me, I often became an object of her frustration.

Wen-shi and his regiment seemed to move from place to place; therefore, he was hardly ever at home. Ke-ming had bought an attractive two-story house in Changsha, capital of Hunan Province. One day, Ke-ming announced we would be traveling to Changsha and the new home. During the train trip, I developed motion sickness. I threw up from the upper bunk and sprayed the lower seats. My aunt was livid. She slapped me in the face and continued to beat me. An outraged passenger yelled, "Stop punishing her. She can't help it. She is just a kid!" Beset with her own insecurities and miseries, Ke-ming was not about to show sympathy for a child throwing up in the train.

We finally arrived at our new house which was protected entirely by a high wall. In the front there was a wide carport and a large garden. The second floor of the house had a spacious parlor and dining room with two large rooms in each wing. The bathing room, utility room, and toilets were located behind the main building, on one side. The other side had a well with trolley and buckets for drawing water. Further back were the kitchen and living quarters for the maids, an adjutant, and the guards. The house even had electricity, a novelty for many at the time.

A new house did not automatically improve my life. Spankings became routine when I was even slightly mischievous or if I fought with Yuan-cheng. Then, one winter evening, during one of the beatings, I rebelled. I ran to the stairway, took off some of my clothes, threw them at Ke-ming, and screamed that she would never beat me again. I did not want her clothes, I would run away, and she would have to deal with my father regarding anything that would happen to me. To my amazement my outburst shocked and frightened her. She remained aloof but she did not beat me again. It was a revelation for me! I could actually achieve a bit of power with my wrath! To my astonishment, my "home" conditions improved. My aunt provided me with decent food, clothing, and schooling, but with no trace of affection.

During the Chinese New Year festivities, games were played with real money. I had never seen so much of it in a pile. I stole and hid a large bill. My aunt suspected me and demanded we search for it. I was frightened. During the "search" I pretended to discover the bill in a corner of the room. I gave the bill to her. It did not spare me the inevitable punishment.

Yuan-cheng and I had to share the bedroom with Ke-ming while the house was filled with guests for the New Year. One evening I took to bed some candied nuts I had hoarded, and ate them secretly. The crunching sound as I chewed seemed like the crack of thunder in the quiet room. Of course, I received another tongue lashing. I wondered if I did these things in anger due to the years of deprivation. However, I now was receiving good food and clothes. I was even given vitamins, fish liver oil, and delicately fried liver dishes for nutrition.

Yuan-cheng continued to harass me. One day when I was taking a bath, he tore off the doorknob and violently opened the door wide to see me naked in the tub. I was furious and complained to Ke-ming with the torn-off doorknob. She took the metal knob and threw it at me with force. I dodged swiftly and was not hit. I understood I was not to lodge any more complaints with her. Ke-ming treated the servants in the same way, throwing things at the maids and striking them when they made a mistake or displeased her.

Aunt Ke-ming frequently entertained with small dancing parties. She wore her hair like the Japanese women, with high buns in front. She instructed the hairdresser to give me a permanent and a similar hairstyle. She also had western dresses made for me. A teacher at school shook her head and clucked at me, probably disapproving my hairstyle. I learned to dance and soon could sing just about every popular song from the record player. The servants called me their little singing star. My aunt, however, rarely taught me things. One of her lady friends told me to smile when I was dancing and even while walking.

A young man who attended these parties seemed to take a special interest in me. He would dance with me and occasionally take me to the movies. It was all quite innocent. My aunt said nothing at first, but later commented wryly, "I heard that man hugged you in the movie house!" Her tone showed disapproval and disdain, but I did not care. The man was sweet and he showed a measure of affection I missed and craved. I began to notice my appearance in a vain, silly way. I decided I must have a slim waistline like the movie stars in the magazines. I made myself a belt and tied it around my waist when I went to bed at night. Ke-ming grew curious and asked me if it was a female sanitary belt. I had a vague idea what she meant, but I wondered, "Could a nine-year-old really need one?"

Wen-shi was promoted to brigade commander of the 1st Brigade of the 205th Division in 1946, and we joined him in the city of Guiyang in Guizhou Province. One day he took the family on a brief vacation trip. The trip was originally intended to appease my aunt, who constantly complained about his absence and infidelity. However, they continued to quarrel in the hotel. For some reason my uncle and I shared a bed in a separate room. I was innocent and in good spirits. When I saw him changing his underpants, I even giggled, saying, "I see you, I see you!" However, when he got into the bed, he began to fondle and molest me. I was petrified and cried silently and miserably in the darkness. Wen-shi said to me, "This stays between you and me. Don't tell anybody!" When I saw my aunt the next morning, I dared not complain to her.

Wen-shi had a complex personality. He was an incurable womanizer and sexual predator, with a temper. He had developed the coarse language and tough demeanor of a field soldier. Yet, strangely, he seemed kind and gentle at home. He came home to spend the night more often now, at least for a while. During these periods, things improved in the family. Yuan-cheng did not blatantly taunt me. He continued to be a menace, however. He would ride a bicycle over a little puppy. He kicked the servants, but he stayed away from me. On two occasions my uncle came to my defense, in a way. I burnt myself slightly on the upper arm as I was playing with a hot iron the maid was using. My uncle noticed the burn mark. He turned angrily to my aunt and said, "You should take better care of the children!" Several days later I was sitting in the back of a jeep driven by an adjutant. My uncle sat next to the driver. The adjutant parked on a busy street. I jumped out on the street side. A car driven by a doctor grazed me, knocking me down. Though I was unhurt, the adjutant pulled the doctor out of his car, slapped him, and proceeded to beat him. One did not resist a militiaman. Wen-shi had his say too, in army language, "I'll blast you dead, you son-of-a bitch!" I was afraid he might mean it.

My uncle continued to molest me whenever he had the opportunity. One day Wen-shi said to me, "Let us go upstairs later, and I will show you how to do a French kiss." I was terrified and wanted to throw up. My aunt called me and I ran out of the room. I had escaped another indignity. Fortunately, the degree of my uncle's molestation was constrained by a fear of the consequences if my father were to learn of his conduct.

Wen-shi and his Family Move to Taiwan

In the spring of 1947, Uncle Wen-shi and his division had been battling the Communists in northern China. Suddenly he was ordered to Fujian Province to take command of the 205th Division of the Youth Corps. He was ordered to proceed with his troops to Taiwan, following the bloody events of the previous weeks, to maintain stability on the island and suppress any future revolts.

The trouble had begun in 1945 when the early contingent of mainland Chinese arrived in Taiwan. At first, they were greeted as liberators by the Taiwanese. However, during the 18 months under the inept rule of Governor General Cheng Yi and his corrupt government and ignorant troops (some of whom considered the Taiwanese as Japanese or Japanese sympathizers), whatever goodwill had existed earlier had turned to disillusionment, resentment, sense of betrayal, and hostility. On February 27, 1947, the seething tension on the island exploded over a small incident in which a police officer confiscated a supply of cigarettes from a woman peddler, knocking her unconscious with the butt of his pistol. The crowd of angry Taiwanese bystanders in Taipei grew into a mob that stormed the police station and government offices. The uprising spread throughout the island on February 28. Governor Chen Yi summoned military reinforcements from Fujian Province on the mainland to quell rioting and anti-government demonstrations by "Communists and radical groups." Military retribution spread to organizers, intellectuals, teenage students and random population. The February 28th or 228 Incident left within many Taiwanese a deep, lasting bitterness and hatred toward mainlanders. Wen-shi's 205th Division arrived in April with the task of maintaining calm.

Uncle Wen-shi, Ke-ming, Yuan-cheng, and I flew to Taiwan in a small military airplane. This was my first experience in a plane. I was nine years old, thrilled, but afraid of the height and noise. My ears plugged and I suffered impaired hearing for several days. Upon landing, we were greeted courteously and escorted in a caravan of cars to Taichung, a major city in central-western Taiwan. The ringing in my ears did not stop me from feeling an awed admiration for the beautiful property that would be our home. We rode past the guards at the gate and through a circular driveway, finally stopping in front of an exquisite house. It resembled a Japanese shrine, with gracefully flared roofs and intricate wooden walls and windows. We entered the spacious foyer lined with maids and servants, then the living room. We were all overwhelmed by the grandeur and beauty of the room. The furniture and accessories were magnificent. Through glass doors on one entire side of the living room, one could walk into a serene Japanese garden. It contained exquisite bonsai plants, orchids, and a picturesque pond consisting of water cascading from a low terrace, a bubbling fountain, intricate stone features, and exotic colorful fish. It was Shangri La!

The formal dining room-ballroom was huge. Yuan-cheng and I were agog with excitement, and we ran from room to room, gawking at the floor-to-ceiling windows. The area next to the rear bedroom was adorned with curving verandas and a garden delicately landscaped with winding stone paths. From the house we had a full view of a lovely municipal park across the street, with a large lake and pagodas. I learned, later, that "our" house had once been the official residence of a prominent Japanese officer of the highest rank in Taichung, who had escaped to Japan.

Our stay in Taiwan was the highlight in each of our lives, including Wen-shi's. We were served by an attentive, well-trained staff, happy to be employed during those chaotic times. Natives from Hunan would show up from time to time to cook us Hunan delicacies to relieve any homesickness. My uncle often entertained colleagues and visiting dignitaries from mainland China. Occasionally, I would be asked to sing a popular song for the guests. The parties were usually formal. On one occasion a distant relative who was the chef-of the-day proudly presented two fat, live chickens to the assembled guests, as a preview of the scrumptious dinner in store for them. My uncle was livid and my aunt aghast at this crude display.

In June my father arrived in Taiwan, one of several investigators sent by Chiang Kai-shek during this period, to gauge the nature of the unrest and develop suggestions for reforms that would ease the tensions of the population. Leaders of the island, including General Peng Meng-chi, deputy commander-in-chief, greeted him on his arrival. The whole family accompanied Wen-yi on his sightseeing tour of the island. My father was relieved to see I appeared to be doing well. He gave me fifty US dollars which I kept for many years. Our lifestyle and the island impressed him so deeply that he sent my brother Yuan-zhong and oldest sister Yuan-ping to spend the summer with us.

I could not get over the enormous contrast between this exotic island and the mainland. Taiwan was neat and orderly with lush subtropical growth and sparse population, while the China I knew was chaotic with litter everywhere and packed with despondent people. The local Taiwanese people seemed always polite, pleasant, modest, and patient, remnants of earlier Japanese influence.

In the fall I entered grammar school with little enthusiasm. I faced a language barrier, since I didn't understand the Taiwanese dialect. Classes were conducted in an oppressively rigid atmosphere similar to the earlier Japanese schools. As the daughter of a military chief, I became the "leader" of a group of girls in after-school activities. We usually played in the remote part of our immense garden. Our favorite pastime was playing house. We did real cooking, with food and ingredients pilfered from the kitchen, in tiny tin cans on a fire set up secretively among the rocks. We ate our cooked fare from crude metal containers.

Perhaps as a result of the many hours of running and playing amidst the hot and humid vegetation, I became infested with head lice, nothing new to me. I combed out the lice with a very fine comb. Our proper, elegant Taiwanese maid saw what I was doing and was appalled. Ignoring my pleas, she informed my aunt, who scolded me and immediately sent for the medical officer. He freed my hair of lice with some chemicals.

Curiously, Ke-ming became morose and prim in our elegant surroundings. What little gaiety she had, subsided, including any between her and my uncle. Their relationship appeared distant and formal, like that of many Chinese couples. I had heard the gossip. Apparently Wen-shi had several concubines and other transient affairs with women.

I shared a large bedroom with eight-year-old Yuan-cheng. Our beds aligned head to toe in one side of the room, both fitted with mosquito nets in the evening. This arrangement did not deter my uncle from entering the room and reaching inside the net to fondle me. Why a highly positioned man with concubines and endless women at his disposal would resort to molesting a defenseless little girl has always remained a mystery to me. I tried to pretend a deep sleep and dared not make a sound during such violation. I was afraid to tell Ke-ming since I feared the consequences.

Oddly enough, other than displaying this one despicable trait, Wen-shi was always kind to all in the family. Ke-ming was resentful that my uncle favored me over their adopted son. My rebellious and mischievous nature frustrated her. She frequently showed her negative attitude by scolding and striking me to alleviate her bad mood. However, she seemed to think that having Wen-yi's daughter in her charge should strengthen her position in the extended family. I was well fed and clothed, but there was always a distance between me and my aunt. Sensing her frustration and hostility, I never trusted nor confided in her.

While we were enjoying our luxurious lifestyle in Taiwan, the civil war between Chiang Kai-shek's Nationalist regime and Mao Ze-dong's Communists had been escalating at an alarming rate. Wen-shi was promoted to commander of the 205th Division at the end of 1947. The 205th Division was ordered back to Qingdao to fight the Communists in May 1948. Wen-shi assigned an adjutant and a distant relative to escort the family back to our home in Changsha. How I hated to leave this beautiful setting!

Back in Changsha

Changsha was still calm when we arrived. Ke-ming reunited with her acquaintances, but they appeared to be distant and engaged with other activities. Yuan-cheng and I went to a neighborhood school. I was an instant celebrity with my western dresses, different dialect, and frequent military escort. The class president, a cute boy with beautiful calligraphy skills, seemed to be very fond of me. One day, our teacher, tired of my restlessness and inattention, ordered me to stand up. I could not do so. Out of boredom, I had wrapped and tied my shoelaces to the desk legs! As punishment I was forced to stand against the wall in the back corner of the classroom. As the students were leaving at the end of class, my hero, the class president, approached the teacher to plead for my release.

My uncle sent us some fur coats from the front line, as well as a large sum of money through a military friend. Ke-ming asked Adjutant Hsu to fetch it and instructed me to go with him. Because of the raging inflation and radical depreciation of currency, we received several huge sacks of money and had to cart them home by rickshaw. Hsu felt insulted that my aunt had me tag along on this errand and grumbled to me, "If I wanted to walk away with the money, does she think a ten-year-old kid could stop me?" Actually, Hsu helped us through some difficult times and fulfilled his duty with high integrity. A more pragmatic reason for his loyalty may have been that he had nowhere else to go, like most of the Chinese people at the time.

1. Deng Wen-yi, Cadet - First
Graduating Class, Whampoa
Military Academy, 1924

2. Gwen's parents, Deng
Wen-yi and Li Bai-jian,
1930

3. Deng Wen-yi in full regalia - Military Attaché to Moscow, 1940

4. Wen-yi remarries: 4th from left, Aunt Deng Bi-xia, bride Shen Wen-ying, and groom Wen-yi, Chengdu, Sichuan, 1940

5. Deng Wen-yi and Generalissimo Chiang Kai-shek, 1946

6. Gwen, Aunt Ke-ming, Cousin
Yuan-cheng, Guangdong, 1946

7. Wen-yi unites with family during an inspection tour of Taiwan.
(left to right) Aunt Ke-ming, Uncle Wen-shi, Gwen, local girl,
Cousin Yuan-cheng, Wen-yi, 1947

8. Yun-fu National Elementary School, 6th grade, graduating A-Class. Gwen's 6th grade teacher Mr. Yen (front, fourth from right), Gwen (back row, seventh from right), 1950

9. Wen-yi visits daughter
Gwen at Tainan Provincial
Girls' Middle School, 1952

10. (Left to right) Li Zong-ren (later, Acting China President) and Wen-yi, 1949

11. Chiang Ching-kuo (left), Kai-shek's son and future successor, and Wen-yi, 1960

12. Wen-yi, General and Mrs. Gu Zhu-tong, and wife Wen-ying, 1960

13. Family Portrait with my siblings and half-siblings, (front): 2nd from left, Wen-yi, 4th, Grandma Ho, 5th, Wen-ying holding baby Yuan-yi, (back): 2nd from left, Gwen (Yuan-yu), 3rd, Brother Yuan-zhong, 1955

14. Wen-yi and his sister Bi-xia (sitting), and his first family with Bai-jian, 3rd from left is Gwen, 1982

15. China Paramount Leader Deng Xiao-ping and my father Deng Wen-yi, 1990

16. Deng Xiao-ping's Successor, President Jiang Ze-ming and Deng Wen-yi, 1991

Chapter 17

One War Ends, Another Begins

The Allies' war against Japan was approaching a critical stage. The US military command estimated an invasion of the Japanese mainland could result in one million American casualties.[1] The USSR's active participation in the war against Japan was vital. At the Yalta Conference in February 1945, Roosevelt, Churchill, and Stalin agreed that the Soviets would be granted concessions in Manchuria in exchange for the Russians' entry into the war against Japan. Chiang Kai-shek had not been consulted. Patrick Hurley, then American ambassador to China, disliked the Chinese Communist Party (CCP). He was furious. He called the Yalta agreement "a cowardly surrender to the Communists."[2] He returned to Washington to tell an ailing President Roosevelt the treaty would destroy the territorial integrity and political independence of China. However, Roosevelt died on April 12, 1945, before he could act on Hurley's recommendations.

Russia declared war on Japan two days before the Japanese surrender, and immediately took over Manchuria, with its 50 million people, natural resources, and industrial capabilities. Wen-yi had been in the field for four years as a senior officer sharing responsibilities with the commander-in-chief of the 3rd War Zone and its five provinces. He was acutely aware that grim times were ahead. The economy was in near ruin. Inflation soared uncontrolled amidst blatant corruption and profiteering, contributing to an increasingly resentful population. The quality of the troops had dropped steadily as the combat losses of trained soldiers were replaced by untrained, inferior, unwilling draftees. The Communist ranks were increasing. Soviet Russia's presence in Manchuria, thanks to the Yalta agreement, enabled the Communist armies to re-supply themselves with arms and equipment left behind by the Japanese. Wen-yi had to admit Mao Ze-dong was proving to be an astute military man and administrator with more than his share of able generals.

When World War II ended in 1945, the people's support for the Nationalist government was in steady decline, while the Communist Party had been busily building up a grassroots following among the peasantry. There was little time for celebrations with the rest of the world. After ten years of internal strife and eight years of war against Japan, the country faced the prospect of a civil war. Both the Nationalists and Chinese Communists rushed to take over territory Japan had occupied, especially the prize of Manchuria. The US Air Force air lifted 500,000 Nationalist troops to North China and Manchuria. US Marines established a force of 55,000 in Manchuria until June 1947.[3] Ambassador Hurley was ordered to try to mediate an agreement that would lead to a united and democratic Chinese government, under the Nationalists.[4]

This was not what Chiang Kai-shek wanted. The Generalissimo really wanted a continuing military alliance with the US to support his government in the event of a civil war. He reluctantly accepted American mediation, believing that if mediation failed, the US would continue to support the Nationalists. Mao was aware of the American support of the Nationalists, but wanted to forestall any US military intervention while the CCP built up its own forces. Both the Nationalists and CCP agreed to the meetings, each with the ultimate goal of complete control of the country.

In August 1945, Mao Ze-dong and Zhou En-lai flew from Yanan to Chongqing with Ambassador Hurley to confer with Chiang and the Nationalists in what turned out to be a futile effort to avert a civil war. In November 1945, an angry Hurley returned to Washington and resigned abruptly, charging that America's China policy was being changed by a State Department with Communist leanings.[5] Truman sent the distinguished soldier and statesman George C. Marshall to China as the President's special envoy with the personal rank of ambassador to mediate for peace between the two parties.

General Wedemeyer warned Marshall that hardliners on each side held intractable positions and simply would not make any compromise. Sixty-six-year-old and much revered Marshall, accustomed to success in his many endeavors, was less pessimistic. The Chinese people appeared to support Marshall's mediation upon his arrival. However, Marshall was caught in a no-win position. The ambassador did manage to arrange a temporary truce between the two adversaries.

The New National Assembly

Meanwhile, reassured by some early victories, and responding to the country's demands for "peace, democracy, unification, and reconstruction," Chiang plunged into the development of a new National Assembly and a constitution for a new elective government. Delegates to the National Assembly were elected to represent county or municipality areas. If the population of the electoral district exceeded 500,000, one additional delegate would be elected for each additional 500,000 population. The duties of the National Assembly included electing the president and vice president, amending the Constitution, and adopting regulations for the counties and municipalities of the country, subject to referenda in their respective jurisdictions.

My stepmother Wen-ying was persuaded by area inhabitants to seek election as a National Assembly member representing Sichuan Province. Wen-ying lost in a close race, and became an alternate. (Later, when Chiang's Government moved to Taiwan in 1949, the Sichuan representative did not move; therefore, my stepmother Wen-ying, as the runner-up, assumed the seat in Parliament.)

The Constitution was adopted by the National Assembly on December 25, 1946. The angry Communists refused to recognize the new Constitution and announced they would not accept any further American mediation or negotiations unless the National Assembly were dissolved and the Nationalists withdrew to their positions during the January truce. The truce collapsed and Chinese civil war began again. Marshall realized he could not succeed. In his January 7, 1947, statement he observed that "the National Assembly has adopted a democratic Constitution," but it was "unfortunate that the Communists did not see fit to participate in the Assembly." He added that neither side showed a true inclination to compromise. Marshall left China, and the American mediation groups were disbanded. Chiang's attempt at democratization did not attract the desired popular support. Government corruption, political bickering, and chaotic inflation had taken their irretrievable toll.

The New Ministry of National Defense
General Albert C. Wedemeyer had noted that the old Military Affairs Committee had become bloated with too many bureaus with identical or overlapping responsibilities. The result was confusion, inaction, and duplication of effort. In January 1946 a draft was produced for a complete reorganization of the Military Affairs Committee into a new National Defense Ministry partly modeled after the US military reorganization.[6] In March 1946, my father Wen-yi was assigned to a design group to restructure the old committee and work out the details for the new Defense Ministry. It was intended to separate army and party duties and responsibilities, as well as civil and military authorities. Wen-yi was unhappy with the initiative, feeling directives for the new ministry were ill-advised. Nevertheless, lack of coordination among various departments of the military, the party, and the government, as well as the fighting forces in the field, was a serious problem.[7]

In April 1946, Wen-yi and his colleagues in the Political Department flew from Chongqing to Nanjing where the Nationalist government was being re-established. Despite Chongqing's devastation from continued Japanese bombings Wen-yi felt a tinge of sadness in bidding farewell to the city that had been his home for the past number of years. However, as the plane descended into Nanjing, Wen-yi's excitement grew as he viewed the city he loved, nestled next to the Yangtze River.

Suddenly the magnificent Zhongshan Tomb Park emerged, sparkling in the sunset. Everyone in the plane burst into emotional applause. They had waited so long for this moment.

Wen-yi spent several days exploring familiar places and having many emotional reunions with old friends he had not seen for almost ten years. However, he felt depressed to find that his house had been completely destroyed. It was the house his first wife, my mother Bai-jian, had painstakingly built when Wen-yi was in Moscow as the military attaché.

The country had begun its reconstruction, and he was anxious to re-build his own home. He wrote to wife Wen-ying and asked her to come to Nanjing to help with the project. Wen-ying had just had her fourth child, finally a son, but she shared her husband's excitement in rebuilding the home and their lives. She first returned to her hometown Wuxiang, to place her three older daughters, aged one to six, temporarily in her parents' care. She also thanked the local people who had campaigned and voted for her. She then left for Nanjing with her new son and a wet nurse.

When house construction was well underway in the fall, Wen-ying accompanied my father and several friends to West Lake, Hangzhou for a three-day tour. They welcomed the serene and calm country sites amidst tensions evident between the Nationalists and the Communists to the north. Finally the house in Nanjing was completed. An elated Wen-yi felt a sense of confidence about the future of the country. He decided to have a house built in his hometown of Liling, in Hunan Province, as their retirement home.

The new Ministry of National Defense was now under the control of the civilian administration of the Executive Yuan. General Bai Chong-xi was appointed defense minister. Since the president would have command of the armed forces, the new Defense Ministry, and the civilian Executive Yuan, the real power was in his hands. President Chiang decided to exercise his control through his chief of staff, General Chen Cheng, a man of great personal integrity, a capable field commander, and a ranking member of the Whampoa clique. This gave him a huge advantage over Defense Minister Bai Chong-xi, who had to act through the Executive Yuan. In effect, Chen would command the six key departments of the new Defense Ministry. Minister Bai was left with actual control of a public relation and publicity bureau directed by Wen-yi, and several other bureaus within the ministry.

The lines were drawn. Powerful conservative hardliners within the Nationalist party and government strongly opposed the new views on China's path forward. They opposed any negotiations with the Communists, insisting their forces had to be eliminated militarily before any representative government could be considered. A more liberal faction within the Nationalists, represented by Sun Yat-sen's son, Sun Po, felt that unity could only be achieved politically, rather than militarily. The CCP should be invited to join the national government, but should give up its armed forces to a new coalition government, rather than to the current Nationalist government. This was not far from the US State Department's view. However, for the CCP, appeals for unity were painfully reminiscent of the 1927 Shanghai Purge, resulting in the collapse of the first united front or coalition between the Nationalist Party and CCP. [8]

Particularly galling to Wen-yi was the directive that stated, "All political parties shall be forbidden to carry on party activities in the army, whether open or secret. The army shall be strictly forbidden to interfere with political affairs."[9] Wen-yi had devoted most of his career and political skills in behalf of the party, the military, and the government, and as head of the powerful Lixingshe organization. Isolating the activities and skills of the various organizations seemed to him a step backward.

Wen-yi Assumes his New Duties

My father now headed the News Bureau within the Political Department of the Defense Ministry. The News Bureau was in charge of military news and nonmilitary education for the troops. Wen-yi assumed the role of military spokesman for the Nationalist government. Speaking for the Defense Ministry, he would provide news and analysis to the commander-in-chief and chief of staff. My father had three deputy directors overseeing five departments. The whole bureau had over 300 employees, so it was much smaller than the old Political Department and wielded less power and authority.

Wen-yi found it extremely difficult to establish and implement a news policy and a political-propaganda strategy for the News Bureau in the absence of direction from higher authority. The chain of command through Defense Minister Bai was simply too ambiguous. Caught between events on the military front, truce talks at the rear, and the pressure for coalition from the US, the News Bureau decided to take an optimistic tone in reporting events from the field, and a hard line regarding the stalemated negotiations.

In addition to his personal contacts with the party, the government, and news reporters, Wen-yi and the News Bureau developed a comprehensive system to collect and analyze news. The Bureau issued carefully screened intelligence and military news for the public from the Defense Ministry. Wen-yi often stayed up through part of the night trying to make sense of the confusing materials available.

Meanwhile the Communists were aggressively building their military forces and winning over the masses, including many demoralized Nationalist military defectors. Communist propaganda continuously attacked the corruption of the four big Nationalist families of Chiang, Soong, Kung, and the Chen brothers, accusing them of enriching themselves at the expense of the country.

The Defense Ministry was also plagued by Communist moles who had infiltrated the ministry, the field officers corps, and all segments of the government and party. This intelligence leakage caused tremendous damage to the military operation. Yet, there seemed to be little anyone could do to stop the flow of information or defections to the CCP.

Wen-yi and the Media

The News Bureau and the Intelligence Department of the Foreign Affairs Ministry held weekly news conferences to provide background regarding current events. Between 30 and 50 domestic and foreign reporters attended. Wen-yi did not fare well at these sessions. He had the unenviable task of casting unfavorable developments in an optimistic light. He knew he spoke too fast, and was often too passionate and quick-tempered in discussing prickly issues with reporters. Chiang Kai-shek once asked Hu Shi, a famous scholar and diplomat present at some of the news briefing sessions, "What do the foreign reporters think of the News Bureau director?"

Hu Shi responded, "The foreign reporters often find him hard to take."

Chiang repeated this criticism to Wen-yi, telling him to be more objective and control his emotions. Wen-yi accepted the criticism as valid, but added, "Sir, our party, the people, as well as the reporters are deeply divided regarding the direction that our government moves with the Communists. Many do not like what we have to say." Wen-yi silently wondered how the volatile Generalissimo would react under similar circumstances.

Hu's view is seconded by John K. Booth in his book, *Fabulous Destinations,* in which he describes the scene of a Wen-yi press conference he attended with Harold K. Milks, Associated Press chief in China.[10] They entered a room with cloth-covered tables arranged in a horseshoe, around which sat about two dozen Chinese newspapermen. Also present were Jean Lyon of the New York Times and H.K. Tong, director of the Chinese Government Information Services. Tumblers of hot tea were set on the tables. Booth says the press conference was conducted by General Deng Wen-yi, official military spokesman for the government, whom he describes as a youthful looking man who could pass for a 23-year-old lieutenant in the American Army. Wen-yi stood before a wall map with a pointer which he used to outline how the military situation had changed from the previous weekly conference. Booth wryly observes that the young General had been suitably picked for his role as spokesman since "his analyses were masterpieces of ambiguity and deception."

"Our armies in this sector are making a successful advance south against great opposition," Wen-yi stated.

Booth added, "That's a beautiful way of saying they are retreating in their territory."

Wen-yi then repeated the report in Chinese for the native newsmen.

At a party in Nanjing the secretary of the Russian Embassy said to Wen-yi, "Your job must be hell. If I were you, I would have quit it a long time ago."

Wen-yi said, "It is difficult and not always pleasant, but it's certainly not hell."

The Russian said, "You often dispatch war news. When your troops have lost the battles at the front, you often make it sound as though they had won. That must be hard to do!"

Wen-yi retorted, "I acquired that skill from your Soviet colleagues when I was the Chinese military attaché in Moscow." Unsmiling, the Russian walked away.

One evening Chiang Kai-shek met with Wen-yi and Zheng Jie-min to discuss the propaganda and news work. The president criticized them both. "I feel that your presentations and analyses of events are neither deep nor thorough enough. Your work must improve if you are to achieve the expected results."

Wen-yi was tempted to give his leader a detailed analysis of why the situation existed, but he was all too familiar with the result if he did. However, he decided to tell the president about two core problems.

"We are working under very poor conditions. We have little guidance on our overall propaganda strategy and policy, and a lack of good people and funds. While troops fight the Communists savagely at the front, the government carries on empty talks of truce and democracy. Minister Bai has made you aware of our Department's view of these prolonged talks, with which views, I'm told, you are not in total disagreement. When the coffin of a division commander from the battle line passed through Nanjing, we were told to keep it a secret. We are isolated from our troops.

"Secondly, Communist propaganda and slogans are focused on the evildoings of the four big Nationalist families, the Soongs, the Kungs, the Chen brothers, and, with respect, even your own family. The masses are simple and can be easily fooled and bought by such tricks. Would it be possible for Mr. Soong and Mr. Kung to leave China for a period?" Wen-yi was sure that Chiang would be apoplectic. Instead, he detected a ghost of a smile.

Wen-yi's concerns, like those of most officials in the Ministry, proved legitimate. The expected benefits of the military reorganization were not realized. Instead, the changeover disrupted organizational continuity and caused confusion and dislocations throughout the entire military forces. Chinese military representatives abroad suffered long delays in contacts with the Central government. Still more seriously, communications between field commanders and the central command were dangerously inefficient. Many combat units were cut off, for all practical purposes, from the new supreme staff and received little ammunition, funds, or replacements for several months.[11]

The year 1947 had started well for the Nationalists. But the CCP had launched a summer offensive and toward the end of the year the tide had turned in favor of the Communists. Government forces were weary from two decades of nearly continuous warfare, senior leadership was rent by internal disunity, and the economy was paralyzed by spiraling inflation. The price of a 22-gallon can of cooking oil was 25 yuans in the summer of 1937. By the summer of 1948 it had risen to 190 million yuans![12] The Ministry of Defense was greatly hampered in doing its major task of distributing materials and manpower to the areas where they were most needed, because the

Generalissimo was making these day-to-day decisions himself, with poor results.[13] At a Cabinet meeting in November 1948, George Marshall said, "The Nationalist Government is on its way out and there is nothing we can do to save it."[14]

By mid-June it was apparent civil war was inevitable. As talks continued through the weeks, the Communists were growing in strength while Nationalist forces were deteriorating, along with the economy and the morale of the army. In the second half of 1947, military initiative passed to the Communists, and in the summer of 1949, Nationalist resistance collapsed.

Chapter 18

Goodbye China

Yielding to the fear that our area would be the site of a battle zone soon, my aunt Ke-ming reluctantly abandoned our lovely home in Changsha, Hunan, leaving the property in the care of the servants. Carrying only minimal necessities our little group of five, including two military escorts, glumly departed for Nanjing to seek my father's help. On our way north, Ke-ming decided she would pay her respects to her mother and relatives in a remote country area in Jiangxi Province, next to Hunan.

As we moved away from Changsha to the countryside, many of the grim reminders of war gradually faded. The terrain became steep and rough, and there were hardly any paved roads. We were now forced to travel either in a primitive sedan chair carried by two men, or on one-wheel "rooster cars." The ingenious rooster car had one large wheel in the center with seats on both sides and two handles in the back, to be pushed forward like a wheelbarrow. It was so named because the large wheel looked like the crown of a rooster and it moved with relative ease on narrow dividers among rice fields. My cousin Yuan-cheng and I loved to ride on it with our legs stretched out on the low seats. We bickered and played with leaves and twigs as we plowed through the growth in the fields. When I finally got off, I fell to the ground; my stretched legs had become numb during the long, jolting journey. Several minutes were needed to restore feeling to my legs.

There were no hotels in the remote countryside. We stopped at a crude, farm "eating house" for supper. People squatted on benches as they ate, spitting out bones on the dirt floor. The squatting habit was probably due to lack of chairs at home and in the field. That night, Ke-ming, my cousin, and I were lodged in the only room available. Other guests pushed the table aside and spread bedding on the dirt floor.

Finally, to our great relief, the journey ended. We had arrived at Ke-ming's childhood home. We were greeted by a huge crowd headed by Ke-ming's mother, and a deafening blast of firecrackers. The house behind them was massive. I later learned that, after their prosperous father died, Ke-ming's three brothers further expanded the house and sectioned it to provide separate quarters for each of their families.

After the ritual welcome we entered a huge atrium that seemed vast and dark despite the open skylight in the center. The atrium branched into four wings. My "Grandma" and her servants lived in one, and each of the brothers lived in the remaining three wings with their families. Each family took turns sharing meals with Grandma, fulfilling the ancient Chinese tradition of four generations living in the same home. Aunt Ke-ming arrived home with fanfare, since her husband was a general for whom several of their relatives worked. The presence of the two children and two military aides enhanced her position. Everyone listened avidly for any new information on current events.

We stayed in Grandma's quarters. After the first big communal banquet, we joined Grandma for dinners at each of the three uncles' quarters. I sensed each family was carefully observing what was being served during meal times to be sure their own meals would be equivalent or better. Grandma had a huge square canopy bed, and she kept sweet snacks near the bed. While in her room I tarried near her bed until she gave me some sweets from her cookie jars.

We children amused ourselves in the huge and dark place. It was exhilarating yet terrifying to pass through the center atrium, where Grandma's big coffin was placed in full display at one corner. Wealthy people in the country customarily flaunted their wealth by securing and displaying high quality coffins for their elders. At night I had no problem passing through the dark hall with adults or a group of children. On the rare occasion when I had to cross the atrium alone with a lit candle, I found myself trembling at the possible appearance of a ghost.

Cousin Yuan-cheng delighted in sneaking up on me and blowing out the candle. Surrounded by utter darkness I screamed, ran aimlessly, and became disoriented. It was like Halloween in an ancient mansion in remote Jiangxi!

I heard the gossip and subtle rivalries of the families. Number One Uncle, Da Jiu Jiu, was not quite right in the head and often acted oddly. Number Two Uncle, Er Jiu Jiu, and his lovely family were prosperous and the favorite of the clan. Number Three Uncle, San Jiu Jiu, was somewhere in between the two extremes. Number Two Uncle's beautiful daughter was my favorite; I liked her and insisted on sleeping with her in her large bed. She gladly accepted me since I was like an exotic and glamorous doll to the country folks. During our turn to dine with Number Three Uncle, his daughter asked if I might sleep in her room. I declined the offer. I was sorry to see her look hurt because my refusal made her lose face.

It was time to depart. Grandma and the entire household seemed apprehensive about our uncertain future. Aunt Ke-ming told me the large family felt secure in their home in a remote part of Jiangxi. I cherished the visit and the traditions of these relatives. I felt bad, later when I learned that the family had been forced out of their magnificent house and punished as evil landlords by the Communists.

We journeyed to the town of Pingxiang for a brief stay at the home of Ke-ming's sister, whose husband was mayor of the town. Through his influence I was allowed to attend the local school during our stay. This aunt had a lovely 15-year-old daughter. One night I heard the parents discussing how hard it was to find a husband for their daughter during this difficult and unsettling time of war. I heard the name of the male teacher mentioned. In class the next day, I stood up and announced loudly and proudly that my aunt was planning to marry their daughter to our teacher. The teacher was stiff with embarrassment. The news spread quickly through the whole town. The daughter was too mortified to attend school. We were no longer welcome in that home. We hastily resumed our journey to Nanjing. Our escort Adjutant Hsu taunted me, "So you are a matchmaker now!" His tone was sarcastic. I was not surprised. Interestingly, my aunt never uttered a word about this to me.

My Stepmother Wen-ying

We finally arrived at my father's home in Nanjing. It was a lovely two-story house with a garage for Wen-yi's chauffeured automobile. The regular household included Wen-yi, Wen-ying, their four children, a cook, and two maids. The reunion with my stepmother was cool. She inspected my clothing critically and sniffed, "So these are the clothes your aunt bought you." I thought she was surprised I dressed so well. However, she chatted amiably with Ke-ming and pointed out various interesting scenes on our brief sightseeing tours.

My aunt took me on her endless visits with relatives and friends, many of whom were strangers to me. One day, as we were leaving a crowded house gathering, an old lady stared at me and exclaimed, "You, Tiny Sis! Don't you even remember your grandmother?" It was Grandma Pan! Four years had passed and much had happened; she had changed and I did not recognize the grandmother who had raised me, however resentfully, for seven years! She hugged me and gave me some money and snacks. This was not the grandmother Pan I remembered. She had made me feel worthless and alone. She told me she would be returning to her hometown of Liling, Hunan. It was the last time I would see her. Later, when the whole family prepared to leave for Taiwan, my brother was sent to fetch her. She refused to leave her home and possessions. She vanished from our lives.

One morning I noticed an unusual excitement in the household. My stepmother was preparing for a large dinner party for my father's friends and colleagues. The elaborate dinner would be followed by dancing. My stepmother, in her lovely gown, was extraordinarily beautiful. Many of the women wore long silk gowns. The men were dressed in uniform or western-style suits. The children were not allowed to attend, but we observed everything from our secluded positions. I was proud of my parents and awed by the elegant guests who arrived in their chauffeured automobiles.

When my stepmother married my father she had every intention of helping him advance his career. However, she became apprehensive about the uncertain political situation in China at the time, with good cause. (She and the whole country had been shocked to learn about the mysterious assassination of a brilliant and popular politician, Yang Yong-tai, who had just assumed the position of governor of Hubei province. Yang had once been my father's immediate superior. Yang's grandson would later marry Wen-ying's oldest daughter.) Wen-ying had quickly learned the virtues and limitations of my father. He was efficient, perceptive, hardworking, energetic, and optimistic. He was rabidly loyal to Chiang Kai-shek, who had taken Wen-yi under his wing since he was nineteen. Chiang had always been fond of her husband Wen-yi despite frequent irritations that arose when they were in daily contact.

However, she also recognized my father did not possess the guile to defend himself or his activities against many of his predatory colleagues, who were always vigilant in taking advantage of opportunities to acquire additional power at the expense of other officials or organizations. Wen-yi lacked the ruthlessness or ambition to play this game, placing himself at a disadvantage amidst the constant intrigue. His trusting nature made him well-liked, but also, a tempting target. Wen-yi had recovered some ground in his relationship with Chiang, though it was not as it had been. My stepmother sensed that Wen-yi's career and influence, though high, may have reached their limit. Higher positions would expose him to further intrigues and he was not equipped to deal with them. In fact, she often thought that my father's life, several times in jeopardy, was spared because he did not represent a threat to a few ruthless officials in the most senior positions. Wen-ying found she disliked many of her husband's friends and their lifestyles. She decided to become less involved with promoting his career. She actually tried to discourage him from pursuing further advancement. She never regretted her decision. However, his family, who had always been suspicious of Wen-ying, questioned her motives. Their resentment was barely concealed.

Our stay in Nanjing turned out to be brief. The situation of the Republic of China (ROC) against the Communists was deteriorating rapidly. Nationalist troops were exhausted from eight years of bitter war against Japan. The whole country was angry that it had to continue to fight another savage, internal war instead of savoring the victory over Japan. Chiang's government and military organizations were deeply infiltrated by Communist members. More and more, Nationalist troops refused to fight or to die in the unpopular civil war. Troops surrendered to the Communists or deserted. The once powerful Nationalist force, with weapons and supplies from the US, was eroding rapidly.

My father and uncle decided it was time for my aunt, cousin, and me to move to Taiwan. Our transportation was arranged. As we said goodbye to my parents, I saw some fear in the eyes of my stepmother, perhaps due to the uncertainty of her own future. The seriousness of the situation that caused our exodus finally hit me. It was the end of 1948 and I was eleven years old. My uncle was now with his division, trying to prevent the loss of Beiping to the Communists. The sense of chaos and despair was becoming increasingly evident.

As we began our journey, the train station and trains were packed with people with grim faces. Armed soldiers tried to maintain some order among the desperate, short-tempered mob. Even with first class tickets, we needed the intercession of our two fully attired military attendants to get us and our luggage on the train to Guangzhou. Arrangements had been made for our lodging while we waited for the ship that would take us to Taiwan. We all felt strange and uneasy arriving as guests in a stranger's home. However, our host was amiable and polite. Most of his family had already left for Taiwan, leaving an empty house.

Ke-ming was edgy. She would relieve her tension by striking me with her large chain of keys at the slightest perceived transgression, whether I spoke too loudly, or spilled something, or temporarily misplaced my red sweater! That red sweater seemed to disappear and reappear on its own free will, due to the constant packing and unpacking in strange places. How I suffered for it! Despite her unpleasantness I remained obstinately close to my aunt. I was afraid if I got lost or was not there, they would leave without me, and I would be caught and killed by the Communists.

Finally we were cleared to board the ship to Taiwan. The dock was a scene of mass confusion with people hurrying in all directions. On board we were crowded into tiny bunks in an open cabin. As we passed through the South China Sea and Taiwan Strait, the water turned rough and violent. I became sea-sick and threw up continuously into the nearest container I could find. When I finally recovered, Ke-ming asked Adjutant Hsu to clean the container. I could see his flash of anger. He was an officer, not a lowly hired hand to clean up such things! The sea voyage seemed endless. Finally, we landed in Keelung, the major northern port of Taiwan. My aunt Ke-ming, her adopted-son Yuan-cheng, and I were the first of the Deng family to flee from the Chinese Civil War in the mainland.

Taiwan

We arrived at Taiwan in November 1948. The dock-side scene was dramatically different from our departure from the mainland. The piers were empty except for passengers and goods discharged from our ship. The warm and humid evening breeze was like a soothing balm. After retrieving our luggage, we checked into a small hotel near the dock. We found a nearby restaurant for a much needed supper. Ke-ming kept looking about her with eyes glistening with tears. As she had done during our voyage, she lamented the loss of her properties, gone forever, and her dear relatives and friends she would never see again. She constantly wondered what she would do if her husband did not return to take care of her.

In sharp contrast, our two escorts were finally in good spirits and were looking to the future with much hope. They had now left the old military service and were free to strike out on their own. Cousin Yuan-cheng and I were bursting with curiosity and anticipation. We kept asking, "Are we going back to our lovely Japanese house in Taichung?" Alas, the lovely house was no longer available to us.

Our new refuge was located in Tainan, a major city in southwest Taiwan. The home belonged to Mr. Lu, an ex-commander of the 2nd Regiment in my uncle's 205th Division. He had retired from the army six months earlier and had remained in Tainan to start a rice milling business. We received a lukewarm reception. At least, we had a roof over our heads, however awkward and uncomfortable the situation.

Suburban Tainan turned out to be home for other military families. There were many children in the neighborhood. I immediately became part of a group of energetic children bent on mischief. We climbed trees and stole fruit from our neighbors' trees. We chased each other on the roofs of the low Japanese-style houses. We teased the younger children and taunted some of the meeker adults. Ke-ming paid little attention to me. Since we were guests in an uncomfortably crowded household, she just could not punish or discipline me properly. She also had other more urgent problems at hand. I was left free to do what I pleased. We stayed in Mr. Lu's home and waited for my uncle Wen-shi to arrive. However, my uncle Deng Wen-shi was busily engaged in a deadly struggle against a powerful Communist army.

Chapter 19

The Civil War - Part 1

The Chinese Civil War, with its dizzying 150 battles and campaigns over a vast country, involved many millions of military and civilian death and casualties. The story of the Civil War has been told and retold and is beyond the scope of this book, except for events in which my father Wen-yi was engaged. At the end of the long war against Japan, Chiang Kai-shek and the Nationalists held a significant advantage in manpower, equipment, territory, and financial assistance from the US. However, popular support remained low because of government corruption, and a chaotic inflation and economy. The Communists had improved their position considerably since the beginning of the united front against Japan. They continued to bide for time to increase their strength and military resources. The areas under Communist control were mostly rural. The Communist political and military personnel took care to win support of the masses. However, Chiang's longtime obsession to wipe out or subjugate the Communists to Nationalist rule remained intact.

The Nationalists Capture Yanan, the Communist War Capital

My father traveled to Xian in Shangxi Province with President Chiang Kai-shek to meet with the area commander General Hu Zong-nan. There they discussed military and political issues for an offensive campaign to capture Mao's Communist headquarters at Yanan, in Shaanxi Province. General Hu had been one of Chiang Kai-shek's most trusted generals during the war with Japan. He was also Wen-yi's friend. Yanan was the end point of Mao's famous "long march" and had served as the Communist war capital for 10 years. Its capture would provide a huge surge in morale for the people and the Nationalist Party.

In March 1947, General Hu's forces attacked Yanan from three directions, forcing the Communists to retreat east and north of the Yellow River. On March 19 the 1st Army occupied Yanan with 10,000 prisoners in tow. The outcome might have been disastrous for Mao and the CCP if they had not been alerted to the impending attack by General Hu's trusted assistant, Major General Xiong_Xiang-hui, a Communist spy. Mao had been receiving daily reports from Xiong concerning Nationalist plans. Therefore he and Zhou En-lai, who was also in Yanan, had two weeks to carry out an orderly evacuation, taking with them all military, communications, and medical equipment.

Wen-yi remained in Shaanxi for a month, through much of the Yanan campaign, analyzing intelligence reports on the enemy and issuing news items to help the local government, civilians, and troops to understand the significance of the campaign. The battle had not been fierce. Nevertheless, the victory had a huge political, symbolic, and uplifting effect on the people and troops. Wen-yi was elated at this opportunity for his bureau to distribute news, analysis, and propaganda pieces throughout the country, and raise the morale of Nationalist China while depressing the spirits of Communist military and supporters.

Shortly after the victory Wen-yi flew to Yanan to meet with General Hu. The tiny Yanan airfield was hidden in a deep valley and the plane spent much time circling to locate it. When they finally landed General Hu was there to greet Wen-yi. As my father visited troops and officers in Yanan, he saw signs of Communist propaganda proclaiming Yanan a heaven. Wen-yi stared at the desolate, isolated town dotted with hundreds of cave dwellings dug out by survivors of the "long march." He reconnoitered the town with two officers, and visited the modest structure where Mao Ze-dong had lived with his earlier wife, He Zi-zhen. Shortly after the start of the war against Japan, Yanan had become a target for Japanese bombers, forcing Mao to move into a cave. After Japan's defeat, Mao and his current wife Jiang Qing moved into a large multi-room cave in a lovely hill. Zhou En-lai and his wife resided in a cave next to Mao. A short distance below Mao's old house was the yellow brick headquarters of the Communist Central Committee. The dusty town had few trees or greenery. A small liberal arts university with meager facilities had also been moved before the attack. Civilians who followed the Communist retreat left with their belongings, with instructions to burn everything else.

Two planeloads of reporters arrived from Nanjing to report further on the victory. Their curiosity was mixed with amazement at the stark, barren landscape. Wen-yi gave the reporters background information about the town, and the battle, interspersed with elements of propaganda he hoped would be included in their reports. The reporters toured the village and wrote their stories, duly describing in detail how the Communists had oppressed and deceived the people in the area. After two more days Wen-yi left Yanan with the press group. Gradually, over a thousand civilians in rags returned to their caves, with no food. The Nationalist government flew in foodstuff and supplies.

The Communists Gain Momentum
The tide began to turn in the second half of 1947. Mao Ze-dong and his generals planned and conducted a strategic defense battle that evolved into a series of successful offensive campaigns in northeastern and northern China, spreading into the central plains.

Menglianggu - Shandong Province
Shortly after the Yanan victory, the Nationalists developed a plan to lure the Communist People's Liberation Army (PLA) into the Menglianggu Mountains, where General Zhang Ling-fu and his 74th Division would allow themselves to be surrounded. Meanwhile two Nationalist armies would converge in the area and surround the Communist PLA. It was a battle the Nationalists expected to win decisively. The battle plan was

sound but its execution was not. Careless delays resulted in the Nationalist troops being outraced to their planned positions on a strategic height called Yellow Cliffs. As a result, the PLA rained rifle and cannon fire on the vulnerable Nationalist forces. Commander Zhang Ling-fu was killed along with 15,000 men of the 74th Division. The Nationalists were soundly beaten.[1]

Morale of the military and the people sank to another low. A stunned Generalissimo ordered Wen-yi, who was increasingly taking on the role of "trouble shooter," to the Menglianggu area to determine what had gone wrong. My father talked to many wounded soldiers, officers, and commanders. In a report to Chiang, Wen-yi outlined the key factors that had doomed the battle. However, he concluded that Zhang Ling-fu, of all the commanders, had conducted himself in a manner beyond reproach. A saddened but grateful Chiang ordered a warship to be renamed Zhang Ling-fu, to honor the dead commander. Surprisingly, the Communists also paid rare tribute to an enemy by giving Zhang a burial with full military honors.

The tide was turning. In June 1947, Communist General Liu Bo-cheng, with 100,000 troops, crossed the Yellow River into the vast Central Plains in Nationalist territory and moved south to link up with General Chen Yi's army. Mao Ze-dong sent a message to his PLA commanders urging them to "kill the enemy and destroy the morale of survivors who escaped."[2] The two Communist armies began attacks on Nationalist brigades with surprising success. The Central Plains incursions convinced Mao it was time for the Communists to change their strategy to a nationwide offensive.

Battle at Linqu

The Communist onslaught was temporarily stymied in July 1947, when two Communist columns attacked the town of Linqu. Nationalist commander Li Mi's two brigades successfully beat back the enemy. Hampered by a continued heavy rain and flooding, the enemy nonetheless attempted another assault on the town, but again was driven back. After three days and three nights, the defeated PLA troops were forced to withdraw. The Nationalist victories in the Linqu Campaign provided a much needed emotional boost for the people and government.

My father went to Linqu to discuss the situation, troop morale, and the next mission with General Li Mi. Thousands of Communist corpses remained scattered and unburied. Wen-yi spent much time with the troops. As he sat with the exhausted Nationalist soldiers he felt a rush of sympathy for these men who had borne the unending burdens of war for an uncounted period of time, far from the comforts of family and home, or even the temporary comfort of a military base. Loneliness and death were their constant companions.

Wen-yi questioned the local people for information about the fleeing PLA troops. He learned the Communists had mobilized tens of thousands of shoulder-pole carriers to move their wounded toward the Yellow River. The exhausted Communist main force was still at the Yellow River bank. My father sent an urgent message to Nanjing describing the situation and urging that Nationalist troops be allowed to attack the Communists troops at the Yellow River, to prevent their escape across the river. Central Command responded there was no objection to the action; it was a decision to be made by the field commander. However, Commander Li Mi decided not to press the Communists. He felt his Nationalist troops were too exhausted from the fighting and punishing weather they had endured. The troops needed rest and the army to be re-supplied. A disappointed Wen-yi knew the PLA would have wasted no time pressing its advantage. As a result, Chen Yi's Communist troops safely crossed the Yellow River. Three months later, with his ranks reinforced, Chen Yi came back south to harass the JinPu and LongHai Railways.

Wen-yi Heads the Political Work Bureau

Chiang instructed my father to organize and head the task force to develop a new, expanded Political Work Bureau. The main duties of the new bureau were to strengthen interaction with the military, to monitor and raise the morale of the troops and people, and to launch an effective propaganda campaign against the Communists. The new Political Bureau was established in April 1948, headed by Wen-yi. He moved rapidly to build and train a cadre with which to expand the responsibility and authority of the new organization. To rectify the recent untimely reduction of military manpower, Wen-yi used members of the Youth Corps to build a country-wide organization of 40,000 people. They were to be deployed in villages, cities, and military units to increase recruitment, morale, and to root out enemy spies.

Earlier, in the winter of 1947, Wen-yi, now the presumptive director of the new Political Bureau, and Defense Department Minister Bai, flew to the Shanxi capital town of Taiyuan in North China, where they encountered a bad snow storm. The ancient airplane circled repeatedly above mountainous terrain trying to line up a landing into the almost hidden airport. The old plane lost one wheel as it made an emergency landing. The shaken men were warmly greeted by the once infamous warlord Yan Xi-shan, now Shanxi provincial governor and Northwest military chief. A spare wheel was requested for rapid delivery from Nanjing. General Bai and Wen-yi inspected the defenses of the densely populated city. The isolated but prosperous walled city seemed secure with castles and trenches; however, Communist troops in the area represented an increasing threat.

For three evenings, after fine and elegantly served dinners, the three men discussed the flagging morale of the civilian population and plans for military defense against the rising Communist threat. As they talked, my father studied the two men and thought, "What irony! I am sitting and talking strategy with two warlords who have led their troops in battle as enemies and as allies of Chiang Kai-shek's Nationalist government." Now in his mid-sixties, Yan had ruled Shanxi Province for three decades. As a warlord he was a bit of an oddity. He was an aggressive yet progressive ruler, having instituted a number of social, educational, and infrastructure reforms throughout his territory. Yan showed my father several hundred poison pills spread atop a disc, which he said he and his officers would use if the Communists ever captured his domain. (However, when it came to pass, he did not take the pills; instead, he followed Chiang to Taiwan.[3]) My father found him to be polite, hospitable, and even gentle. But Wen-yi was familiar with the toughness and ruthlessness Yan had displayed during his rule. In return for his friendship Yan sought more weaponry and increased food and other supplies for the civilian population. My father secured Yan's promise to improve the exchange of intelligence concerning political and military activity of the Communists.

My father and Defense Minister Bai then traveled to North China to assess the military and political situation in the newly formed North China Bandit Suppression Headquarters, with its new commander-in-chief General Fu Zuo-yi. When Bai and Wen-yi stepped off the train at Zhangjiakou, the headquarters of the North Army, Commander Fu Zuo-yi was there to greet them along with a large crowd of curious citizens. Wen-yi very soon realized the political climate among the local population was anything but encouraging. The Nationalist Party and military had managed to create the same corruption, inflation, and disregard for civilian welfare as in South China. As a result the same feelings of anger, disillusionment, and hostility were clear. These feelings were exacerbated by the strong presence of Japanese troops, the earlier deadly enemy, moving about freely. Adding to Fu Zuo-yi's problems was the destructive rivalry between the Youth Corps and the Nationalist Party, which had recently merged.

General Fu asked Wen-yi to question a Communist regiment commander who had defected, to see if he might receive any valuable intelligence. The Communists had ordered the commander to take action against his wife's wealthy landlord family. The distraught officer could not inflict such cruelty on his wife and her family. He also had helped his brother-in-law to leave Communist territory secretly. The CCP discovered this betrayal and arrested the commander's wife and two children. His wife was later executed. The commander knew he was a marked man and defected to the Nationalists with a large number of his troops. The defector told Wen-yi all Communists felt unsafe and vulnerable under the Communist "Investigations Movement," which brought victims in indiscriminately for interrogation and punishment. He felt the Nationalists could exploit that fear to encourage large-scale Communist desertions. Wen-yi discussed the information with Commander Fu Zuo-yi, who expressed support for jointly developing a propaganda campaign for the Northwest theater of operations.

Manchuria: Northeast Army, R.I.P.

Northeast China, especially Manchuria, had long been coveted by Japan, Russia, and the Communists due to its strategic location, richness in minerals, and agricultural productivity. Immediately after Japan's surrender, both Nationalists and Communists sent political cadres and troops into Manchuria (Northeast). It was the one region of China where the Communists' military strength was greater than that of the Nationalists. For the Communist Military Committee (CMC) it was the logical area to mount a major offensive to wrest control of the entire Northeast, as a springboard for subsequent campaigns to take control of all of China. Command of the Communist Northeast forces was given to General Lin Biao and political commissar Luo Rui-qing. General Lin Biao developed a plan to sever railways and roads, isolating important cities such as Shenyang, Changchun, and beyond from Jinzhou. Lin Biao had already captured Liaoyang and begun deployment to close the trap, by approaching and encircling strategically important Jinzhou. With Jinzhou taken, Nationalists in Shengyang and Changchun would be cut off from supplies, as well as a reinforcement and retreat route.

Before the Storm...Shenyang

On September 19, 1948, a concerned Chiang Kai-shek flew from Nanjing to Shenyang with Wei-yi to discuss with Commander Wei Li-huang and his generals the alarming PLA activity around Jinzhou. Wen-yi's objectives were to discuss morale of the troops with the field generals, and enlist their aid recruiting local candidates to do intelligence and propaganda work for the Political Bureau. Chiang was not happy. Lin Biao had taken control of the Beining Railway lines and had begun his campaign to seize possession of all Manchuria.

Wen-yi listened to the sharp disagreement among the high command concerning how to proceed. Chiang's inclination was to withdraw from Shenyang and Changchun, and deploy those additional troops to secure Jinzhou, thus protecting the troops' safe withdrawal route into North and Central China.[4] Area commander Wei Li-huang opposed Chiang's strategy, feeling that the loss of these cities would make the Nationalists vulnerable to ambush. My father spent an evening in a private train car discussing the military situation in the Northeast with General Liao Yao-xiang, commander of the 100,000-man 9th Army. Wen-yi asked Liao whether it might not be better, under current circumstances, to move all the troops in the area to a safer place to fight another day. Liao replied that an all-out drive to secure Jinzhou followed by withdrawal by sea would be his personal option.

Battle of Jinzhou

While Chiang and his commanders argued about the preferred course of action, PLA commander Lin Biao and his troops slowly began to encircle Jinzhou. Chiang again ordered General Wei to immediately launch a strong force to Jinzhou. To Chiang's disgust Wei did not act until October 9. Wei finally ordered General Liao Yao-xiang to move his troops along the rail line toward Jinzhou. Wei gave General Liao only 11 Divisions instead of the 15 Chiang had ordered. As Liao's 9th Army moved toward Jinzhou it encountered a PLA force that had been ordered to ambush the Nationalist army and stall its advance.

Meanwhile, the Nationalist garrison at Jinzhou, with slightly more than 100,000 men under General Fan Han-jie, had been under constant bombardment by Lin Biao's forces. Finally, on October 14, a fierce all-out attack was launched by the PLA. After one and a half days of fierce fighting, the Communists took control of the city. Fan Han-jie's army had been destroyed, with 20,000 troops killed and 60,000 taken as prisoners. General Fan was captured as he was fleeing the city.[5]

When Liao Yao-xiang received word Jinzhou had fallen, he urgently requested permission to withdraw and escape by sea to north China. He received three different directives from three members of the High Command in Shan-yang. Du Yu-ming agreed with Liao's request. Chiang, furious at this turn of events, ordered Liao to break out and proceed to Jinzhou. Another order urged Liao to bring his troops back to Shenyang immediately. It was too late. Lin Biao quickly sent a large part of his Jinzhou troops north, linking up with the PLA forces in the Heishan area. Now the balance had tipped in favor of the Communists. On October 26 the combined PLA troops surrounded the Nationalist troops and attacked Liao's army from the north and south. General Liao was trapped in a marshland. The Nationalist troops were easy prey for the large army that now surrounded them. During the next three days, more than 100,000 Nationalist troops were captured or killed. Commander Liao Yao-xiang and three corps commanders were captured.

The news of Jinzhou hit the Nationalist bases throughout the entire region like a tidal wave. Demoralized troops at Tashan gave up the fight and retreated. Morale at Shenyang plummeted. The soldiers and people in Changchun had been under siege by PLA troops encircling the city. Now the 5-month siege was over. Food and supplies had been depleted. Many thousands of civilians had died of starvation. Some barely survived by eating insects, rats, and even flesh from the dead bodies scattered about. On the news of Jinzhou's fall, the Nationalist garrison at Changchun surrendered to the PLA.

Wen-yi left Shenyang two days before its fall, on a military plane from Pai Ling Field. Planes were constantly landing and leaving, loaded with whole military companies and civilians fortunate enough to have secured a ticket. The city seemed empty except for hordes of soldiers at the train depot waiting to load on for a trip to Yingkou and the sea.

Communist forces launched a coordinated attack on Shenyang on October 29 that ended with surrender of the city on November 1. Commander Wei Li-huang left the city before the fighting was ended, leaving a subordinate in charge. Fearing he would be punished for dereliction of duty, Wei made his way to Hong Kong. Nationalist agents found him and he was placed under house arrest in Nanjing. Yingkou was captured on the same day as Shenyang. On November 2, all Manchuria was in Communist hands. More than 470,000 Nationalist troops had been lost in the campaign.

Wen-yi - Introspection and Frustration

On his flight to Nanjing, a depressed Wen-yi thought of his recent evening spent with General Liao, now a prisoner of the Communists. He wondered about the fate of the Nationalist Party and his own ability to conduct political activities under present circumstances. He thought with envy how effectively General Lin Biao and political commissar Luo Rui-qing had led the Northeast army on a series of offensive campaigns to destroy the Nationalist forces. They had rallied hordes of workers and peasants to their support through land reform and many promises. The Communists had also imbued officers and troops with a greater sense of loyalty and discipline. Mao had repeatedly stated that in war, winning the hearts and minds of the people was more important than winning a battle.[6]

Ironically, Chiang Kai-shek held a similar view, in principle. However, a large segment of the people had been virtually ignored by Chiang and the Nationalist government for years, except for the bourgeoisie. The primary Nationalist interest in workers and peasantry was to impose a series of taxes and conscript their young men for the army. Military commanders were told to live off the land and countryside by "requisitioning grain and other foodstuffs," though it sometimes meant starvation for the people. The Nationalists also rapidly lost support from the general population by constantly printing money, bringing on a horrendous inflation that reduced the value of money to zero.

A substantial part of the Nationalist military was made up of warlord armies who had been enemies or allies as it suited the interests of the warlords. Hence, the loyalty of these troops was to their respective warlords. Nationalist officers and troops often suffered from low morale and lack of loyalty. Some of their pay was siphoned off by senior officers. Line officers frequently received battle orders that were quickly contravened.

This unfavorable environment greatly limited political activity as an effective tool. There had been moments of elation and satisfaction resulting from the work of Wen-yi's organization, but these were all too few. Wen-yi could not restrain the feeling of frustration and sadness at what could never be.

Chapter 20

Civil War - Part 2
Bad News, Like Falling Snowflakes

Wen-yi left Shenyang for Beiping on October 29, 1948. Two days later Shenyang, the last Nationalist stronghold in the Northeast (Manchuria), was lost to the Communists. With Manchuria now in Communist control, General Lin Biao and the People's Liberation Army of one million men set out on a second major campaign to take possession of all of North China including Tianjin and Beiping.

Chiang instructed Wen-yi to spend a week with the North China Commander General Fu Zuo-yi, his troops, officers, and the local population, to assess the political situation and the attitude and mood of each group. He was not pleased with what he observed. The situation had worsened since his earlier visit in 1947. He noticed a broad and deep hostility toward the Nationalist Central government among military and civilian population, because of the lack of urgency in providing strategic military support, supplies, and financial assistance. Corruption was rampant.

Then, suddenly, General Fu and Wen-yi were summoned to Nanjing by Chiang Kai-shek for strategy discussions. On the plane trip to Nanjing, Wen-yi tried to share his observations of the situation in the northeast with General Fu. As Fu began to get the tenor of Wen-yi's remarks he showed disinterest in further discussion.

The Generalissimo gave a dinner to which he invited, in addition to Fu and Wen-yi, members of his top military staff. During the social period before dinner Chiang Kai-shek drew my father aside to ask his personal assessment of the situation in the North. Wen-yi knew Chiang would not be happy with what he had to tell him. Chiang listened impassively as Wen-yi told him the political climate among the local population was anything but encouraging. The Nationalist party and military had managed to create the same corruption, inflation, and disregard of civilian welfare as in South China. Feelings of anger, disillusionment, and alienation were clear. The continuing strong presence of Japanese troops, recent deadly enemies, moving about freely, added fuel to the resentment. Wen-yi had no choice but to tell the Generalissimo of the destructive rivalry between the Youth Corps and the Nationalist Party. Although they had merged, each was determined to act on its own.

With a feeling of unease Wen-yi then added, "Your Excellency, we seem not to have learned the hard lesson from the Manchuria debacle. Most of the well equipped and trained Nationalist troops are scattered in garrisons in northern China rather than in field operations." My father felt a momentary pang of anxiety that he might have overreached, since this had been the strategy Chiang himself had adopted, but Chiang showed no visible reaction. Wen-yi added that the troops and headquarters had been seriously infiltrated by Communist spies and propaganda agents. Discipline was lax. The people were too absorbed with daily survival to be concerned with, or supportive of, the Nationalist cause. Wen-yi sensed Chiang knew much of this. He now appeared unhappy, and listened with barely restrained anger to the unwelcome confirmation of the dismal state of things. However, the Generalissimo thanked my father for his candor, adding that he knew it had been difficult for Wen-yi to lay out his opinion. My father felt a wave of relief. He was very familiar with Chiang's unpredictable temperament from earlier times.

In the strategy discussions after dinner Chiang Kai-shek and the staff decided that General Fu faced three options. First, abandon northern China and deploy large army forces to assist the Nationalists against General Chen Yi's Communist troops in Shandong. Second, redeploy his troops west to link up with the forces of former warlord Yan Xi-shan in Shanxi Province. Finally, fight the Communist troops in Beiping and Tianjin.

Following the meeting, Fu Zuo-yi returned to Beiping to ponder his next move. Wen-yi was ordered to proceed to Xuzhou in the Central Plains region of China where a major battle was about to take place.

Shandong Province is Lost

Several months earlier, US Ambassador Leighton Stuart had reported in a letter to Secretary of State George Marshall that Lt. General Wang Yao-wu was being relieved of his military command and governorship of Shandong Province. A great admirer of Wang, Stuart added that General Wang had been considering establishing an autonomous regime of Shandong under his leadership.[1] Stuart said there was the possibility Wang Yao-wu would be succeeded by General Deng Wen-yi who had never commanded troops and had done a poor job as the military spokesman. However, Wen-yi was a Whampoa man solidly loyal to the Generalissimo.

In mid-September, General Wang's army of 100,000 troops was soundly beaten by General Chen Yi and the PLA in the battle for Jinan, provincial capital of Shandong. Wang was captured and imprisoned until 1959.[2] During his imprisonment, Wang urged his fellow commanders to defect to the Communist side. The Communists were now in total control of Shandong. The door was open for a Communist push into central China.

The Million-Man Battle Huai-Hai Campaign

The stage was set for the do or die battle that would determine the destiny of China. The huge area in Central China north of the Yangtze River was suddenly the scene of a rapid convergence of one million Communist and Nationalist troops, like ominous thunder clouds. The Communist objective was to destroy the remaining large Nationalist force, control the territory north of the Yangtze River, and capture the strategic town of Xuzhou with its railway lines. This would open the country south of the Yangtze, and the road to Nanjing about

100 miles to the south. Chiang deployed his armies of 600,000 men into the Xuzhou-Huai River area, like pushing a huge stack of chips into the pot of a no-limit poker game. Mao Ze-dong met the challenge with 600,000 PLA troops as General Liu Bo-cheng and political commissar Deng Xiao-ping arrived from Shandong with 400,000 troops, and General Chen Yi with his 200,000 men. The Communist army was supported by more than five million peasants and laborers hauling material to the front and relieving the PLA of many needed non-military tasks.[2]

Nationalist field operations were controlled from both Xuzhou garrison headquarters by garrison chiefs Liu Chih and Du Yu-ming, and by Chiang Kai-shek from Nanjing. Chiang's Nationalist force had superiority in military ground forces and air power but they suffered from poor generalship, ill-conceived strategies, and many contradictory orders from Chiang. The Nationalist commanders had neither flexibility nor cohesive battle plans. The Communist army was better organized, with a defined strategy that often resulted in Nationalist forces being outmaneuvered.

Chiang Kai-shek's headquarters and the army field units were heavily infiltrated with Communist spies. A furious Chiang Kai-shek vented his frustration on Wen-yi, ordering him to the front line to eliminate infiltration problems immediately. This was, by now, an impossible task. Wen-yi took a team of trained agents to Xuzhou with a plan to uncover sources of widespread espionage. Small task forces were placed in many units to find and interrogate enemy agents discovered within the military.

Wen-yi's team arrested two dozen agents and Communist sympathizers, and interrogated them to obtain further information concerning the identity and location of other agents in the Nationalist ranks. The number of "suspects" increased rapidly. But the Communist network had become too pervasive.

Meanwhile, as Nationalist General Huang Bai-tao's 7th Army was crossing the Grand Canal, about 50 miles east of Xuzhou, two Nationalist corps commanders defected to the Communists, exposing the east flank of Huang's army. Communist General Chen Yi launched a fierce attack on the vulnerable flank and soon surrounded Huang and his army. Chen Yi's losses were also heavy but he received continuous Communist replenishment and support. Huang's army lost over half of its men and received no re-supply of its dwindling food, water, and ammunition. The Communists continued their relentless attacks and broke Huang's defense lines.

Wen-yi was heartsick since General Huang Bai-tao was his good friend. He knew Huang would never surrender or allow himself be captured. President Chiang sent an urgent order to Commander Liu Chih to send troops from Xuzhou to rescue Huang, even at the risk of losing Xuzhou. Chiang asked Wen-yi to fly to the battlefield and ask Huang to hold on and wait for the reinforcements. Wen-yi flew over the next morning and talked with Huang through radio communication. He gave General Huang Chiang's message and told him that Qiu Qing-quan's 2nd Army Group would reach him within a day. General Huang responded, "I appreciate the President's recognition and concerns. I will try my best to hold on one more day. The situation here is desperate. I hope relief will arrive by noon tomorrow."

On his return from the front Wen-yi angrily told Garrison Chiefs Liu Chih and Du Yu-ming of Huang's extremely precarious position. "Our 2nd and 13th Army Groups are intact and rested. We should be able to rescue Huang and even win the battle," Wen-yi said. After a hurried conference with Nanjing, Chiang Kai-shek ordered General Qiu Qing-quan's 2nd army and General Li Mi's 13th army to help Huang's troops to break out. The staff conferred for three hours. The decision was made. Qiu's 2nd Army Group would rescue Huang and his troops in the morning. Chief Du Yu-ming and Wen-yi would be at Qiu's headquarters to supervise the deployment. By 3:00

a.m., General Du and Wen-yi were ready to depart. However, they noticed General Liu Chih's reluctance to send out his garrison troops. Du asked Liu, "Is it more important to defend Xuzhou or save Huang Bao-tao?"

Commander Liu responded crisply: "If we cannot defend Xuzhou, what's the purpose of saving Huang Bao-tao?!"

Wen-yi was dumbfounded. He protested, "But the President's order is to save Huang Bao-tao at all costs... the security of Xuzhou is not an issue. By saving Huang, we defend Xuzhou!"

Without another word, they piled into the jeep and drove to Qiu's headquarters. They met with several corps and division commanders, all of whom said they were ready and could move in half an hour. However, General Qiu Qing-quan, still irritated and jealous of the special honor given Huang by Chiang Kai-shek, deliberately slowed the progress of his 2nd Army troops. He is said to have remarked, "Now Huang can prove whether or not he was indeed worthy of the honors bestowed on him." Instead of reaching the battle site early in the morning, Qiu's army arrived in the late afternoon. By then the opponent had received intelligence of his approach and had reinforced their troops. Qiu's troops could not break through.

Huang led his last three regiments in an attempt to break through the siege but was repulsed. His troops were destroyed. At 6:00 p.m. General Huang Bao-tao committed suicide. Receiving the news, Wen-yi was overcome with sorrow for his valiant friend. After the destruction of Huang Bao-tao's army, Xuzhou was besieged on all fronts. The Nationalist troops were exhausted, low on ammunition and without reinforcements. The People's Liberation Army, however, had also sustained severe losses.

The Curtain Begins to Fall on the Nationalist Army

The Nationalist 12th Army commanded by General Huang Wei was marching toward Suxian to recapture the town, 10 miles from Xuzhou. The Nationalist 8th army and 6th army were sent from Xuzhou to link up with the 12th army. However, the march was hampered by bad weather and poor roads, and was stopped by attacks of the Communist guerillas. Nationalist efforts to push on to reinforce the besieged 12th Army were delayed.[3] The 12th Army was surrounded by the Communist Eastern China Field Army. The besieged Nationalists fought a series of bloody skirmishes, but their doom was inevitable. PLA forces completely destroyed the 12th Army, captured much needed supplies, and conscripted the Nationalist prisoners to their ranks. On December 15, 1948, the 12th army was wiped out.

On December 17, 1948, Mao Ze-dong broadcast an ultimatum to field commanders of the two Nationalist armies and to Garrison Chief, General Du Yu-ming. Mao said: "Now that Huang Wei's army has been completely wiped out...I immediately order all your troops to lay down their arms and cease resistance. Our army will guarantee life and safety to you, high-ranking officers, and to all officers and men. This is your only way out."[4]

The message was ignored by the Nationalists. Their troops continued to resist desperately. But the outcome was inevitable. The high stakes game was over. The Nationalist had lost almost all of their chips. The Huai-Hai Campaign began on November 6, 1948 and ended on January 10, 1949, after 65 days, in a crushing Nationalist defeat. A total of about 1.4 millions troops had engaged in the battle from both sides. The large Nationalist force was almost entirely destroyed, including 155 General officers and countless items of war equipment.[5] Qiu Qing-quan was killed; Du Yu-ming, deputy commander-in-chief of the Xuzhou garrison, was captured. Two senior generals escaped.

My father flew out of Xuzhou on November 29, 1948. He felt a sense of guilt at having escaped the cruel fates of the troops and officers. A Communist general told American journalists, "Huai Hai was like your Gettysburg."[6] Chiang wrote that the Nationalists had failed, not because of external enemies but because of disintegration and rot from within.[7]

The Communists were now in control of all territory north of the Yangtze River. The way was open for a final PLA drive on Wuhan, Nanjing, and Shanghai.

Chapter 21

The North and Beiping in Jeopardy

My uncle, General Deng Wen-shi, was ordered to move his 205th Division from the coastal city of Qingdao to Beiping to support General Fu Zuo-yi. Commander Fu had returned to his headquarters from Nanjing in torment, caught in the grip of conflicting pressures from the Nationalists and the Communists to order his force of 500,000 men into very different actions. Fu, among the more capable of the Nationalist generals, had taken steps to fortify the main garrisons in the region.

Mao Ze-dong and his agents mounted a strong effort to persuade General Fu to surrender his 200,000 troops in Beiping to the Communists, promising fair treatment to the troops and retention of rank for the officers. By doing so, they argued, Fu would be sparing the lives of his soldiers and civilians, and the precious cultural antiquities in the museums in Beiping. As he pondered the offer, the unfortunate General was being whip-sawed by a stream of emissaries from Chiang Kai-shek urging him to retreat west, or south. Mao, informed of these intentions through key members in Fu's inner circle, decided to reduce Fu's options and increase the pressure. The Communist PLA, commanded by Lin Biao, launched a campaign that captured the critical western gate city of Zhangjiakou and proceeded to encircle Beiping. Communist forces then captured Tianjin, a strategic economic center of north China, on January 15, 1949, following a 29-hour long battle. Both sides sustained heavy losses, but Fu's were more severe. Although Fu's 500,000 troops were better trained and equipped than the 800,000 of the Peoples Liberation Army, Lin Biao had been nimbler and more aggressive. General Fu had not learned from the mistakes that lost Manchuria. He sought to conserve his troops by concentrating them in garrisons in several cities rather than in the field.[1]

With the main retreat routes now blocked, Fu Zuo-yi's options narrowed. The Communists then dispatched Fu's daughter to urge him to surrender. How could he guess that his own daughter, Fu Dong-ju, and his trusted personal secretary, Major General Yan You-wen, were moles for the Communists, passing intelligence information to Lin Biao's army? Both were now pressuring Fu to surrender. Fu began secret negotiations with Lin Biao. Ironically, he designated his secretary, General Yan You-wen, as his representative. He did not learn of Yan's perfidy until after the war. Mao was in a position to dictate the terms he sought. Fu Zuo-yi and his Nationalist troops would surrender and become part of the People's Liberation Army. Fu Zuo-yi would not be treated as a war criminal, he would keep his personal property, his political position was guaranteed, and the troops under his command would be treated leniently.[2]

Escape or Surrender?

On January 19, 1949, my uncle Wen-shi, whose troops had steadily engaged the Communist forces, was promoted to deputy commander of the 31st Corps. Fu's secret talks with the Communists had reached a critical stage. As reported in World Journal LLC (worldjournal.com), on January 21, General Fu assembled his generals for a meeting at his headquarters. When they were all seated, he announced, "We have been engaged in a peace negotiation with the PLA for quite some time. Both sides have now reached an agreement concerning the peaceful solution of the Beiping question. You will now listen to the agreement."

Fu had barely finished his remark when army commanders Li Wen and Shi Jue, and my uncle Deng Wen-shi leaped to their feet to protest loudly: "You want us to surrender. We will not!"

Fu replied calmly, "Generals, please listen to the agreement first." After the agreement was read, Fu asked, "What is everyone's opinion? Please speak up."

One of Fu's generals stood up and said, "Only a peaceful settlement can spare the old capital from ruin and relieve its two million people of the horror of war. We should do the best for the people. I am strongly in favor of Commander's decision." There were several nods of assent.

Then, General Shi Jue stood up abruptly and shouted, "Was this event reported to President Chiang? Who is responsible for all this?"

Fu responded, "The decision will be broadcast by radio and reported by newspapers tomorrow. President Chiang will know by then. I, Fu Zuo-yi, will be responsible for everything."

General Li Wen stood and yelled, "If we choose to surrender, how can we face our leader Chiang?"

Many voices shouted agreement with Li Wen. The meeting room erupted into vigorous dissent. As many supported Fu's negotiated surrender as those who opposed, Army commanders Li Wen and Shi Jue rose to leave saying, "This is a serious matter. We must consult with our subordinates." However, they were blocked by Fu's guards and forced to retake their seats.

Li Wen made another try: "We have one request. Allow us to return to Nanjing."

Fu replied, "We will not force anyone to stay. However, you must comply with the following stipulations. You will assist in preparing the troops for the handover to the Communists, insisting that there be no overt resistance, that no one be injured. When you have accomplished this I will see that you leave for Nanjing safely. Anyone who refuses to fulfill this requirement will be court-martialed."

With a sad expression, Fu Zuo-yi looked around the room at his commanders and said slowly, "We all have our own aspirations and ideals. We must now each go our separate ways. For those who want to leave, I will assign airplanes to take you to Nanjing. To those willing to stay in Beiping, I welcome you and I thank you." Two officers, not able to deal with the humiliation, later committed suicide.[3]

The surrender terms were officially signed on January 21, 1949. The agreement and its content were quickly relayed by radio and newspapers. The next day, two planes took the departing generals to Nanjing. My uncle Wen-shi declined the plane trip. He had agreed to lead 1,300 men from his command to Taiwan. It was a fortunate choice, since despite Communist assurances that General Fu's officers would be treated leniently several of the division generals were executed. Wen-shi and his men traveled overland to the coastal city of Qingdao. For the last leg of the trip by sea, Wen-shi arranged to have his young, beautiful, and pregnant mistress, Liu, join him. A grateful Liu cried at her good fortune to be able to leave China safely.

On January 31, 1949, General Fu marched his troops through Beiping's massive gates for "liberation and reorganization."[4] Beiping had fallen to the Communists without a shot, concluding the PingJin Campaign. Beiping became the capital of the People's Republic of China and was renamed Beijing. General Fu was later rewarded by the Chinese Communist regime with a military commission in the Peoples' Liberation Army and, after that, posts in the People's Republic of China government.

When Wen-yi received news of Beiping's surrender, he morosely reflected on the entire turn of events in the civil war. He thought of the many incompetent Nationalist field generals who had led their troops to catastrophic defeats at the hands of smaller, but better organized, PLA forces. The Nationalist military was infested with Communist spies and sympathizers to the highest levels.

President Chiang Kai-shek Steps Down
By the end of 1948, popular resentment against Chiang and the Nationalist Party fostered a series of labor disputes, student demonstrations, and harsh criticism from the intellectual community. The economy was in shambles. The people demanded economic security and the end of destructive corruption.[5] Chiang's lack of funds to meet the huge military

expenses led to a continuing printing of paper money. This hyper inflation spiraled crazily. In June 1937, 3.41 yuans traded for one US dollar; by May 1949, one US dollar traded for 23 million yuans.[6] In July 1948, Chiang issued gold certificates to replace the devaluing Chinese dollar. Within ten days, the government forced people to hand in 27 million US dollars, and an equivalent amount of gold and silver, for the gold certificates, at an exchange rate of 1 gold yuan for 3,000,000 yuans. In the final days of the civil war, the silver dollar was briefly introduced, equal to 500,000,000 gold Yuans.[7] A decent meal cost one million current dollars. Chiang's brother-in-law, economic minister TV Soong, and the Central government, became the focus of scorn. When the gold certificates devalued 20,000-fold in ten months, millions of people lost all their savings and hated the government for it. (During this same period, the New York City Transit Authority announced its own inflation...the subway system fare would increase from five to ten cents.)

The series of huge Nationalist military defeats in Manchuria, the North, and Huai-Hai in the past year had destroyed the bulk of Chiang Kai-shek's armies. Military victory was now remote. The Nationalist Army had been decimated. Almost 800,000 troops had defected to the Communists. At this point, Vice President Li Zong-ren and Defense Minister Bai Chong-xi exerted strong pressure on Chiang to step down from his presidency. This was painful for Bai since he had been, until recently, one of Chiang's good friends. However, Chiang resented the strong role Bai had played in getting Li Zong-ren elected vice president, rather than Chiang's choice of Sun Po. Chiang told the two men he needed time to consider his decision. On January 3, 1949, Chiang visited Li Zong-ren at his home to tell him he had decided to step down, adding briefly "I tried my best."[8]

Chapter 22

Defeat and Exodus

Chiang officially resigned on January 21, 1949... sort of. Li Zong-ren took over as "Acting President." The very next day, General Fu Zuo-yi surrendered at Beiping. Chiang returned to his home in Xikou, where he maintained active contact with many military and government leaders who still considered him their leader. He issued orders and suggestions to senior officers and unilaterally appointed reliable General Tang En-bo as commander of the Shanghai area, charging him with the task of constructing defensive positions around the city.

Chiang quietly floated some suggestions for a possible peaceful resolution of the conflict. Mao summarily dismissed these. Earlier, Mao had put forth his own eight terms for "peaceful negotiation" which, in essence, called for unconditional surrender. A faction of the Nationalists, including Li, was inclined to accept these terms as a starting point, with the hope of later negotiating more lenient terms. Mao observed the Nationalist region was no longer a "total government"... there was much local activity by people in many places trying to achieve peace.

Li offered to negotiate with the Communists, starting with the terms Mao had laid out on January 14. Emissaries were sent to discuss possible compromise terms, with no success. Acting President Li was in an untenable position. He had been pressured by Mao to accept the eight terms of surrender as a starting point for "peaceful negotiations." Li had to deal with his own government with no unity among factions. The patience and support of the people were ebbing daily. For Li, the decision to surrender must have seemed a wrenching far cry from his moment of glory in April 1938 when he and his army had soundly defeated Japanese forces in the battle of Taierchuang, to the joy of the people of the land.

Mao Ze-dong Attacks my Father Wen-yi

Mao Ze-dong's surprised delight at Li's telegram indicating a willingness to negotiate on Mao's 8-point terms, was dampened as he read a Central News Agency dispatch from Shanghai on February 9. In it, my father criticized Mao's idea of achieving peace locally in many places, as a swindle and trickery, a deceit to gain time for Communist military to coerce surrender.[1] Wen-yi had added that the million Nationalist troops south of the Yangtze River should continue to fight to the death. High-level members of the Nanjing government hastened to state that Deng Wen-yi's dispatch was not the government's official opinion. Wen-yi felt he had spoken for the millions, and he remained adamant about his daring act.

Mao turned his wrath on Wen-yi, calling him a war criminal and one of the Nationalist die-hards, opposing local peace and demanding a total peace. Mao added, "The farce of a disintegrating Nationalist demand for a total peace reached its climax in a statement issued on February 9, 1949 in Shanghai by the war criminal Deng Wen-yi, Head of the Bureau of Political Works in the Ministry of National Defense."

Mao said, "Deng Wen-yi repudiated Acting President Li Zong-ren's January 22 statement, which accepted the eight terms of the CCP as a basis for peaceful negotiations; instead, he (Wen-yi) demanded a so-called 'peace on an equal footing,' failing which, he said, 'We will spare no sacrifices in order to fight the Communists to the bitter end.'" Mao added, "But Deng Wen-yi failed to mention with whom we, his opponents, should now negotiate for a 'peace on an equal footing.'"[2]

Mao further pointed out that Deng Wen-yi was asked by a reporter, "Has Acting President Li approved the four points in your public statement?"

Wen-yi answered, "I am speaking from the stand of the Ministry of National Defense, and the four points made today were not submitted beforehand to Acting President Li." Wen-yi, once again, had taken matters in his own hands and acted without the approval or authorization of the Central government.

Mao said, "Deng Wen-yi openly opposes and maligns the peaceful settlement of Beijing,

while the Ministry of National Defense hailed it on January 27 as an act to shorten the war, secure peace, and thereby preserve the foundation of the ancient capital Beijing and its cultural objects and historic monuments." Mao's parting shot: "A Bureau of Political Works of the Ministry of National Defense can contradict the Ministry of Defense as well as the Acting President!"[3]

Wen-yi wondered how Chiang Kai-shek, "retired" in Xikou, must have reacted when news of Wen-yi's statement reached him. He would perhaps have smiled approvingly but he would also have dropped the roof on his errant subordinate for again acting without authority.

Then, on February 13, the Nationalist Central Executive Committee's attitude stiffened. The committee issued a Special Directive saying:

1. Rather than surrender unconditionally the Government should fight to the bitter end.

2. The eight terms Mao Ze-dong put forth in his January 14 statement would ruin the nation, and the Government should not have accepted them.

3. The CCP should bear the responsibility for destroying the peace. Instead, it has drawn up a list of so-called war criminals which includes the Government leaders and many others. (This particularly galled the members of the Central Executive Committee, most of whose names were on the list.)

A surprised Mao observed that, suddenly, the Nationalists had begun to play down their peace tune and were taking up the old cry of "fighting the Communists to the end."

To the Bitter End

Li favored forming a main defensive perimeter on the south bank of the Yangtze. Chiang wanted to defend the cities. General Tang En-bo refused Li's request to make his troops available for Li's defensive plan. Li desperately sought aid and support from the US, but his plea was rejected by President Truman. In February, he flew to Hangzhou to meet with Chiang to enlist his support. He came away only with a statement of support which Chiang was not actually prepared to give. When he returned to Nanjing, Li found the Central government had moved the seat of government to Guangzhou. He hurried south.

On April 1, a Communist delegation headed by Zhou En-lai and a delegation from Nanjing headed by Zhang Zhi-zong met for a do-or-die negotiation. It clearly was not a meeting of equals. The group struggled for 10 days during which the Communist terms did not change significantly. At last, Zhou handed Zhang a final document intended as an ultimatum. The Nationalists had five days, till April 20, to accept the terms, after which, PLA forces would cross the Yangtze for a final drive on Nanjing and other cities.

The Nationalist government was in a quandary. The Communists had shown no inclination to soften their original eight terms for a truce. Acting President Li was unable to arrive at an agreement for a counter-proposal acceptable to the Communists. Li and Chiang rejected Mao's terms.

Communist troops immediately began their offensive, crossing the Yangtze River to the south side. Within three days Nanjing was in Communist hands.[4] The Nationalist government moved its capital from Nanjing to Guangzhou with surprising order and speed on April 22nd. In response to frantic appeals from a threatened Shanghai, Chiang left Xikou for a final visit to his special city, to assist in developing defensive plans, though he realized it was probably in vain. The plan included procedures for an organized retreat. There was still much wealth here to be gathered and shipped to Taiwan. The city was in turmoil amid rumors, disintegrating currency and banks, and fear of the coming battle.

The Shanghai Campaign started in the middle of May and lasted for two weeks. The Nationalists' uncoordinated defense was no match for Chen Yi's army. The governor of Zhejiang defected, and momentum was lost, as was any chance of victory. The city was taken with severe losses to the defenders. Tens of thousands of government workers and civilians managed to escape with strategic supplies. The Nationalist army, navy, and air force were forced to retreat to Zhoushan Island of Zhejiang and Taiwan.

On July 12, Chiang and Ching-kuo made a short visit to Guangzhou to meet with the Central Standing Committee, to develop plans for military operations and launch a party reform movement. The latter was summarily rejected given the present circumstances.

Then, without consultation, Chiang appointed Tang En-bo governor of Fujian Province. The southern generals were enraged, proposing to arrest Chiang as in Xian. They were dissuaded by Acting President Li, who said Chiang had too much financial support and broad military loyalty for the plot to succeed. Chiang then met with General Bai and a reluctant Li to discuss defensive strategy. It was a strained meeting. Li insisted a strong defense along the Yangtze was their best hope. Chiang's defense of the cities had not worked. Li's accumulated resentment of Chiang's actions and lack of support boiled over in a litany of accusations and enumeration of Chiang's many faults. Surprisingly, Chiang listened to this diatribe, then quietly took his leave.[5]

Wen-yi had also come to Guangzhou during the government relocation. As official military spokesman, he was under constant questioning by the media about the safety and future of Guangzhou. Wen-yi pointed out that the Communists had been broadcasting propaganda that Guangzhou would be captured by the end of May. Wen-yi assured the media that the city would still be secure by the autumn moon festival at the beginning of October. The reporters were skeptical. However, on the day of the moon festival my father had a reception for several dozen reporters on a yacht. It was not a gay affair since, by then, the signs of war were sufficient to raise fears that the period of peace was coming to an end in Guangzhou.

On October 13 the Nationalist government moved out of Guangzhou to the new capital in Chongqing. Chiang had returned to Taiwan. Wen-yi managed to board the last military plane out of Guangzhou to Chongqing.

In Chongqing, it was obvious government activity was being conducted amidst a rapid deterioration of morale. By the middle of November, the Nationalist position was bleak. The currency was useless and inflation rampant. Wen-yi suddenly realized escape was becoming more treacherous since no one had expected Chongqing might be lost so soon. Anticipating an inevitable evacuation of the city, my stepmother Wen-ying and my half-brother flew to Haikou, then on to Taiwan. On November 30, Wen-yi collected his three daughters with the intention of driving to Chengdu by car. It took them six hours to travel six miles on the road packed with traffic and panicked refugees. Wen-yi drove to the military airport to see if he could find a plane to take them. There were only two empty seats on the last plane for the legislators. Wen-yi stubbornly squeezed the three young girls and himself into the plane, and they reached Chengdu safely.

Meanwhile, Chiang had left Taiwan for Chongqing, a dangerous place, to resume the post of President. He was accompanied by his son Ching-kuo. Acting President Li Zong-ren was invited to join them in Chongqing. Instead, pleading a need for medical treatment, Li flew to Hong Kong, then the United States. There he remained until he moved back to Beijing on July 20, 1965 through an arrangement with Zhou En-lai.

The situation in Chongqing was hopeless. On November 29, Chiang met with military commanders to prepare for an orderly retreat. At the urging of his staff, he left Chongqing for Chengdu the next morning, arriving at the same time as Wen-yi and his children. By the following day, December 1, Chongqing fell to the Communists.

General Hu Zong-nan was encamped west of Sichuan with several hundred thousand troops. Chiang and other high government officials felt the situation would remain stable for a while. However, within ten days the Communists had reached within sixty miles of Chengdu. On December 11, 1949, the governor of Yunan defected to the Communists. The Communist Army entered northern Sichuan and approached the suburb of Chengdu.

On the evening of December 8th, Chiang Kai-shek had a dinner with Hu Zong-nan, and several high staff officers of the Defense Department, including its chief Gu Zhu-tong, Chiang Ching-kuo, and Wen-yi. Halfway through the meal, Chiang's aide brought an intercepted message, a telegram sent to a Sichuan Nationalist general in Chengdu, instructing him to kidnap Chiang as in the Xian Incident. Everybody present was outraged and appalled over this treasonous attempt. After dinner, they discussed this and other matters for over two hours. There was unanimous agreement Chiang should leave for Taiwan first thing in the morning. Any defensive warfare could be entrusted to General Hu Zong-nan.

Chiang finally accepted this advice. The meeting grew somber and nostalgic, as the officers realized they were about to give up their country for good and that its spirit would never be the same again. Reminiscences and the unbelievably fast downturn of events were discussed well past midnight.

Chief of staff Gu Zhu-tong exclaimed, "After the downfall of central China, the bandit troops entered Sichuan within a month after the loss of Chongqing. Now, suddenly, the Communist bandits are pressing against Chengdu in less than ten days. Several thousand miles of territory ... lost as though under the spell of demons. Is there really such thing as demon and devil? This is unbelievable!"

A restrained Kai-shek twirled a glass in his hand absently and said, "We used to study war history and war strategy. We found the words 'In a defeating battle, soldiers escape and run against oncoming wind!' hard to understand. Sadly, in our Nationalist defeat today, the troops escaped and ran, even without any wind. I wonder how the future war historians will write about this." At this historically tragic moment, Kai-shek glanced about his surroundings. He then looked deeply, one by one, at his favorite followers who had dedicated their lives to him.

Wen-yi arose as the room turned silent. "Commandant," he said, calling his Leader by the title he had held during their years at Whampoa, "for all these years you have been an inspiration and mentor to us all, present and absent. We will serve you proudly in our continuing struggle for victory in Taiwan." There was much applause. When Chiang silently raised his glass in appreciation, everyone jumped to their feet holding a glass full or empty. Later, alone with Wen-yi, Chiang said to him softly "You should teach and help Ching-kuo like your family member." Wen-yi was mystified by this strange request. Several months later, in Taiwan, he would have reason to recall the conversation with Chiang.

Chiang Departs from Chengdu to Taiwan

As dawn arrived, Chiang Kai-shek and Ching-kuo made ready to leave the Chengdu Military Academy for the airport and their final retreat to Taiwan. Wen-yi and several others stood quietly by to see father and son off from mainland China. Communist troops had arrived at the suburbs of Chengdu. Ching-kuo had the car waiting at the back door for the sake of safety. Kai-shek said to him firmly, "That will not do. I came in through the front door and I must exit through the front door." As they prepared to leave, Kai-shek turned to Ching-kuo and said, "Let the two of us sing the national anthem." With the small group they sang:

"The Three People's Principles
Adhered to by our Party
To build the Republic
To promote universal harmony..."

A strained smile and a quick salute by the Generalissimo and they were gone. They flew in a small plane amid heavy clouds.

On December 8, 1949, the Executive Yuan voted to move the Nationalist government to Taipei in Taiwan. Early in the morning of December 10, 1949, Communist troops laid siege to Chengdu, the last Nationalist controlled city on mainland China, where Chiang Kai-shek and Chiang Ching-kuo had directed the defense at the Chengdu Central Military Academy. The Nationalist world came to an end.

Wen-yi left for Haikou on the last plane on December 16. My father remained in Haikou for two weeks to help evaluate whether the island could become a second base to Taiwan. Over 100,000 Nationalist soldiers had come to Hainan. The island offered excellent potential for successful agricultural products. However, it was also vulnerable to attack by the PLA. Wen-yi left the island for Taiwan on December 30.

Chapter 23

My Two Lives in Taiwan

In November 1948 Aunt Ke-ming, cousin Yuan-cheng, and I were domiciled temporarily with Mr. Lu, who had served under Uncle Wen-shi. Four months later, Wen-shi reached Taipei after a long journey with his 1,300 troops along a land and sea escape route from Beijing, following the surrender of all the Nationalist Northern Forces to the Communists. Almost immediately after their arrival in Taiwan, the men dispersed to fend for themselves. Wen-shi looked forward to the immediate future with considerable relish. It was what had sustained him on the arduous journey.

With the end of the civil war in sight, he had gathered the assets of the dissolving Youth Corps 205th Division which he had commanded. "Better that I have them than the Communists," he told himself. At the age of 42, he now had a considerable supply of gold bars that allowed him to be free of the discipline and obligations of military life. He would now dedicate himself to an unbridled libertine lifestyle in Taiwan, especially with many available beautiful women. He bought a house in Taichung for his pregnant mistress Liu and assigned two former staff members to see to her needs. Wen-shi established his own Taipei household with a Taiwanese girl, a former mistress, who had had a child with him. Looking to a source of future income he bought a rice milling business. He would surely prosper meeting the needs of soldiers, military families, Nationalist Party members and associates, and intellectual and business elites, who were arriving in a steady stream. However, the venture would not detract from his dedication to a dissolute life, with little thought of his wife and family in Tainan.

Inevitably, gossip about Wen-shi's lifestyle reached Ke-ming. Already insecure, she was overwhelmed with feelings of devastation and anger. She felt helpless in trying to deal with the situation, other than by writing him bitter letters of condemnation.

The Lu family had taken us in on a temporary basis. With several children of their own, they said they could no longer continue to have us in their household. Finally, after several frantic letters from Ke-ming, Wen-shi sent her some money. She immediately bought a small one-bedroom house located in a narrow alley in the center of the city of Tainan. We left the Lu family with mutual relief, and moved into our own house. Ke-ming began to make a life for herself, joining other displaced friends in daylong mah-jongg games, while Wen-shi continued to lead a playboy's life in Taipei and Taichung.

Our house was located in a quiet residential alley with well-spaced main doors of single-family or apartment houses connected by walls. The residents rarely saw one another. However, we were more fortunate than those living in very narrow alleys with small, densely packed houses, or streets crowded with peddlers and mobile stands of various goods, where the peddlers mingled with residents. Ours was a Japanese-style house with tatamis, old Japanese style straw mats, on the floors. There was electricity and tap water, but no flush toilet. The cesspit of the toilet had an opening to the alley. A man with a dung-cart pulled by an ox emptied the cesspit weekly. Dung was used by farmers to fertilize the land. This collection process with the many large dung carts created an almost unbearable odor on the street early in the morning.

Our lives in the new house suddenly took on a semblance of normalcy. The desperate fear and flight from war was behind us, we hoped.

Early in 1949, Yuan-cheng and I entered fourth and fifth grades at the Eternal Happiness (Yun-fu) National Elementary School. I was not aware my life path would now begin to change. Our school was located along a busy street behind a cement wall with a metal railing on top. Beyond the main entrance was a well-tended garden leading to the classrooms. In the rear of the property was a sports field where the 900 pupils received daily "spiritual" lectures, and performed morning exercises. A water garden with a fountain and beautiful water lilies adorned one corner of the grounds.

There were three classes of 50 students in each of the fifth and sixth grades. The best students and those from influential families were assigned to the A-Class. These classes had the best teachers and received extra tutoring. The remaining 100 pupils were divided into B- and C-Classes. Elementary school education was compulsory. Many poorer parents would have preferred to keep their children home to do chores or pursue trades to bring in money.

Ke-ming knew nothing about the school system, nor did she care. I was escorted to school by an aide. I was placed in the C-Class. Most children in my C-Class were from poor families with heart-wrenching stories. I was among the fortunate ones in the class. Occasionally I received candy with beautiful wrapping paper from Uncle Wen-shi. When the candy was consumed I played with the wrappers, folding them into book marks. One day on the playground, I was chewing bubble gum, aware of the envious glances of my schoolmates. When I spat the spent gum to the ground, a girl asked me timidly if I was done with the candy. I nodded in surprise. She quickly picked it up and popped the dirt-studded gum into her mouth. I was embarrassed and shaken by this incident. I wished I had a fresh piece to give her, but I did not.

Classes were conducted in Mandarin by government decree since it was now considered the national language. This was an advantage for me since I was fluent in Mandarin. I had discarded my strong Sichuan dialect in which I had conversed for my first seven years in Chengdu, Sichuan. Since the written characters are the same for all Chinese dialects, it was possible for people from different provinces to learn Mandarin. However, this presented difficulties for many of the Taiwanese teachers and pupils. Despite their best efforts they spoke the language awkwardly and with a strange accent.

Our textbooks were provided free of charge, but paper and pencils were special and rarely used for routine exercises. Classroom tasks and homework were done on a thin polished slab of slate, 8" x 10" in size, using hard chalks. The schoolwork was not challenging, nor was it taken seriously by students or our teachers.

I was restless and my home life was unpleasant. Uncle Wen-shi remained in Taipei and showed no inclination to return home. Aunt Ke-ming continued to seek distraction from her anxiety by playing endless mah-jongg games. There were often ten people or more in the one-bedroom house. We had to be careful at night not to step on someone sleeping on the floor. I channeled my energy and frustration into the only outlet I had, schoolwork. I particularly enjoyed composition and arithmetic.

The grand examinations for the entire fifth grade came at the end of the semester. These would determine the sixth grade class assignment for each student. Mr. Yen, a teacher of the prestigious sixth grade A-Class, appeared to be watching me as I worked on my exams. He had noticed that while other children were dithering at their desks, I was busily writing. Sensing his attention, I gave an extra effort to write the correct answers. When the new class assignments were announced, I was thrilled to learn I had been assigned to Mr. Yen's A-Class in the fall.

The new class proved to be an entirely different experience for me. Mr. Yen conducted his class with strict discipline. He dispensed corporal punishment in a typical, ruthless Japanese style. This teacher had a grim face, wore his belt below a slightly protruding belly, and swaggered like a Japanese samurai. When a student failed to produce a correct answer, which was often, Mr. Yen would whip the little bare legs of the pupils with a thin, flexible strip of bamboo. Mr. Yen would also hold an unfortunate pupil's head between his two large hands and slap the small face with one hand, then the other. I had never seen such corporal punishment in the schools in mainland China.

Under this rigorous regimen, I made sure all my schoolwork was as perfect as possible. I particularly loved tricky arithmetic problems. I found solving these exhilarating. Mr. Yen appeared to be pleased with me. This strict and forbidding teacher seemed to have singled me out from the 50 elite pupils. He apparently had seen something in me that no prior teacher or adult had bothered to notice. Mr. Yen gave me many challenging tasks and I responded enthusiastically. With his special mentoring, I was selected to compete in a series of inter-school speech, debate, arithmetic, and composition contests. I was thrilled with such competitions and rivalries. They were much more fulfilling than chasing my playmates on rooftops. I was able to win several awards for the school. I was in a daze of happiness. Mr. Yen often held me up to the class, to my embarrassment and pride, as a model student. He told the pupils to notice the way I read quickly with my eyes instead of my lips, and how I used logic in solving arithmetic problems. My compositions were posted on the bulletin board. I eventually won the highest Mayor's Award.

I became a target of some students. As I read some verses aloud, one classmate sneered and said, "Aren't you supposed to read with your eyes only?" Other accomplished students received similar treatment. No one at home showed the slightest interest in my progress at school. However, for the first time I experienced the unfamiliar feeling of being regarded as special by an adult. I even cherished the envy of my peers. The feeling of being like a weed was fading.

I graduated from Eternal Happiness Elementary School with high honors and was accepted to the prestigious Tainan Provincial Girls' Middle School by passing a difficult entrance exam. Only two other girls in my school had been accepted. I lost touch with Mr. Yen after elementary school but I would always remember how this stern, even ruthless teacher, had provided the means to view myself more positively. I felt inspired by the belief I could be much more than I had been. I will always remember him.

By the end of 1949, almost the entire Deng family was safely in Taiwan. Wen-yi and my grandmother had each settled into separate large households in Taipei. In the spring of 1950, Ke-ming, in desperate need of money and emotional support, ventured to Taipei to plead for help from the family. None was forthcoming. Ke-ming was bitterly disappointed at their unsympathetic attitude. Defeated, Ke-ming returned to Tainan even more depressed.

However, Ke-ming's plea and despair had a profound effect on my stepmother Wen-ying. The contrast between the two sisters-in-law was striking. Ke-ming was timid, insecure, and mediocre in every aspect. Wen-ying was highly educated, beautiful, and smart. She was a member of the National Assembly and admired by many, particularly men.

The only thing the two women had in common was that their husbands were avid womanizers. Wen-ying felt humiliated that her husband should seek comfort from women with considerably less to offer. She felt isolated, and regretted that she had not brought any of her four sisters to Taiwan as a source of support. Whenever she learned of Wen-yi's transgressions, she reacted violently, slashing his best suits, and berating him. She even took her young children to confront Wen-yi and his women. When Wen-yi raised the possibility of divorce, her paranoia became full blown. She accused my older brother of procuring women for my father. My brother was so outraged at these irrational accusations that he did not speak to her for several years.

The husbands of Wen-ying and Ke-ming had a number of similarities and sharp contrasts. Both brothers were handsome and had attained the rank of General. Uncle Wen-shi's entire career had been with the military. He had been commander of an Infantry Division and later a Deputy Corps Commander. His brother Wen-yi had made his mark in the political arena with senior positions in several major party organizations and in

Chiang Kai-shek's inner circle as his personal secretary and aide-de-camp. The brothers, both powerful, considered womanizing an entitlement. For Wen-yi, it was a pleasure that he pursued in a more refined way, while for Wen-shi, sex was an addiction that had no boundaries. Wen-shi's speech was coarse and rough, as a result of years spent in the field with the troops. Wen-yi was more literate and polished as a result of dealing with highly placed party and government officials. Both men were spendthrifts. Each felt it was entirely appropriate to use government funds for their personal pleasure. Wen-yi cheerfully gave money to friends or subordinates in need, or borrowed from them, when needed. Neither brother gave any thought to saving money, thereby placing a heavy burden on their wives. Wen-shi was generous with his mistresses, his children by them, and his many casual girl friends. Within two years, his gold bars were gone. He faced the prospect of a radically new lifestyle with little regret.

I entered the Tainan Provincial Girls' Middle School in the fall of 1950. This had once been an elite school for Japanese girls during Japanese control of the island. The school maintained its prestige throughout the 1950s. The school complex, located on the quiet outskirts of Tainan, had three long, two-story brick buildings for classrooms and offices. These were surrounded by lovely gardens, music buildings, sports fields, gym, tennis courts, swimming pool, and teachers' residences. In one section, however, the area was scarred with ruins of bricks, burnt wood, and debris from a bombing by American planes near the end of World War II.

In my 7th grade, only 15% of the girls were from mainland China; the rest were native Taiwanese. Some of my Taiwanese classmates from rural areas were the first in their towns and villages to be admitted to this school. The school had strict codes regarding appearance and conduct. When the teacher appeared at the classroom, the class president would call the class to rise, bow to the teacher at the podium, then sit down. This was standard for all classes. The student bowed upon encountering a teacher on or off the campus. We wore uniforms, carried maroon book bags, and were required to keep our hair straight and short. Make-up, dating, and socialization with the opposite sex were strictly forbidden, to the displeasure of the town boys.

Most of my Taiwanese schoolmates came from well-to-do families. The quality and condition of their uniforms and their mannerisms contrasted sharply with those of the poorer mainlanders. Nevertheless, the struggling mainland families had great expectations for their children. As for thousands of years in China, the children's education was considered a source of good fortune for the family. Yet families paid little attention to how their children conducted themselves at school. I, also, received little support from Ke-ming. The mainlanders were loud, mischievous, and unkempt. Their uniforms were made of coarse material and constantly wrinkled. For many of them, the uniform was their only wardrobe, worn at home and school. However, the mainlanders scored above average scholastically, probably due to the good education they had received in China.

It seemed natural for me to gravitate toward mainlanders. We thought of our Taiwanese classmates as being pretentious and dull. Unlike Taiwanese students, we loved to go to the movies in town. The movie theater was usually packed. Before the movie, everyone rose for the national anthem and remained standing if there was a recorded speech from Chiang Kai-shek. A news film followed, showing heroic battles and retreats of the Nationalist troops during the Chinese Civil War, or the cruelty of the Chinese Communists during the ruthless Korean War. Most of the Chinese films were tragedies, causing tears among the audience when laughter would have been more welcome.

We all admired Principal Yu, who had recruited and brought with her many wonderful teachers from the mainland. The school had a powerful public-address system which sent out beautiful western classical music between classes. With recollections of wars and escapes barely behind us, we were grateful that Principal Yu provided the lovely music and environment, as a haven where we could dream of a better future.

One day during geometry class, I was summoned to the principal's office. On the short walk to the office I apprehensively reviewed the good and bad things I might have done. As I entered the office, Principal Yu said, with a twinkle in her eyes, "Deng Yuan-yu, see who is here to visit you!" It was my father, Wen-yi! I suddenly felt shy and self-conscious.

I finally managed to say, "How are you, Baba?!"

My father beamed with delight to see his abandoned daughter growing into an attractive young lady. He said, "How are you, Yuan-yu? Your principal tells me you are doing well here."

Principal Yu added, "Indeed, she is an excellent student and the president of her class." Turning to me the principal said, "Yuan-yu, you may show your father the school before the crowded recess period."

Flustered by compliments from the principal, I silently led my father out of the office to the school grounds. It had been almost three years since I had last seen him in Nanjing. I was now fourteen and had grown almost to my full height of 5'4", nearly as tall as he. My face was losing its remnants of "baby fat" and beginning to look more like a young lady, with large, shining, almond-shaped eyes. My father appraised me carefully, with obvious approval. It seemed as though he were seeing me for the first time. I was secretly pleased I could actually carry on a conversation with him with little or no nervousness. He asked me about my school and home situation. I answered his questions without hesitation, but was afraid to tell him of my aunt's indifference and neglect.

That evening, my father came to our house. He was staying at a fine hotel. He gave us much news about our relatives and happenings in Taipei. He then took us out for a fine dinner. It was a special event for our household. When I returned to school the next day, the word had spread that my father was an important General. My status had suddenly risen among my classmates. No one thought it odd that I did not live with my father in Taipei, since many students lived away from home.

My father had published a book, *My Journey of Ten Thousand Miles*, which became quite popular. Our Chinese teacher critiqued the book during class, unaware that the author was my father. "The new popular book of Deng Wen-yi is a well-written travel book, but it interjects too much of his political and military experiences and accomplishments," he stated.

My classmates sensed the criticism and prodded me: "Who is he to criticize! Tell the teacher Deng Wen-yi is your father." I did not.

That summer, following my father's visit to the school, he asked me if I would like to accompany him on governmental trips to southern Taiwan. Wen-yi currently held the position of Vice Minister of the Interior. I was speechless with joy and stammered my pleasure and excitement. I was allowed to select new clothes so I would be presentable to people I would meet on the trip. During our many visits he introduced me to his friends and colleagues. While we were in central Taiwan, we spent an afternoon at a beautiful lake called "Sun Moon Lake" surrounded by mountains. One of the women told me it was the largest natural lake in Taiwan; the lake was so named because the eastern part of it is round like the sun, while the Western part is shaped like a crescent moon. Sitting on the beach I found myself staring again and again at the many peaks that rose up in nearby mountains covered with trees and green vegetation.

I was included in the dinner and dance parties, always feeling a sense of unreality. After so many years of being ignored and uncared for, I was now being received and accepted with respect and, yes, with flattering comments regarding what a beautiful young woman I was. The wives were apparently familiar with my family situation. One woman asked me, "How do your adoptive parents handle the situation when you make mistakes and need discipline?" I dared not tell her that I was largely unnoticed at home and treated with little respect.

I felt strange to be with my father for an extended time. I sensed his eagerness and sincerity to amend our relationship, but I felt no love or closeness to him. I did not know how to receive or give love to a parent. After all, I was just one of his seven daughters. How much could I mean to him? I was proud of his position and accomplishments, admired by many. But to me he was merely a man who, at age 45, looked very middle-aged now, not quite the handsome and powerful master he had once seemed to be. I felt only a slight pang of guilt for having no filial feeling toward my own father, though I did cherish and appreciate this brief kindness.

During 9th grade, my views toward my small world began to change. I grew disenchanted with my mainland friends and longed to be a more "cultured person." I had briefly experienced the possibilities life could offer. I began to take private piano lessons; however, it was soon apparent that since there was no piano available to me on which to practice, I could not progress rapidly. It was a wrenching setback for me. I yearned to know more about western classical music but had limited means to hear it.

I found myself preferring the company of my more cultivated Taiwanese classmates. They welcomed me to their group enthusiastically. The Taiwanese students conversed in their native dialect outside the classes. Soon I could speak with them in almost flawless Taiwanese dialect. I conscientiously emulated the mannerisms of my more refined classmates. I was enchanted by their families, and was often invited to visit their country homes, spend a weekend in the beach house of an affluent classmate, and even fish at a lovely family fish farm. My two closest mainland friends, Han and Lu, felt betrayed. They drew closer to each other and distanced themselves from me. I felt guilty and disloyal. The awkward situation ended when we graduated from junior high.

Graduates of the junior high faced an option in our paths forward. We could go to the Tainan Girls' Normal High School, which provided its students with monthly expense money and teaching jobs in elementary schools three years later. Many of my classmates were told or coerced by their family to enter the normal school for financial reasons. In addition, teaching elementary school was considered a good profession for a girl. About one third of my class, including Han and Lu, entered the normal school. For those seeking more intellectual pursuits, the Tainan Provincial Girls' Middle School was the preferred option. As the honor student of my class, I entered the high school with an exemption from the entrance exams.

I was excited by the thought that I was about to be with those students I had admired for three years. In high school, we became more aware of the political environment and tensions on the island. Taiwan was now under American protection with the 7th Fleet of the US Navy stationed in the Taiwan straits, so we did not need to fear any Communist invasion. Our school life shielded us from the harsh life under martial law. We understood we were not to speak or write against the government, nor to form or join any private student or political organizations. We dutifully shouted slogans such as "Retake the Mainland!" or "Exterminate Bandit Mao Ze-dong!" However, we had little enthusiasm for Chiang Kai-shek's many "inspirational" messages.

Our citizenship classes emphasized the Three People's Principles, the mantra of the Nationalist Party. We received military training with real weapons. During one of our military classes I accidentally fired a rifle by not setting the safety properly and got knocked to the ground by the recoil. I did poorly at target shooting because I had difficulty keeping one eye closed. Our teachers and families were not enthused by patriotic exhortations. Many of them had fought against the Japanese and the Communists. Now older, they simply urged the students to study, do something useful, and stay away from political and military arenas. We admired these teachers greatly and empathized with their pain and frustration. It was not surprising that my generation had little fervor or sense of loyalty toward the government. Our priorities were quality of life and career. This was in sharp contrast to the era when my father's generation gave their unquestioned loyalty to Chiang Kai-shek in fighting many battles against the warlords, foreign invaders, and the Communist Party. We had our own yellow brick road to follow.

Upon entering high school, I had to make a decision regarding my future course. Would I pursue science or the liberal arts? Our teachers were adamant that technology was the correct road to the future. Science would lead us to prosperity and utopia. The arts could be embraced later. Girls with no scientific aptitude or those with early marriage prospects entered the liberal arts class. The more academically inclined students selected the science program. We dreamed of getting into the best university and going to America, which promised a prosperous future. The three-year intensive program was intended to prepare us to compete for a place at the National Taiwan University or the few other desirable colleges. This would be our battleground. I arrived early every day at school and remained late in order to memorize a few more English words, Chinese poetry verses, geography, and dates and events in history. I attended the supplementary math and English classes held in our teachers' small homes. I was embarrassed, but secretly delighted, when my diminutive math teacher addressed me teasingly with, "Here comes Dr. Deng Yuan-yu!"

We were becoming young women. Dating was strictly forbidden. With the large influx of military men and male students from the mainland, girls were greatly outnumbered and in demand. Any letter of admiration sent to the school was confiscated. If a student was spotted and reported to be with a man or boy, she would be asked to the dean's office and reprimanded. Principal Yu warned us not to smile at men, to avoid unwelcome advances. Such rules were proper and traditional for most Taiwanese families who arranged marriages for their children. Most of us naively followed and believed in these rules. Whatever adolescent yearnings we had, we released through romantic books, movies, and popular songs. We talked about the new movies and sang the popular songs over and over again. I devoured any book I could get hold of. These were some of my happiest years. Gradually I was becoming a poised, and, yes, even (I was told) a beautiful young lady.

Toward the end of 1950, the Nationalist government launched a number of programs to provide work for the many high-level officers exiled from the mainland. Uncle Wen-shi had squandered all his money and was reinstated as a senior staff officer in the Army's Headquarters in Fongshan. He received only a modest stipend. Now he would come to stay with us on weekends. Ke-ming found little comfort in Wen-shi's return. The continuing dire financial situation did nothing to improve her bitterness. Yuan-cheng and I did not help her. She once sent me to beg for money from Wen-shi's former subordinate Mr. Lu, a humiliating task. I returned empty-handed and refused to go again, much to Ke-ming's dismay.

Wen-shi's return to the house on weekends became a source of aggravation for me. I had been keeping a daily diary, which I hid in the bottom of my small suitcase. Somehow, my uncle discovered it while I was in school and read it for amusement. On one page I had written, "Father was off the last couple of days carousing with his girlfriends." When I opened the diary to write an entry I was stunned to see he had scribbled a note: "It is not fair to accuse me wrongly." I was furious. I threw the sullied diary into the cesspool and never again kept a diary.

However, the worst was yet to come. One night while Ke-ming was playing mah-jongg with three players in the living room, I was asleep in the big bed in the adjoining bedroom. It was separated from the living room by Japanese-style sliding doors, made with fine wood frames and rice paper. The bedroom also contained a smaller bed for Yuan-cheng, and a still smaller one for me. For staying "out of the way," I was permitted to use the big bed during the mah-jongg game. I was suddenly awakened by something touching my leg. I discovered Wen-shi lying naked next to me with a huge erection. I leapt up and stomped to the bathroom, filled with loathing and rage. As I passed through the living room, Ke-ming, facing me from her game table, noticed my distress. I lingered in the bathroom as long as I could. When I finally returned to the bedroom, Wen-shi had donned his underwear. He whispered, "Go back to bed. It will be all right." I moved as far away from him as possible in the large bed and fell back to sleep.

The following Sunday, Ke-ming took me to a quiet park and asked, "What happened the other night? Why were you so upset?"

Embarrassed and also relieved that I could finally confide in someone, I stammered, "Father woke me up. He had taken his underpants off."

"Did he do anything to you?"

"Not this time!"

That set her thinking. She looked at me in alarm. "Were there other times? What else has he done lately?"

"When we went to the movies the other day, he told me he was lonely. He said you were difficult to live with and not loving. And he was very healthy and in the best physical shape." I recalled I was uneasy yet sympathetic toward him then.

"He said those things to you? That animal! Did he say or do anything to you before?" Ke-ming grew angry.

It suddenly dawned on me: I had felt so disturbed by Wen-shi's remarks at the movies because he was trying to seduce me! The realization made me cringe. I decided to tell her everything.

"Yes. When we were in China, he often came in after I went to sleep, and put his hand into my underpants and rubbed between my legs."

Ke-ming's face turned totally white and she said hoarsely, "Why didn't you tell me then?"

"Father told me not to tell anybody. I was afraid, and you did not ask me."

For the next few days, the tension in the house was palpable, but remained beneath the surface. Always timid toward her husband, Ke-ming apparently had not dared to confront Wen-shi. But her festering anger and paranoia flared.

One day, she suddenly grabbed and shook me: "Where were you last night? Why weren't you in your bed?"

"I was in my bed. I did not go anywhere." I was totally puzzled.

"You dirty trash! You were sleeping with your father! You were with him in his bed," she howled.

I was horrified and humiliated by this accusation. I pleaded, "That is not true. I slept alone in my bed last night."

"You are an ungrateful whore! How dare you do such a thing in my house and under my eyes?" she screamed, with a savage glint in her eyes.

I was alarmed and backed away to the kitchen. Ke-ming looked totally unglued. I sat on a small stool, overcome by a sense of helplessness and misery. Years of suppressed suffering and humiliation broke open; I cried uncontrollably.

After quite a while, her sanity restored, Ke-ming came to me and said in a tight voice, "Stop crying, it is not your fault."

For the next three days and nights, she simply sat in a stupor, without sleep. Everyone in the house was worried. On the fourth day when I came home from school I found a disheveled Ke-ming waving both arms in the air and chanting incoherently. She had become insane. The accumulated years of insecurity and abasement had taken their toll.

Wen-shi took her to the mental hospital for various treatments including electric shocks. He then brought her to a Christian retreat in the mountains. Ke-ming never regained her sanity. She sat in the house all day with an empty stare. Although Ke-ming was never close to me and often treated me roughly, I was horrified by her current state. I wondered, with a sense of guilt, if my revelation might have triggered her plight. Deep down, however, I blamed Wen-shi for his libertine lifestyle that had caused such long and deep misery for his wife and me. I hated him all the more for it.

News of Ke-ming's illness elicited little attention since many people had been suffering mental anguish in varying degrees while trying to adjust to the trauma of exile in a new, strange world. Her nephews did not blame Wen-shi since, they said, mental instability had been a recurring family problem. Ke-ming's oldest brother had also suffered from dementia in mainland China. The news, however, frightened my stepmother, since her insecurities were similar to Ke-ming's. Wen-ying's paranoia increased.

Surprisingly, the turmoil did not affect my progress at school, a happy haven of relief where I was able to forget the problems at home. My cousin, Yuan-cheng, had always been the apple of Ke-ming's eye. Her breakdown had been a terrible blow to him. By then, our childhood animosity and rivalry were gone, but we were too young to protect and take care of each other. Wen-shi moved back into the household. He had little money and resorted to borrowing from friends and fellow officers.

I was fifteen years old. As a good high school student ready to leave for college, I now commanded a certain amount of respect at home. I had a tiny room all to myself and usually studied late. On nights Wen-shi came home after his evening card games and other activities, he would bring me snacks such as a soy-sauce egg, a few chicken wings, some dried tofu, or pork head meat. I enjoyed the treats and appreciated his kindness. But whenever I thought of what he had done to me, I would turn angry and flush with rage. Ironically, Wen-shi had no idea he was the source of the problem. He would comment nonchalantly, "It is a shame that Yuan-yu has this frequent facial contortion. She would be much prettier otherwise."

We had always had a maid to do the cooking, laundry, and housework. Now that Wen-shi was in charge of the household, he fired the middle-aged maid and hired an innocent and bosomy seventeen-year-old girl named Ah-tio. From the start Ah-tio complained to me that Wen-shi would grope her when she was cooking at the stove. I warned her about his behavior. However, she soon accepted his advances, and they both appeared happy. Ah-tio became pregnant. Her sister arranged a marriage for her to a veteran soldier who developed orchards of exotic fruits in the mountains, a project sponsored by the government. The isolated life was lonely and hard; it was almost impossible for these soldiers to find a wife. The veteran was elated to have Ah-tio and readily accepted her pregnancy. Ah-tio found contentment in her new life. In a poor Taiwanese family, she would have had to cook, launder, and labor for the whole family and possibly be abused by the mother-in-law and sisters-in-law. The orchard project was successful. Ah-tio occasionally brought her firstborn to visit. Wen-shi had meanwhile obtained another pretty maid.

Through all this, the motherless weed had slowly evolved into a strong young woman. My life at school was bright and filled with promise. During our graduation ceremony, my classmates and I cried openly. I graduated first in my class, which allowed me to enter the Chemical Engineering Department of the distinguished National Taiwan University in Taipei, exempt from the tough entrance exam. I was ready to take on the future.

Chapter 24

Taiwan and Wen-yi in Transition

Wen-yi and Chiang Ching-kuo

When Chiang Kai-shek resumed his former post as president on March 1, 1950, his immediate priorities were to establish his supreme authority in Taiwan, and to continue to expand his loyal son Ching-kuo's influence and power, for his eventual ascendency to the presidency. The relationship between Wen-yi and Ching-kuo had always been one of "restrained friendliness." They had worked closely together on several occasions. Both held the rank of Lt. General. Ching-kuo had listened impassively as Wen-yi described his stay with my mother Bai-jian at the Chiangs' ancestral home, and of his conversations with Ching-kuo's mother, Mao Fu-mei. Ching-kuo may have been irritated by his father's seeming affection for the loyal, sometimes quixotic Wen-yi, and by my father's obvious devotion to the elder Chiang.

Chiang Ching-kuo Replaces Wen-yi in the National Defense Ministry

One day, Chiang Kai-shek asked his son and Wen-yi to dine with him. After the general conversation was done, Chiang turned to my father and said, "Wen-yi, I want to ask you to step down from your position as head of the Political Bureau in the National Defense Ministry so that I can appoint Ching-kuo to that post. He needs the post to acquire additional experience and to expand the scope of its operations. I would like for the two of you to be like brothers. I want you to mentor Ching-kuo on the issues and problems he can be expected to encounter." Ching-kuo remained silent. It may have irritated him that he was to be mentored by someone whose skills as a political leader were beneath his own. After a pause, Wen-yi said he would do his best to smooth Ching-kuo's path. Chiang added,

"There will be other things for you to do to help our government move forward."

Wen-yi reluctantly set himself to the task of putting in order the Political Work Department he had painstakingly built in the past five years, for turnover to Ching-kuo. Wen-yi was not happy with the task and Ching-kuo was anxious to have the mentoring behind him so he could proceed with his ambitious plans for the organization.

Although their friendship was not a close one, both men carefully maintained an air of amity and respect. Ching-kuo had several times come to our house for dinner in Chongqing and Nanjing. The exodus to Taiwan at the beginning of 1950 had resulted in a severe housing shortage in Taipei. Ching-kuo offered the large house next to his to Wen-yi as a gesture of friendship and good will. As my stepmother Wen-ying and Wen-yi were inspecting the house, they saw an attractive young woman, well dressed and made up, passing through the backyard of the house they were inspecting. She then entered Ching-kuo's house. Wen-ying thought it odd. Wen-yi knew the woman was Ching-kuo's girlfriend. Wen-ying decided she would rather live in her own house than a "government house." Wen-yi was relieved. He had already felt some concern that Ching-kuo might be after his beautiful wife Wen-ying. Having made their decision, Wen-yi returned the house key, explaining that they were grateful for his gracious offer but had decided to remain in their current home. At the celebration of the Lunar New Year, Ching-kuo and his wife called on my father and stepmother to offer their good wishes. Occasionally, Ching-kuo and Wen-yi would slip away together to the clubs where they enjoyed dancing, drinking, and some dalliance.

Ching-kuo quickly took over my father's position and became director of the General Political Department of the National Defense Department. This would be a springboard for expanding the scope of his power. He wasted no time launching a series of actions to expand the reach and importance of his newly inherited operation into a widespread, powerful intelligence and security apparatus. He enlisted the help of Peng Meng-chi, commander of Taiwan Provincial Security Command, to take control of the secret police network throughout the island. Ching-kuo then established a commissar system of political officers throughout all levels of the military, followed by a similar system in the university, to monitor and discourage dissent or opposition in these bodies.[1]

My Father Takes Over Ching-kuo's Post
True to his word, President Chiang appointed my father secretary general of the Taiwan Provincial Nationalist Party, a position previously held by Ching-kuo. Wen-yi maintained his rank as Lt. General. His deputy secretary was Li You-bang. The party was still in transition, with only three dozen party workers and a few thousand registered members. Wen-yi immediately initiated a project to recruit and train party workers for a propaganda section. Within three months the now firmly organized party was expanding into cities, counties, and villages. Membership in the Nationalist party grew rapidly to tens of thousands. The party provided services to assist the government in carrying out a variety of projects. Wen-yi worked aggressively and passionately, heedless of resentment and opposition from liberal party members and government officials, especially Dr. K. C. Wu, current governor of Taiwan. Chiang Kai-shek and Chen Cheng, head of the Executive Yuan, praised Wen-yi for his accomplishments.

K.C. Wu
Wu's hostility and Chiang's approval of Wen-yi were not surprising. Wu had replaced Chen Cheng as governor of Taiwan. He had been a surprising choice. Although Chiang disliked Wu he recognized and valued Wu's administrative skills. Wu had a doctoral degree in political science from Princeton University. Chiang had earlier appointed him mayor of Chongqing in 1939, vice minister of Foreign Affairs from 1943-1945, and mayor of Shanghai in 1945. Nevertheless, this

was not a comfortable appointment for Chiang. However, he needed to maintain the appearance of a reformer to the Taiwanese and especially to the US administration.

Wu's appointment was received with hope by the Taiwanese who felt they would, at last, have an ally in the government. K. C. Wu was a man of great integrity. He was also a liberal politician and reformer. He wasted no time introducing a number of reforms to obtain the trust and support of the people. He brought many Taiwanese into his administration, allowed local elections by the people, and tried to reduce coercive actions of the secret police. These actions increased the dislike and distrust of the man by the Chiangs, Chen Cheng, Wen-yi, and party conservatives. Their objectives were to establish political stability, economic development, and modernization through a strong authoritarian government. This meant temporarily shelving the freedoms guaranteed by the Constitution that Chiang had so proudly established.

Wu and party liberals argued Wen-yi was too aggressive and conservative, hindering reform in party and government. Chiang was now under pressure to remove him. He summoned my father to his office. He told Wen-yi he was pleased with the way he was conducting his office. So were Ching-kuo and Chen Cheng. However, he was under pressure, and was now, reluctantly, asking Wen-yi to step down for the sake of party unity. He quickly added that there was still important work for Wen-yi to do. He said he would deal with Wu and others.

My father was angry. He felt he had made important contributions to the party. Now, once again, Chiang had removed him from a post in which he had accomplished much, for political expediency. My father decided to spend some time at a remote retreat in the mountains, where he wrote a long memoir of his travels, *My Journey of Ten Thousand Miles*. The book was published and received favorable comments and reviews. This was the book critiqued by my teacher when I was in the eighth grade.

My Father Is Appointed Vice Minister of the Interior

One day, the newly appointed Minister of the Interior, Huang Ji-lu, visited Wen-yi to inform him Chiang Kai-shek wanted him to be the vice Interior Minister. Wen-yi received this news with exhilaration and apprehension. He felt he knew little about the issues of the Ministry. Yet, fortunately, Wen-yi knew Huang well and had worked closely with him on several occasions in the past. Huang had served as Sichuan Nationalist Party Chief at Chengdu where Wen-yi headed the political department of the Central Military Academy. Huang was the best man at Wen-yi's wedding to my stepmother Wen-ying. My father knew Huang would lend cooperation and support in their mutual mission.

Wen-yi took the office in the spring of 1952. The Interior Ministry was lax and disorganized, with a limited budget and staff after two years of operation in Taiwan. Wen-yi and the Interior Minister set out to streamline the ministry, and to develop policies and guidelines for supervising the establishment of local self-rule and land reform. Nationalist authorities had launched the first phase of a broad and successful redistribution of land from large landowners to small farmers. Over 150,000 tenant farmers bought land at below market price.

My father spoke out forcefully in favor of a "land-to-the-tiller" program that was to follow the successful first phase sale of public land to the farmers. The landlords would retain a portion of their land. The tenants who were actually working the land could now purchase it at a price set at 2.5 times the value of the crops produced on that land annually. The new "tenant landowners" could obtain interest-free loans to repay the loan over a ten-year period, with money or rice or other crops. Wen-yi felt it would be tragic to repeat the mistakes of the past, ignoring the plight of farmers and peasants, thereby offering another opportunity for the Communists to become active in agitating the people in the rural area.[2] He worked with his staff to develop plans for training a large cadre of field agents, with whom he spent much time in the villages and farms throughout the island, helping farmers and tenants to understand their rights and opportunities presented by the new land reform policies. Landowners were encouraged to start commercial and industrial enterprises as well as small businesses. Taiwan's economy slowly but steadily moved from predominantly agricultural to industrial,[3] on its way to the Taiwan Miracle.

Wen-yi loved to give talks, write, read, and publish. He achieved modest recognition in the literary field. However, the authoritarian government was still applying strict censorship with little freedom of speech, press, and publishing. Creativity was stifled. A newly formed "Library Association of Taiwan" appealed to Wen-yi for his support in obtaining the government's approval for their project to promote and advance librarianship and to encourage research in Library Science. They felt that his literary interest and earlier activities as a publisher and bookseller would offer their best opportunity to obtain official status. Wen-yi suggested the society submit a petition to him with detailed plans for their new organization. The Ministry of the Interior gave its approval for this initiative. During inaugural ceremonies Wen-yi and R. C. Krugerm from the US Information Services were guest speakers.

Ching-kuo had now solidified his power and began to flex his muscles and settle old debts. His first major target was Governor K. C. Wu. Dr. Wu detested Ching-kuo and had courageously chastised the Executive Yuan, and the actions of the Chiangs. He compared Ching-kuo's Youth Corps and secret police to Hitler's Youth Group and Gestapo, declaring Taiwan virtually a police state. The personal affront to Ching-kuo was the last straw. Wu barely escaped assassination on April 3, 1953, and was dismissed from his position as governor seven days later. Wu and his family escaped from Taiwan to the United States, but were forced to leave their young son behind as a hostage for more than a year.

Ching-kuo then moved to control the Interior Ministry. He took caution due to Wen-yi's status with the Whampoa Clique and closeness with Chiang Kai-shek. Wen-yi suddenly found himself with no major tasks or assignments in the Ministry. This was difficult for my father, a workhorse who needed to be busy all the time. Suddenly, Wen-yi and General Hu Zong-nan were asked to attend a World Moral Re-Armament Movement meeting abroad. It was still standard practice to send officials on such missions when their presence was inconvenient. Wen-yi did not object since he loved global travel and interaction with people in different lands.

While my father was traveling abroad, Interior Minister Huang Ji-lu suddenly resigned. Then, three agents appeared at Wen-yi's home with a prepared written request for his retirement, sweetened by a substantial amount of retirement money. They asked his wife Wen-ying to sign for Wen-yi. By now a longtime member of the National Assembly, Wen-ying was not in the least intimidated. She simply told them they must deal with her husband directly. The three men dared not argue with her. Wen-yi received her letter while he was in the Philippine Islands. He decided he would not stay in a job where he was not wanted. He sent a telegram to Chiang Kai-shek resigning his position. When he returned to Taipei, Kai-shek summoned him and told him he need not resign; there were other positions in the government. Wen-yi expressed his genuine desire to teach, write, and pursue religious and moral services. In 1958, after Wen-yi had worked six years in the Interior Ministry, Chiang accepted his resignation. Later, Wen-yi quit his position as adviser to the Executive Yuan. Three years later he formally retired from his military association at the age of 56.

Chapter 25

Wen-yi: Entrepreneur, Diplomat

During the exodus from mainland China, my older brother Yuan-zhong was shocked to learn that our maternal grandmother Pan, who had cared for him all his life, refused to leave the mainland. He watched in tears as she packed her belongings to return to her home in Hunan with my oldest sister Yuan-ping. This decision cost them dearly. My Aunt May and Yuan-ping were tortured, hung by the hands as water was continually forced down their throats. As they recovered from their ordeal some sympathetic friends arranged for their escape to Taiwan.

My stepmother Wen-ying had left her six-month-old daughter, Yuan-ming, to her mother in Chengdu, Sichuan. When the local Communists became aware she was the mother-in-law of Chiang's close ally, Deng Wen-yi, she was subjected to constant harassment and mistreatment. When she could stand it no longer she committed suicide. Her granddaughter Yuan-ming was taken to a remote area of Guizhou to be raised by an aunt.

My Stepmother, Wen-ying

In February 1954 Wen-ying gave birth to a son, Yuan-yi. Several months later she was seated as a member of the National Assembly, a position she would hold until 1991 when President Li Teng-hui finally dissolved the Assembly. Li asked Wen-ying to serve on a reconstruction committee to reshape the new legislative body. For this she received a handsome stipend in addition to her generous pension.

Many of her friends envied her life of prestige as a member of the Assembly, her great beauty, and good income. But Wen-ying was not happy. She was obsessed with acquiring and holding onto her money. Of greater concern was her great insecurity and jealous rage at Wen-yi's frequent womanizing. It did not matter that this was a common practice among high-level officials. She also suffered a lingering sense of guilt over the plight of her family on the mainland. She had made no effort to bring any of her sisters to Taiwan. She remained aloof, even hostile, toward Wen-yi's side of the family.

Shortly after their arrival in Taiwan, Wen-ying bought a second house into which she could move with my father and their children, leaving the other house for the family. Now she could complain bitterly to her husband about his indiscretions without incurring the criticism of the family. Wen-yi's casual attitude toward sexual liaisons infuriated her. Whenever I visited Taipei during my high school years in Tainan, I stayed with my grandmother, Aunt Bi-xia, and the rest of the family in the first big house. Wen-yi would often stop by to visit with his mother and the rest of the family. Although the two houses were within walking distance, Wen-ying would invite the family only for special occasions.

I Enter Taiwan University

In 1956 I entered the National Taiwan University. The dormitories were primitive. Twelve girls shared six bunk beds in a modest room. There were six large desks, each shared by two students, leaving little walking space. A two-foot shelf between the bunk beds and the space under the bed were our storage places. There were sufficient shower stalls, and the weather was subtropical and comfortable. In chilly winter, the hot water supply was limited and unpredictable. The communal toilets often did not flush, or they overflowed. The meals were meager, usually consisting of vegetables and rice. We did not complain since the facility was better than most on the island. Male callers were not allowed in the girls' dormitory. They were required to be announced, very loudly, to the entire dormitory by the guard at the gate. It was the only means of communication for the guard. The procedure was an embarrassment to the girls and a deterrent to young men of faint heart.

There was no tuition at the National University, and all other fees, including board, were modest. However, I could not count on receiving money regularly from my father. He grumbled that there were too many family members and friends asking him for money. He often reminded us he had not gotten much help from home when he went to school; therefore, he expected us to be on our own. I could not win money through gambling as he did. Therefore, I began to tutor. Tutoring was a common vehicle for the university students to make money.

I think my father was proud of me. He may also have felt bad that I had not been properly cared for. One day, he took me to visit his mistress, June, and asked her to take care of me. June and her ex-husband, a well known artist, had known my father from earlier days on the mainland. She was in her thirties, attractive, gracious, but not really beautiful. She lived in a small apartment on the third floor and was extremely kind to me. I visited her often, and I enjoyed our lively conversations and fine meals. Wen-yi introduced my brother Yuan-zhong, his favorite son, to several of his girlfriends, and he would sometimes take my youngest half-brother to the movies with a girlfriend. None of us dared to mention a word of this to my stepmother Wen-ying .

I began to feel uncomfortable with my father's lack of propriety in the presence of women. On one occasion, he took me to a wedding banquet. I felt embarrassed as he blatantly ogled a beautiful woman at our table. One day as my father and I were rowing a small boat on a lake in a park, chatting aimlessly, he said proudly, "I've had some of the most beautiful women in my time."

I frowned and said, "Baba, this is not a right thing for a married man to be doing."

He laughed dismissively. "What do you children know? Those were brutal and dangerous war times. A man must seize the opportunity to enjoy life since he may die at any minute." The war was over but his behavior had not changed.

After he resigned his post as Vice Minister of Interior in 1958 Wen-yi remained busy doing serious reading, writing, and teaching courses at the defense and cultural institutes, and of course, womanizing. These were for him, sanctuaries. Through the years Wen-yi had continued to write and accumulate notes. He wrote a column about his travel in Taiwan for the *Shanghai Daily Newspaper* in Hong Kong. In 1961, he published a large 300,000 word volume entitled *Traveling in Taiwan, Vol. I.*, which he presented to me as a wedding gift in 1962.

Wen-yi had refused several offers of employment that seemed too ordinary to be of interest. Then one day, a Hong Kong syndicate, aware of Wen-yi's excellent contacts with the government, approached him with a proposal to develop a racetrack in Taipei. My father was excited. This was a business challenge, and horse racing represented recreation and adventure. The Taiwanese economy was growing. There was a large influx of people from the country to cities and towns where better paying jobs were available.[1] The population was now more actively seeking cultural and leisure activities.[2] Wen-yi seized this opportunity. With some assistance from the governor, Huang Jie, and syndicate money, the corporation bought a large tract of land in the city of Taipei. However, Wen-yi had underestimated the number of people in the layers of government that needed to be bribed. He ran into endless delays and problems obtaining the necessary permits and licenses. Soon, powerful Chiang Ching-kuo heard of this venture and expressed his displeasure concerning horse race gambling. The corporation dissolved. The syndicate recovered most of its money.

Meanwhile, Wen-yi had become smitten with a serious, spirited young woman from Hunan. She reminded him of the passionate revolutionary woman, Bai-jian, in his younger days. Assured by Wen-yi's obvious affection for her, she pressed him to divorce his wife or have her as his second wife. She had not taken into account the reaction of my stepmother Wen-ying. When Wen-ying learned about Wen-yi's mistress she relentlessly berated him, allowing him no moment of peace. Wen-yi, in despair, suggested a divorce. A furious Wen-ying immediately left Taiwan to visit her children and stepchildren in the United States to ask their opinion about her problems. Her daughters each told her it was a decision only she could make. Receiving no satisfaction from her own daughters, she came to visit me in Delaware. She screamed at me as though I were the cause of her problem. She demanded I turn over to her any letters from Wen-yi. My husband, shocked by her erratic behavior, explained that Wen-yi rarely wrote to us. Her ferocity frightened both of us. Wen-ying realized she could not live by herself or with her children in the US. She decided to go back to Taipei. We gathered for a farewell dinner with her. When someone offered a critical comment about our father to placate her during the dinner, she immediately reacted, angrily demanding, "How dare you criticize your father? None of you can be compared to him!" We were astounded by her outburst. I realized that she loved our father deeply, in her way.

Back in Taipei, Wen-ying decided to bring the intolerable situation to a resolution. She told Wen-yi that under no circumstances would she agree to a divorce after devoting the best part of her life to him. She warned that she could bring public embarrassment to him and physical harm to the woman. She reminded him that most of their money had been placed in her care. She demanded Wen-yi break up the affair or suffer the consequences. With a heavy heart Wen-yi explained the situation to his mistress. They could not see each other anymore. She looked at him, unbelieving, then fell into uncontrollable sobs as she pleaded with him not to leave her. She could not live without him. Wen-yi's eyes filled as he saw the pain on the face of the woman for whom he had developed a deep affection. She tried in various ways to reach my father in the next two or three weeks with no success. Left with no other recourse she committed suicide. Wen-yi was in complete shock, with waves of grief and guilt. He had not felt such pain since the death of his young wife Bai-jian. He was left only with the solace of arranging a proper burial for her, and an occasional visit to her grave. Her suicide gave Wen-ying a sense of closure.

Wen-yi Develops an Amusement Park

Excited by his brief entrepreneurial experience with the racetrack, Wen-yi set out to find another venture. He decided to build an amusement park like those in America. He carefully developed a plan he would present to investors, government officials, and banks. Aware of Wen-yi's deep resentment toward her, my stepmother tried to win back his favor by supporting his amusement park project that she had previously opposed. She used her position in the National Assembly to smooth the way for government approval. They found a small mountain location in Bi-tan, a prime piece of real estate located in the southern suburb of the capital city, Taipei. The site was a perfect setting for an amusement park, beautiful and accessible. Wen-yi had little difficulty obtaining initial funding, a major loan from the Taiwan Land Bank, through his friend, Senior Vice President Li of the bank. He bought the mountain site. An exultant Wen-yi took friends and relatives to the site to show them the scenic beauty of the mountain.

After the initial euphoria, the enormity of the task began to frighten him. He was not a disciplined, detail person. Worse, he was not astute in selecting competent, experienced business people to participate in the venture. The task before them was daunting... clearing the mountain site, developing the architectural design, construction, equipment selection, purchasing, installation, operations, maintenance, staff training and supervision, etc. This required careful management skills, and a great deal of capital.

My father began a search for investors, including friends, relatives, and old colleagues from whom he could borrow funds. Many were flattered to be asked and offered modest amounts of money from their meager assets. However, his working capital could not keep up with the escalating expenditures of the construction. His checks bounced due to insufficient funds.

The Bi-tan Amusement Park was finally forced to open prematurely. The anticipated large crowds did not materialize. Wen-ying stopped paying wages to the operators. After a year Wen-yi was forced to shut down the park. The nightmare now began. The small debtors were desperate to get their money back. They pounded on his front door screaming for their money. Wen-yi was forced to go into hiding. When an influential, desperate debtor applied heavy pressure on Wen-yi for the immediate return of his money, Wen-ying was forced to sell a house to pay him. The amusement park debacle wounded Wen-yi deeply. He now had to restart his life from scratch. He and Wen-ying traveled to the United States to visit their children. During his stay at my home, I took my father to my place of employment, and gave him a tour of our facilities and operation.

On April 5, 1975, Chiang Kai-shek passed away at the age of 85. Millions of people attended the viewing of this major Chinese leader. Wen-yi was devastated. He kept remembering the many good experiences they had shared together, sliding quickly past the less pleasant moments. The following year Wen-yi published a book, *The Spirit of Whampoa Military Academy,* in memory of Chiang. His spirits rose when he was presented with an honorary doctorate in Chinese literature from Hong Kong World University in 1976.

Wen-yi's luck began to turn. The real estate market in Taipei suddenly escalated. The value of his mountain in Bi-tan increased steadily. An excited Wen-ying went repeatedly to check on the property. She could hardly sleep at night in her excitement. The value of the site had been estimated at over one million dollars. Impatient for needed revenue, Wen-yi and his wife allowed the property to be auctioned off. They received $200,000, a fraction of the value. However, this revenue paid up all the remaining debt and left Wen-yi with a modest profit. Wen-yi's mother, who had suffered through her son's ordeal, died at age 88 shortly after receiving the good news of Wen-yi's financial recovery in 1977. Wen-yi was able to give an extravagant funeral and burial site for his beloved mother.

After some soul searching, Wen-yi turned to philosophy and religion. His parents were both dedicated Buddhists. In the late 1970s he focused on Taoism, the only authentic Chinese religion and second most popular religion next to Buddhism in Taiwan. He wrote a new version of the *New Life Movement Guidelines* he had drafted in 1934, this time for the Moral Maintenance Movement initiated by the Mediums' Association in central Taiwan. My father participated in Tao rituals and even officiated at some of them. In 1988 Wen-yi joined the Taiwan Tao committee, who were invited to attend President Reagan's inauguration.

On November 22, 1985, an elaborate reception was held to celebrate my father's 80th birthday. A stunning array of guests came to wish him well. These included Chiang Ching-kuo, president of Taiwan, as well as cabinet leaders, ministers, Whampoa friends, and his students over the years. Also present was the aging General Xu Pe-gan and his wife. Xu was commanding general of the airfield in the Nanchang air base when it was destroyed by fire. Xu now told Wen-ying how her husband had saved his life at the risk of his own reputation.

To the great joy of the island population, martial law in Taiwan was finally rescinded in 1987, lifting the ban on other political parties, and censorship of publications, media, and speech. It was an exciting time. People in Taiwan were now allowed, for the first time in forty years, to visit relatives on mainland China.

President Deng Xiao-ping Invites Wen-yi to Beijing
The year was 1990. Deng Xiao-ping was into his 13th year as paramount leader of the Peoples' Republic of China. He had received international and national acclaim for reforming China to a market economy, from which China has emerged as one of the world's leading economies. He had also developed a "one country, two systems" approach in dealing with the

unification of Hong Kong, Macao, and Taiwan. The latter was the most difficult and controversial undertaking.

One day, my father was amazed to receive an invitation from Deng Xiao-ping to come to Beijing for personal discussions on the future relationship of China and Taiwan. After consulting with government officials, my 85-year-old father accepted the invitation with delight. Wen-ying decided not to join him, to avoid any potential conflict with her position as National Assembly member. When Wen-yi arrived in Beijing, he looked at the land he had left 40 years ago, and was moved to tears. His sentimentality was intensified when he found his surviving Whampoa classmates and friends waiting on the tarmac to greet him. After an emotional welcome, Wen-yi's old friends accompanied him on a sightseeing tour of the many famous places that had been on his mind all these years. Then it was time to meet the leader.

Deng Xiao-ping greeted my father with much warmth in the presence of a number of senior officials. The two men were the same age. Xiao-ping was quite familiar with Wen-yi's career and his role as Chiang's private secretary, military attaché in Russia, and his political leadership position in several organizations in the Nationalist Party. At first they reminisced about their younger days as fellow students at Sun Yat-sen University in Moscow. Xiao-ping pointed out how similar some aspects of their careers had been. He said both had served in military field units as high ranking military officers (Lieutenant Generals). He added that neither of them was, at heart or in fact, a professional soldier. They were politicians. Wen-yi was well aware that Xiao-ping's career in both fields had been considerably more illustrious than his own. Xiao-ping had also been badly treated by Mao Ze-dong and his gang during the reconstruction of the People's Republic. Wen-yi suspected these friendly allusions to their common paths might be a prelude to discussions of a subject of common purpose. This was confirmed when the talk turned to mainland China and Taiwan.

Xiao-ping told Wen-yi the two sides should strive to make more contacts in order to better understand each other. That was why he looked forward to talks with his old classmate. His position appeared to be that any and all suggestions were on the table for discussion, except that of complete autonomy for Taiwan. Xiao-ping said to Wen-yi, "We are all people from the same family. There should be no war between us. War is unfavorable to both sides." His approach to unification with Hong Kong, Macao, and Taiwan was one of "one country, two systems." He expressed his strong belief there should be only one united China; thus, he could not agree with complete autonomy for Taiwan. Other than that, he said Taiwan could maintain its special identity, practice its own system, and maintain its own forces. He insisted that talks between the two parties should be conducted on an equal basis. However, behind the reasonable, friendly demeanor lay the underlying steel-lined caveat "anything but complete autonomy." Wen-yi later told his wife Wen-ying, "What he had to say to me took twice as long as what I had to say to him."

The visit was filmed and shown on television that evening. As a gesture of friendship, Deng Xiao-ping personally ordered Wen-yi's two houses in Nanjing and Liling to be returned to him. When Wen-yi returned to Taiwan he formed the "China Global Whampoa Unification Association in Taiwan" to pursue closer ties with mainland China.

Deng Xiao-ping retired the following year. The new leader, Jiang Ze-min, again invited Wen-yi to Beijing to continue the newborn relationship. Wen-yi later headed a contingent of over a hundred people from Taiwan to China, to demonstrate friendship and connection to their one-time enemy.

In 1992, my brother Yuan-zhong took a dozen colleagues of the National Normal University to visit China. When they reached Xinjiang, no hotel rooms were available for them. A disappointed Yuan-zhong told the hotel manager that his father Deng Wen-yi had never run into such a complication when he visited. Suddenly, comfortable quarters were miraculously made available.

Mainland China and Taiwan were still at odds after four decades, but Wen-yi and his oldest son were able to witness the closer trade and social ties that Xiao-ping told my father he hoped to see.

Epilogue

When I arrived in America after college, I found home in this vast, promising land. I broke away from the shadow of my sad childhood and severed any emotional ties with relatives back home. I received a doctorate degree in chemistry and enjoyed a fruitful career as a research scientist. I am blessed with a lovely family, with two accomplished daughters and a husband who continues teaching in college well into his seventies. I now enjoy a fulfilling and rewarding retirement. I love gardening, reading, continually learning the language and art of writing, and deriving pleasure from discussion with dear friends in our book club.

My father's retirement was more difficult. Like many of his colleagues and his mentor Chiang Kai-shek, he experienced the loss of mainland China as a constant source of regret and second-guessing. For Wen-yi the tide of new technology and democracy required a difficult accommodation. However, his steadfast loyalty to Chiang Kai-shek and the Nationalist cause never faltered.

I came to realize that my father loved his children in his own way. Unsurprisingly, given Chinese culture, his genuine love centered on his first son, Yuan-zhong. My stepmother Wen-ying loved her husband deeply, though she often treated him badly because of insecurities related to his womanizing.

My father spent many of his remaining years pursuing his lifelong passion to travel. His journeys took him to five continents and sixty countries. He toured the United States and visited with his children. While he was in my home in Wilmington, Delaware, I often caught him casting furtive glances in my direction. It was as though he were seeing me for the first time as a truly worthy daughter. The little girl he had virtually ignored for so many years had transformed into an attractive and successful young woman with a lovely house and a garden filled with exotic plants.

During a visit to the technology center where I worked, I introduced him to my co-author Rudi Carboni. Their animated exchange placed a heavy burden on my role as translator.

One day, I accompanied my father to see the spectacular "Longwood Gardens" in nearby Pennsylvania. We strolled through sunlit paths surrounded by exotic plants and luxuriant flowers and lotus ponds. We paused to watch the multicolored Koi as they swam toward us, then away, in the beautiful artificial lake. Still staring at the fish, he asked, "Do you hate me?" The question startled me because I was having almost the same thoughts as those that prompted the question. My first impulse was to deny. But I could not; I remained silent. I felt no love or closeness to him. I did not even like him. Perhaps I did not know how to receive or give love to a parent. The awkward silence continued as we resumed our walk.

"You were not a father who cared for or loved me," I finally said.

Surprised, he answered, "I gave you life, what more can you possibly ask from me?"

Wen-yi died on July 13, 1998 at the age of 93. Over 200 guests attended the memorial service. His coffin was covered with the flag of the Nationalist government. The first native Taiwanese President, Lee Teng-hui, sent a short poem to honor him, and the Taiwan newspapers gave detailed accounts of his achievements.

Notes and Selected Bibliography

Notes

Chapter 1. The Beginning - From Countryside to Moscow

1. Guomindang (GMD) was the founding and ruling party of the young Republic of China. The name translates to "Nationalist Party." The designation of Kuomintang (KMT) is also used. At the 1924 GMD Party Congress in Guangzhou, influential Russian adviser Borodin helped to reorganize the party as a coalition that included Communists. In order to distinguish between the two major factions in the party we will use the GMD translation "Nationalist" to refer to the conservative pro-Chiang faction, and "Communists" for the anti-Chiang Communist supporters.

2. Warlords were powerful provincial leaders or governors emerging after the downfall of the Qing Dynasty. Warlords mostly built their own armies, and ran their territories like fiefdoms. There were a series of on-off allegiances between the warlords and Chiang's Nationalists. Chiang's Northern Expedition was intended to subdue the warlords. He succeeded, partially. On occasion, they became allies to fight a common enemy.

3. Comintern, or Communist International, was an international Communist organization founded in 1919 by the Soviet Union., Under Soviet control, Comintern served to "export revolution abroad," overthrow legitimate regimes, and use foreign Communist parties for espionage and subversion to further Communist goals.

4. International Press Correspondence, March 18, 1926. Chiang gave Soviet representatives good reason to be favorably disposed to his candidacy, by uttering the following words in his speech at the 1925 Guomindang Party Congress: "Our alliance with the Soviet Union, with the world revolution, is actually an alliance with all the revolutionary parties which are fighting in common against the world imperialists to carry

through the world revolution." Isaacs, *Tragedy of the Chinese Revolution,* Chapter 4.

5. Deng Wen-yi, *Mao Xian Fan Nan Ji, I (The Journal of Challenging Risks and Dangers, I)*, Taiwan, Student Book Corporation, March 1973, 44-54.

6. Deng Wen-yi, *The Spirit of Whampoa*, Taipei: Li Ming Cultural Affair Company, October 1967, 56, 57, 100-103, 160.

Chapter 2. A General at 22!

1. Much of the information of the Guangzhou (Canton) Purge in which my father, Wen-yi, participated is based on his memoirs and private communications with family members.

2. Chang, H.H., *Chiang-Kai-shek - Asia's Man of Destiny*, 168.

3. China Press, April 14, 1927. "An appeal by the Communist Party for a general strike as a protest against the anti-Communist coup was obeyed at noon on April 13 by no less than 111,800 workers." Shanghai Municipal Police Annual Report for 1927.

4. *People's Tribune,* May 15, 1927.43. Ibid- X. The Coup of April 12, 1927. A delegation of Soviet trade unionists en route to Hankow arrived at Guangzhou on April 14. They were treated the next day to the spectacle of raids on the trade unions, mass arrests, and executions in the streets carried out at the orders of General Li Chi-sen. Li, only a few months previously, had been listed in the Stalin-Bukharin directory of "revolutionary Generals."

5. *People's Tribune,* May 6, 1927.

Chapter 3. Wen-yi and the Bandits

1. Seagrave, *The Soong Dynasty*, 239.

2. Ah Xiang, "*China's Wars,*" Second Northern Expedition, Part 2.

3. Ibid, *Battle of Longtan*, excerpts from "Campaign: 1927-1937."

4. Zhou En-lai, *"The Comintern and the CCP,"* Vol 2.

5. Eastman, *The Abortive Revolution*, 1974.

Chapter 4. Chiang vs. the Warlords and Wen-yi

1. In Chiang's armies, the political officer was almost the equal of the senior military officer.

2. Van de Ven, *"War and Nationalism in China,"* 238.

Chapter 5. Chiang and Wen-yi In Exile

1. Chang, Myers, *The Memoir of Ch'en Li-fu.* Li-fu said to Chiang, "If anyone lost his temper with me I would resign at once." Li-fu went on to say that Chiang took him seriously on the remark, 24.

2. Xiao Zuolin, *Fuxingshe shulue*, 37.

3. Chang, Myers, *The Memoirs of Ch'en Li-fu*, 102-106. Hu Han-min was taken into custody on March 1, 1931 because of his opposition to Chiang's proposed "provisional constitution." He was released from house arrest on October 13, 1931. Most members of the National Government Council secretly disapproved of this punishment of a highly respected member.

4. Chang, H.H., *"Chiang Kai-shek - Asia's man of Destiny,"* 236.

5. Fenby, *"Generalissimo,"* 22.

6. Ibid., 24.

Chapter 6. A Powerful Force Emerges

1. The genesis, actions, and demise of this major, secret political organization has received the attention of a number of historians. I have been fortunate to have my father Wen-yi's notes and his memoir, which offer an eyewitness account of his own active participation in the entire event. As the personal

secretary to Chiang Kai-shek, Wen-yi was required to take notes of the three-day founding meeting and to speak at these meetings. In addition, my brother, Deng Yuan-zhong, has been a valuable source. In writing his authoritative book *Sanminzhuyi Lixingshe Shi,* (*The History of the Three People's Principles' Lixingshe, or The History of the Society of Vigorous Practice of the Three Principles of the People*), my brother had the rare opportunity to discuss the events associated with the founding of Lixingshe with its creator, Teng Jie. He conferred with other key players in its formation and subsequent development, including our father Wen-yi, Gan Guo-xun, and Xiao Zan-yu.

2. Wakeman, *Spymaster Dai Li and the Chinese Secret Service*, 57.

3. Deng Yuan-zhong, *Sanminzhuyi*, 117.

4. Wakeman, *Spymaster*, 62.

5. Eastman, *Fascism and Modern China*, 841.

6. Chang, Maria Hsia, *The Chinese Blue Shirt Society: Fascism and Nationalism*, No. 30, 1985, 35, 130.

7. Deng Yuan-zhong, *Sanminzhuyi*.

8. The late Lloyd E. Eastman described Yuan-zhong's research on the history of the Lixingshe as "one of the most objective studies of the Nationalist period to have been published in Taiwan." See my brother's book and his interview with my brother in Xu Youwei and Billingsly, *"Behind the Scenes at the Xian Incident: The Case of the Lixingshe."*

Chapter 7. Wen-yi's Intelligence and Strike Force

1. Seagrave, *The Soong Dynasty*, 331. Chiang decided to derive his return from the opium trade by letting Du Yueh-sheng, criminal head of the powerful Green Gang syndicate, control the opium trade undisturbed.

2. MacKinnon, *War, Refugees, and the Making of Modern China*, Ch.1, 14-15.

3. Wakeman, *Spymaster,* 468n2, says that Chiang established a detective bureau in the Wuhan Mobile Garrison in 1930 headed by Yang Qing-shan, who was also chief of the Triad gangster organization in Wuhan.

4. Wakeman, *Policing Shanghai*, 126.

5. Deng Yuan-zhong, *Sanminzhuyi*, Chapter 8, 313.

Chapter 8. Disgrace, Vindication

1. De Bary, *Source of East Asian Tradition*, 694.

2. Wakeman, "*Spymaster,*" 44.

3. Ibid.

4. Deng Wen-yi, *Conjun Baoguo Ji (My Military Career: a Tribute to My Country)*.

5. Xiao Zuo-lin, *Fuxingshe shulue*, 66.

Chapter 9. Wen-yi, Military Attaché in Russia

1. Deng Wen-yi, *My Journey of Ten Thousand Miles*, 178-179.

2. Ibid., 176-7.

3. Johnson, David, *Johnson's Russia List Newsletter*, JRL 7036-# 9, January 28, 2003.

4. Kuromiya, Hiroaki, *Stalin's Great Terror and Espionage*, Indiana University Research Paper: September, 2009 attributing the quote to Ian Kershaw, *Hitler: 1936-1945: Nemesis* (New York, NY: 2000), 44.

5. Chang, Myers, *The Memoir of Ch'En Li-fu*, 123.

6. Ibid., 124.

7. Ibid.

Chapter 10. A Kidnapped Generalissimo, a Disgraced Rescuer

1. Chiang Kai-shek, *Soviet Russia in China*-Rev., Abr., The Noonday Press, New York, 1965, 50-1, 52-3. Kai-shek's version

of events is self-serving. However, the basic facts are reasonably consistent with other reports.

2. Chang Jung and Halliday, Jon, *Mao, the Unknown Story*, 2005, 175.

3. Fenby, *Generalissimo*, 5.

4. Epoch Time Staff, *Commentaries on the Communist party*, December 13, 2004.

5. Chiang Kai-shek: *A Fortnight in Xian*, 152.

6. Spence, *The Search for Modern China*, 423 [Stalin's letter].

7. Deng Wen-yi, *Conjun Baoguo Ji*, 89.

8. Deng Yuan-zhong, *Sanminzhuyi Lixingshe Shi*, 327-28, paraphrasing Teng Jie's quote: Policies should be determined by the executive committee and not by the Secretary General alone. The Lixingshe should improve its relationship with Central Headquarters of the Nationalists.

9. Chiang Kai-shek, *A Fortnight in Xian*, II, 71.

10. Chiang Kai-shek. *Soviet Russia in China*, 52.

10a. Epoch Time Staff, *Nine Commentaries on the Chinese Communist Party*, 45.

10b. Seagrave, *The Soong Dynasty*, 441-42. Chiang Kai-shek had fled to Taiwan in a gunboat in May, 1949. Then, in August, Chiang returned briefly to the mainland. One of his stops was in Chongqing which was still in the hands of the Nationalists. Then, just before returning to Taiwan, Chiang stopped at police headquarters to sign a death warrant for General Yang who had conspired with the Young Marshal to kidnap Chiang. Gen. Yang had spent the last eleven years in Dai Li's concentration camp, with his family and secretary, outside of Chongqing. They were all taken out and shot to death.

11. Deng Wen-yi, *Conjun Baoguo Ji*.

12. Wakeman, *Spymaster*, 129.

13. Li, Laura Tyson, *Madame Chiang Kai-shek*, 123, 130.

14. Chiang Kai-shek, *A Fortnight in Xian*, I, 154.

15. Xu Youwei and Billingsley, *Behind the Scenes at the Xian Incident: The Case of the Lixingshe*.

16. Booth, *Fabulous Destinations*, 71.

17. Seagrave, 357. Chiang said, "Remembering that Jesus Christ enjoined us to forgive those who sin against us until 70 times 7 times, and upon their repentance that they should always be allowed to start life anew."

18. Hoyt, *The Rise of the Chinese Republic, From the Last Emperor to Deng Xiaoping,* 159.

Chapter 11. Amid the Horror a Bundle of Joy

1. Boyle, *China and Japan at War,* 67. The Chinese army felt confident of victory, since it had been trained by the Germans, and much had been done to modernize it. The Japanese army was confident that after the first strike the Chinese would crumble. The Japanese had underestimated the Chinese army, and the latter had overestimated itself.

2. Fenby, *Generalissimo,* 306.

3. "The History Place - Genocide in the 28th century," The Rape of Nanjing:1937-1938. [http://www.historyplace.com/worldhistory/genocide/index.html]. More than 20,000 females (with some estimates as high as 80,000) were gang-raped by Japanese soldiers, then stabbed to death with bayonets or shot so they could never bear witness.

4. Wen Hsin-yeh, *Wartime Shanghai,* 3. Between 1929 and mid-December 1937, nearly 10,000 of the 25,000 officers graduated from the Central Military Academies had been killed in the fighting.

5. Di Wang, *Street Culture in Chengdu,* 286.

6. Wang Qing-yuan, 29-30, 1944.

Chapter 14. WWII, Wen-yi in the 3rd War Zone

1. Sherry, *WW II Campaigns: China Defensive,* 3.

2. Eastman, Ch'en, Pepper, Van Slyke, *The Nationalist Era in China,* 89-107.

3. MacKinnon, *China at War,* 337.

4. Deng Wen-yi, *Mao Xian Fan Nan Ji* (*The Journal of Challenging Risks and Dangers, A Memoir of Adventures and Risks-II*), Chapter 105, P. 137.

5. MacKinnon, *China At War*, 293.

6. Harris, *Factories of Death: Japanese Biological Warfare*, 102.

7. Mangold, Goldberg, *Plague Wars*, 22.

8. The two branches of training were created for the new Youth Army. The first was referred to as the Central Level Cadre Academy and the other, more advanced level, as Political Work Cadres Training Class.

9. Marks, *Counter revolution in China*, 55.

Chapter 17. One War Ends, Another Begins

1. Boyer, Paul S. et.al., *The Enduring Vision: A History of the American People*, Chapter 25, P. 610.

2. Buhtie, Russell, D., *Far Eastern Agreement*, 343.

3. Paterson, *Meeting the Communist Threat*, 71.

4. For an outstanding work relating how various factors (such as cultural perceptions and values translated into policies, on the part of the Nationalists, CCP, and US) affected the outcome of US mediation attempts, see Qing Simei, *From Allies to Enemies*, 66, 70.

5. Beck, Sanderson, *China at War*, Chapter: "Jiang, CCP, US and USSR, 1945-1946."

6. F.F.Liu, *A Military History of Modern China, 1924-1949*, Princeton University Press, 1956.

7. Liu, section C-125.

8. Qing Simei, *From Allies to Enemies*, 66, 70.

9. Liu, section C-235.

10. Booth, *Fabulous Destinations*, 74-76.

11. Liu, section C-235.

12. Spence, *The Search for Modern China*, 502.

13. Westad, *Decisive Encounters*, 150.

14. Paterson, 71.

Chapter 19. The Civil War - Part 1

1. Taylor, Jay, *The Generalissimo: Chiang Kai-shek and the Struggle for Modern China, Vol. 39*, P. 373.
2. Westad, *Decisive Encounters*, 170-171.
3. Rowan, Roy, *Chasing the Dragon: A Veteran Journalist's Firsthand Account*, 216.
4. Taylor, *The Generalissimo*, 388.
5. Chang Jung, *Wild Swans: Three Daughters of China*, 112.
6. Mao Ze-dong, *"On Protracted War,"* 1938; *Selected Writings of Mao Zedong*,
   Beijing Foreign Language Press 1967, 226-228.

Chapter 20. The Civil War - Part 2, Bad News, Like Falling Snowflakes

1. Van Slyke, *The China White Paper,* US Department of State, August, 1949: letter153b from Stuart to Secretary Marshall, Nanjing, May 19, 1948, 867.
2. Bjorge, *Moving the Enemy: Operational Art in the Chinese PLA's Huai Hai Campaign*, 103.
3. Lanning, *The Battle 100,* 28.
4. Mao Ze-dong, *Selected Works of Mao Tse-tung*, Dec. 12, 1948.
   http://www.marxists.org/reference/archive/mao/selected-works/index.htm.
5. Bjorge, *Moving the Enemy*, 245.
6. Rowan, Roy, *Chasing the Dragon: A Veteran Journalist's First-hand Account*, 239.
7. Eastman, *Seeds of Destruction*, 203. In January 1948, Chiang observed bitterly, "To tell the truth, never, in China or abroad, has there been a revolutionary party as decrepit and degenerate as we in the Guomindang are today: nor, one as lacking in spirit, lacking in discipline, and even more, lacking standards of right and wrong as we are today. This kind of party should long ago have been destroyed and swept away."

Chapter 21. The North and Beiping in Jeopardy

1. Bevin, Alexander, *The Strange Connection: U.S. Intervention in China*, 80-82.
2. Dai Qing, "1948: How Peaceful Was the Liberation of Beiping?" The Sixty-eighth
Morrison Lecture, 5 September 2007, The Australian National University.
3. Li Yan-ju, World Journal LLC (worldjournal.com), October 11, 2009.
4. Time Magazine, January 31, 1949.
5. Pepper, *Civil War in China: The Political Struggle*, 423.
6. Ebeling, "The Great Chinese Inflation," *Foundation of Economic
Education*, Vol.54, Issue 12, December, 2004.
7. Allen, *The Encyclopedia of Money*, 214.
8. Westad, *Decisive Encounters*, 215.

Chapter 22. Defeat and Exodus

1. Deng Wen-yi, *Development of Peace and War*, Central News Agency, Shanghai, February 9, 1949.
2. Mao Ze-dong, *Selected Works of Mao Tse-tung: Volume IV*, 343-344.
3. Ibid., 344.
4. Van Slyke, *The China White Paper*, US Dept. of State, 304. From there on, the Eastern cities fell to the Communist forces like bowling pins, with the capture of Nanjing on April 24, 1949; Hankow on May 16-17; Shanghai on May 25; Tsingtao on June 2.
5. Fenby, *Generalissimo*, 495.

Chapter 24. Taiwan and Wen-yi in Transition

1. Roy, *Taiwan: A Political History*, 91.

2. Chiang Jung-liang, *Economic Transition and Changing Relation Between Income Inequality and Mortality in Taiwan,*" British Medical Journal, July, 1999.

3. Tai Hung-chao, *Land Reform and Politics: a Comparative Analysis,* Berkeley, CA: University of California Press, January, 2004, 87.

Chapter 25.Wen-yi: Entrepreneur, Diplomat

1. Hsiau A-chin, *Contemporary Taiwanese Cultural Nationalism*, 73, note 19.

While the Taiwanese population increased by 35 percent during the 1960s, the large cities experienced a growth of 86 percent and the towns 73 percent.

2. Liu, Jerry, *Leisure Governance in Transition: The Case of Taiwan*, 11.

Selected Bibliography
(Books and other references consulted)

Alexander, Robert, J. *International Trotskyism: Trotskyism in China, 1929-1985*. Durham, NC: Duke University Press, 1991.

Allen, Larry. *The Encyclopedia of Money*. Westport: ABC CLIO Greenwood Publishing Group, 2009.

Barenblatt, Daniel. *A Plague Upon Humanity*. New York, NY: Harper Collins Publ. January, 2000.

Benton, Gregor. *New Fourth Army*. Berkeley, CA: Univ. of California Press, 1999.

Berkov, Robert. *Strong Man of China: The Story of Chiang Kai-shek*. Boston, MA: Houghton Mifflin, 1938.

Bertram, James M. *First Act in China:The Story of the Sian Mutiny*. New York, NY: Viking Press, 1938.

Boorman, Howard L. et al. *Biographical Dictionary of Republican China*. New York, NY: Columbia University Press, 1979.

Booth, John Nicholls. *Fabulous Destinations*. New York, NY: Macmillan, 2007.

Boyle, John Hunter. *China and Japan at War: 1937-1945; The Politics of Collaboration*. Stanford, CA: Stanford University Press, 1972.

Bradley, James. *Flyboys: A True Story of Courage*. New York, NY: Back Bay Books, 2004.

Braun, Otto. *A Comintern Agent in China, 1932-1939.* Stanford, CA: Stanford University Press, 1982.

Bjorge, Gary. *Moving the Enemy: Operational Art in the Chinese PLA's Huai Hai Campaign,* Leavenworth, KS: Army Command Combat Studies Institute, Paper 24, 2004.

Byrne, Paul J. *The Chinese Revolution: The Rise of Communism.* Mankato, MN: Capstone Press. Inc., January, 2007.

Chang, Maria Hsia. *The Chinese Blue Shirt Society.* Boulder, CO: Westview Press, 1994.

Chang, H.H. *Chiang Kai-shek-Asia's Man of Destiny.* Garden City: Doubleday, Doran and Co., Inc., 1944.

Chang, Iris. *The Rape of Nanking: The Forgotten Holocaust of World War II.* New York, NY: Penguin Press, 1999.

Chang Jung. *Wild Swans: Three Daughters of China.* New York, NY: Touchstone Books, 2003.

Chang, Sidney, and Ramon H. Myers, *The Storm Clouds Clear over China: The Memoir of Ch'En Li-fu, 1900-1993.* Stanford, CA: Hoover Press, 1994.

Cheng Pei-kai, Michael Lestz, and Jonathan Spence. *The Search for Modern China.* New York, NY: W.W. Norton & Co., 1999.

Chiang Kai-shek. *Soviet Russia in China.* New York, NY: Farrar, Straus, and Giroux, 1957.

Chiang Kai-shek, *Resistance and Reconstruction, 1937-1943*. New York, NY: Harper and Bros, 1943.

Chiang Kai-shek and Madame Chiang Kai-shek. *General Chiang Kai-shek*. New York, NY: The Book League of America, Inc., 1937.

Corcuff, Stephane. *Memories of the Future: National Identity Issues and the Search for a New Taiwan*. Armonk, NY: M.E. Sharpe, Inc., 2002.

Dai Qing. "1948: How Peaceful was the Liberation of Beiping?" The Sixty-eighth
Morrison Lecture, Camberra: The Australian National University, 5 September, 2007.

De Bary, William, T. *Source of East Asian Tradition*. New York, NY: Columbia University Press, 2008.

Deng Wen-yi. *Congjun Baoguo Ji (My Military Career: a Tribute to My Country)*. Taipei: Zhongzheng shuju, Cheng Chung Book Company, 1979.

Deng Wen-yi. *The Spirit of Whampoa*. Taipei: Li Ming Cultural Affair Company, October, 1967.

Deng Wen-yi. *Lessons from Struggle Against Communists*. Taipei: Shi Jan Publishing Company, 1984.

Deng Wen-yi. *My Journey of Ten Thousand Miles*. Taipei: Li-ming Cultural Affair Company, 1951.

Deng Wen-yi. *Mao Xian Fan Nan Ji (The Journal of Challenging Risks and Dangers, A Memoir of Adventures and Risks-I, II)*. Taipei: Student Book Corporation, March, 1973.

Deng Wen-yi. *Memoir of My Travels*. Taipei: Shanghai Printing Company, October, 1986.

Deng Yuan-zhong. *A History of the Three People's Principle's Lixingshe*. Nelson T. Johnson Papers, Library of Congress, Memorandum on "Conversation with G. W. Shepard," Nanking: May 17, 1937.

Deng Yuan-zhong, *Sanminzhuyi Lixingshe Shi (A History of the Three People's Principle's Earnest Action Society)*. Taipei: Shixian chubanshe, 1984.

Deng Yuan-zhong. "The First Secret Discussion between Nationalists and Communists." Taipei: Taiwan Normal University History Periodicals,Volume 23, June, 1995.

DeRouen, Karl, Jr., and Uk Heo, Editors. *Civil War of the Worlds: Major Conflicts since World War II-Vol.2*. Santa Barabara, CA: ABC-CLIO, 2007.

Dimitrov, Georgi. *Kommunistichasti International i Kitiaskaya Revolyutsiya Documenti Material*. Moscow: 1986. Translation by Tahir Aschar, and collected by Singh Vijay. *Georgi Dimitrov and the United front in China, June 1995*.

Dong, Stella. *Shanghai: The Rise and Fall of a Decadent City, 1842-1949*. New York, NY: HarperCollins, 2001.

Durdin, Pegg. "The 228 Massacre." *The Nation*, May 4, 1927.

Eastman, Lloyd E. *The Abortive Revolution. China under Nationalist Rule, 1927-1937*. Cambridge, MA: Harvard University Press, 1974.

Eastman, Lloyd E., Jerome Ch'en, Suzanne Pepper, and Lyman P. Van Slyke. *The Nationalist Era in China, 1927-1949.* Cambridge, Mass.: Harvard University Press, 1991.

Eastman, Lloyd E. *Seeds of Destruction: National China in War and Revolution, 1937 1945.* Stanford, CA: Univ. of Stanford Press, 1984.

Ebeling, Richard M. "The Great Chinese Inflation." *Foundation of Economic Education,* Vol.54, Issue 12, December, 2004.

Epoch Time Staff. *Nine Commentaries on the Communist Party.* Broad Book Publ., 2005.

Esherick, Joseph E. (Ed.). *Remaking the Chinese City: Modernity and National Identity.* Honolulu, HW: University of Hawaii Press, Nov, 2001.

Fairbank, John, and Merle W. Goldman. *China - A New History.* Cambridge, Mass.: Harvard Univ. Press, 2006.

Fenby, Jonathan. *Generalissimo.* London: The Free Press (Simon and Schuster Ltd), 2003.

Fenby, Jonathan. *Chiang Kai-shek.* New York, NY : Carroll & Graf Publishers, 2003.

Ferretti, Valdo. "Chinese Views of the Soviet Union." Tokyo: CHIR Tokyo Conference, 2004.

Garver, John W. "The Soviet Union and the Xian Incident." Camberra: The Australian Journal of Chinese Affairs, No. 26, July, 1991.

Garver, John W. *Chinese-Soviet Relations, 1937-1945.* Oxford: Oxford University Press, January, 1988.

Goldman, Merle and Andrew Gordon. *Historical perspectives on Contemporary East Asia.* Cambridge, MA: Harvard University Press, 2000.

Grasso, June M., Jay Corrin, and Michael Kort, *Modernization and Revolution in China: From the Opium Wars to World Power.* Armonk, NY: M.E. Sharpe, 2004.

Harris, Sheldon H. *Factories of Death: Japanese Biological Warfare, 1932-1945.* London: Routledge (Taylor and Francis Group,) 2002.

Henriot, Christian, and Yeh Wen-hsin, *In the Shadow of the Rising Sun.* Cambridge: Cambridge University Press, 2004.

Hofheinz, Roy. *The Broken Wave: The Chinese Communist Movement, 1922-1928.* Cambridge, MA: Harvard University Press, 1977.

Howard, Joshua H. *Workers at War: Labor in China's Arsenals, 1937-1953.* Stanford, CA: Stanford University Press, 2004.

Howe, Christopher. *The Origins of Japanese Trade Supremacy.* Chicago: Univ. of Chicago Press, 1995.

Hoyt, Edwin P. *The Rise of the Chinese Republic, From the Last Emperor to Deng Xiaoping.* New York, NY: McGraw-Hill Publishing Company, 1989.

Hsiung Shih-Hui, *An Insider's Account of Modern Chinese History, Memoirs of Governor and General Hsiung Shih-Hui.* Mirror Books, 2008.

Isaacs, Harold R. *The Tragedy of the Chinese Revolution.* Stanford, CA: Stanford University Press, 1961.

Jespersen, T. Christopher. *American Images of China, 1031-1941.* Stanford, CA: Stanford University Press, March, 1999.

Jordan, Donald A. *China's Trial by Fire: The Shanghai War of 1932.* Ann Arbor: University of Michigan Press, 2001.

Kent, Allen, Harold Lancour, and Jay E. Daily. *Encyclopedia of Library and Information Science.* W. Palm Beach, FL: CRC Press, 1980.

Kerr, George H. *Formosa Betrayed.* Boston: Houghton and Mifflin, 1965.

Kristof, Nicholas D. "Decision in Taiwan: The Nationalists; Party Undone by Liberty It Nurtured." New York Times (Intl.), March 18, 2000.

Langer, William L. (Ed.). *Encyclopedia of World History: Ancient, Medieval, and Modern.* London: 1972.

Lanning, Michael. *The Battle 100: The Story Behind History's Most Influential Battles.* Naperville, IL: Sourcebooks, Inc., 2005.

Leng Shao-chuan. *Chiang Ching-kuo's Leadership in the Development of the Republic of China.* Lanham, MD: University Press of America, April, 1993.

Liao Cheng-hung, and Martin M. C. Yang. *Socio-economic Change in Rural Taiwan, 1950-1980*. Southeast Asian Studies, Vol. 18, No.4, March, 1981.

Li Fu-jen. *Lessons and Perspectives of the Sino-Japanese War*, Fourth International, February 1941-51. Transcribed by Ted Crawford.

Li, Laura Tyson. *Madame Chiang Kai-shek*. New York, NY: Open City Books, 2006.

Li, Lincoln. *Student Nationalism in China, 1924-1949*. Albany, N.Y.: SUNY Press, 1994.

Li, Peter (Ed.). *Japanese War Crimes*. Piscataway, NJ: Transaction Publishers, March, 2006.

Lin Hsiao-ting. "Nationalists, Muslim Warlords, and the Great Northwestern Development in Pre-Communist China." Forum Quarterly, Volume 5, No. 1, 2007.

Litten, Frederick S. "Chiang Kai-shek and the Fujian Revolution." Asien, No. 58, Jan., 1996.

Lubell, Pamela. *The Chinese Communist Party and the Cultural Revolution*. Houndmills Hampshire, UK: Palgrave Macmillan, 2001.

Mackerras, Colin. *China in Transformation: 1900-1949*. Harlow, UK: Pearson Education, Ltd.

MacKinnon, Stephen R., Diana Lary, and Ezra F. Vogel. *China At War*. Stanford, CA: Stanford University Press, Oct., 2007.

MacKinnon, Stephen R. and Robert Capa. *Wuhan, 1938: War, Refugees, and the Making of Modern China*. Berkeley, CA: University of California Press, May, 2008.

Mangold, Tom, and Jeff Goldberg. *Plague Wars: The Terrifying Reality of Biological Warfare*. New York, NY: St. Martin's Press, April, 2001.

Manwaring, Max G., and Anthony James Joes (Eds.). *Beyond Declaring Victory and Coming Home*. Westport: Praeger Publ., 2000.

Marks, Thomas A. *Counterrevolution in China*. New York, NY: Taylor and Francis, Inc., February, 1998.

Mao Ze-dong. *Selected Works of Mao-Tse-tung. Volume IV: The Third Revolutionary Civil War Period*. Peking: Foreign Language Press, 1961.

a. McCurry, Justin. Tokyo Guardian Co., U.K. dispatch, October 28, 2004.

b. St. Louis University School of Public Health, August 10, 2005, ANSER, Inc. Newsletter, September, 1942.

Mao Ze-dong. *The Concept For Operations for the Liaoshen Campaign*. Selected Works of Mao Tse-tung: Foreign Languages Press, Peking, 1969, Vol. 4.

Myers, Ramon H. and Hsiao-ting Lin. *Breaking with the Past: The KMT Central Reform Committee of Taiwan, 1950-52*. Stanford, CA: Hoover Institution Press, Stanford University, 2007.

Overstreet, Gene D., and M.Windmiller. *Communism in India*. Berkeley, 1960.

Paterson, Thomas G. *Meeting the Communist Threat: Truman to Reagan*. Oxford : Oxford University Press, November, 1989.

Pepper, Suzanne. *Civil War in China*. Lanham, MD: Lanham, Rowman and Littlefield, 1999.

Qing Simei. *From Allies to Enemies: Visions of Modernity, Identity, and U.S.-China Diplomacy*. Cambridge, MA: Harvard University Press, January, 2007.

Roberts, J.A.G. *The Complete History of China*. Stroud, Gloucestershire, UK: Sutton Publ. 2003.

Roy, Denny. *Taiwan: A Political History*. Ithaca, NY: Cornell University Press, 2003.

Saich, Tony. *The Chinese Communist Party During the Era of the Comintern 1919-1943*. Cambridge, Mass.: Harvard Univ. Press.

Seagrave, Sterling. *The Soong Dynasty*. New York, NY: Harper and Row Publishers, 1986.

Shackleton, Allan J. *Formosa Calling: An Eyewitness Account of Conditions in Taiwan During the February 28th, 1947 Incident*. Taipei, Taiwan: Taiwan Publishing Co., 1998.

Sherry, Mark D. *WW II Campaigns: China Defensive*. Brochure CMH 72-38, Publ. U.S. Army Center of Military History, 2003.

Slack, Edward R. "China and the Soviet Union against Japan." In *Opium, State, and Society: China's Narco-Economy and the Guomintang*. University of Hawai Press, 2000.

Spence, Jonathan D. *The Search for Modern China.* New York, NY: W.W. Norton Co., 1990.

Starr, S. Frederick. *Xinjiang.* Armonk, NY: M.E. Sharpe, Inc., March, 2004.

Stevenson, Gary P. "China: War and Revolution." Cal Poly 315 Lectures.

Stuart, J. Leighton. Department of State Publication, 3578, P. 867.

Sun You-li. *China and the Origins of the Pacific War, 1931-1941.* Hampshire, UK: Palgrave Publ., 1996.

Tai Hung-chao. *Land Reform and Politics: a Comparative Analysis.* Berkeley, CA: University of California Press, January, 2004.

TIME Magazine Archive Article. "Grudge Government." Nov. 27, 1933.

Taylor, Jay. *The Generalissimo's Son: Chiang Ching-Kuo and the Revolutions in China and Taiwan.* Cambridge MA: Harvard University Press, 2000.

Terrill, Ross. *Madame Mao: The White-Boned Demon.* Stanford, CA: Stanford University Press, 1999.

Tsai Yi-Jia. "The Writing of History: The Religious Practices of the Mediums' Association in Taiwan." Taipei: Taiwan Journal of Anthropology 2 (2), 2004.

Van de Ven, Hans. *War and Nationalism in China, 1925-1945*. Routledge, 2003.

Van Slyke, Lyman. *The China White Paper*. US Department of State, August, 1949: letter 153b from Stuart to Secretary Marshall, Nanjing, May 19, 1948, p. 867. Also, Stanford, CA: Stanford University Press, 1967.

Wakeman, Frederic, Jr. *Spymaster: Dai Li and the Chinese Secret Service*. Berkeley: University of California Press, 2003.

Wakeman, Frederic, Jr. *Policing Shanghai*. Berkeley, CA: University of California Press, 1995.

Wang Di. *Street Culture in Chengdu*. Stanford, CA: Stanford University Press, 2003.

Wang Ke-wen. *Modern China: An Encyclopedia of History, Culture, and Nationalism*. New York, NY: Routledge (Taylor and Francis Publ.), 1998.

Westad, Odd Arne. *Decisive Encounters: The Chinese Civil War, 1946-1950*. Stanford, CA: Stanford University Press, March, 2003.

Wikipedia. "The Blue Shirt Society."

Xiang Lan-zin. *Mao's Generals: Chen Yi and the New Fourth Army*. University Press of America, 1998.

Xu Youwei and Philip Billingsly. "Behind the Scenes at the Xian Incident: The Case of the Lixingshe." China Quarterly 154, June 1998.

Yang, Mike Kai-kan, "The Origin and Evolution of Taiwanese Nationalism." Thesis: Vancouver, CA: Dept. of History: University of British Columbia, 1997.

Yaung, Emily. "The Impact of the Yalta Agreement on Chinese Domestic Politics, 1945-1946." Doctoral Dissertation, Kent, OH: Kent State University, 1979.

Zheng Yang-wen. *The Social Life of Opium in China.* Cambridge, UK: Cambridge University Press, 2005.

Zhou En-lai. *The Comintern and the Chinese Communist Party, Vol.2.* Beijing: Foreign language Press, 1989.

Zhao Suisheng. *Power By Design: Constitution-Making in Nationalist China.* Honolulu, HW: University of Hawaii Press, 1990.

Discussion Questions

1. Why did the authors select the book title *Shadows in the Lotus Pool*? Are there symbolic meanings for the title?

2. What is the purpose of this book?

3. How would you characterize the writing style? Objective? Passionate? Is it written in a way that is easily accessible? Are unfamiliar terms and concepts explained?

4. Do the historical elements in the book enhance or detract from the personal stories of the protagonists? In what way?

5. Was there anything that surprised you about the culture and events in China's struggle?

6. What was the most touching, humorous, or interesting account described in the book?

7. What are the central themes of the book? Are the major issues personal, sociological, political, economic?

8. What are the most important factors contributing to the downfall of the Nationalist regime?

9. How do you characterize Deng Wen-yi overall?

10. What were the converging factors that prompted Chiang Kai-shek to elevate Wen-yi to Major General at the age of twenty two? What does this reveal about Chiang that would remain a constant throughout the book?

11. Given Wen-yi's close association with the Nationalist cause, are controversial issues involving major players and events described largely from the Nationalist position or do the authors include views from other sources to attain a more balanced story?

12. Why would the President of China, busy and notoriously short-tempered, endure a turbulent, yet close relationship with a quixotic young subordinate like Wen-yi?

13. During the aftermath of the Xian kidnapping of Chiang Kai-Shek, why was Wen-yi treated less harshly for his bold action than were other members favoring military action?

14. Why did Wen-yi ask for reassignment from his duties as head of the political department at Chengdu Military Academy, to active duty in the field?

15. What do you think was the single most significant action taken by Wen-yi throughout his life? The worst action?

16. Why would the paramount leader of the People's Republic of China invite Wen-yi to Beijing for talks, when he could choose from among many more highly placed officials in the Taiwanese government?

17. How would you characterize Wen-yi's first marriage with Bai-jian, compared to marriage with his second wife, Wen-ying? Similarities and differences?

18. Was there something especially surprising about Yuan-yu's story? What was it and why?

19. Who should bear the major responsibility for the difficult fate of Yuan-yu?

20. Why did Yuan-yu wait so long to tell someone that she was being molested? What would you have done under those circumstances?

21. What character traits helped Yuan-yu to first endure and later triumph?

22. Why did Yuan-yu develop friendships with native Taiwanese girls, angering her mainland Chinese friends?

23. What problems and challenges, good or bad, did the prevailing school system in Taiwan present?

24. Of the characters involved in Wen-yi's story and Yuan-yu's story, which two did you like the most in each story and why? ...the least and why?

25. What do you think is the answer to the question posed in the Author's Note: did recalling events of the past bring Yuan-yu pain or liberation?

CPSIA information can be obtained at www.ICGtesting.com
Printed in the USA
266586BV00003B/1/P